Move Forward

*Ministry is not something we do,
it's the life we live.*

Jim Coursey

Copyright © 2017 Jim Coursey

All rights reserved.

No part of this publication may be reproduced, stored in a retrieval system, or transmitted in any form or by any means – electronic, mechanical, photocopying, recording, or otherwise - without the prior written permission of the publisher.

Unless otherwise noted, all Scriptures are taken from the New King James Bible (NKJV)

Move Forward
Ministry is not something we do, it's the life we live.

ISBN 9781943852789 (paperback)
ISBN 9781943852796 (e-book)
Library of Congress Control number: 2017957612

True Potential, Inc.
PO Box 904, Travelers Rest, SC 29690
www.truepotentialmedia.com

Printed in the United States of America.

Move Forward

Jim Coursey

Dedication

A very special thanks to my wonderful wife Tonya, who is my best friend, and has remained loyal to me even through the toughest of times. Tonya's enormous love for the Lord, and me has been steady as we have learned to grow together, and love together.

Thank you Tonya for being such a wonderful wife as we journey through this side of heaven.

Special Thanks

To those who have chosen to faithfully serve the Lord every day. The following servant's of the Lord are very special to Tonya and I. It has been through their hands that brought about a mighty work of God in our lives.

Gary & Gail York Founders of Give God Glory Ministries
www.gggministry.com
Waterman, Illinois

Apostle Charles Green
Senior Pastor Christian Faith Fellowship Church East
724 S. Layton Blvd. Milwaukee, Wisconsin
(414) 383-8533
www.cffceast.org

Solomon Kepkey
Founder/International Director
www.gomissionsafrica.com
info@gomissionsafrica.com
(630) 465-5627 (USA)
073 822 0027 (South Africa)

Paramel Chummar Verghese (PC)
India

For without these blessed servants of the Lord who answered the call of taking the Kingdom of God outside of the confines of the church building, this testimony would have never been possible.

Thank you, and may the Lord bless each of you!

Jim & Tonya Coursey

Move Forward

Table of Contents

Introduction		ix

Section 1

Chapter 1	This is a New Season	13
Chapter 2	The Early Years	33
Chapter 3	My Own Way	53
Chapter 4	Move Forward	81

Section 2

Chapter 5	Our Walk in Him, The Newness of Life	107
Chapter 6	Intimacy & Identity	129
Chapter 7	Life in the Spirit	151
Chapter 8	As You Go	177
Appendix A	The Father is waiting for you	197
Appendix B	Dreams and Visions	199

Introduction

This book is not merely an autobiography of a Christian who fell away, lived a carnal life, and then God intervened. Although such a story is a remarkable testimony of God's love, this book is much more than that. This book is a call to every believer to take their faith into the world around them. We each have our own realm of influence where we can demonstrate that the Kingdom of heaven is indeed at hand.

Sunday morning, August 2016 I arrived at GGG (Give God Glory), an annual three-day tent meeting in Waterman, Illinois. This event was founded, and hosted by Gary and Gail York of Give God the Glory Ministry. I married Gary's sister, Tonya. So, as a family, we all pitched in to help. That morning I was assigned to ensure that ice was in the coolers for the water. As I went about my business, I clearly had the impression that the Lord was telling me to "move forward." What? Then, the Lord gave me: "Your testimony is not always about where you have been but, where I am taking you. So, move forward." Whoa!

The evening before at GGG, Tonya and I got up and gave a brief testimony of how God had intervened in our lives, at the altar at GGG two years prior. We gave thanks to Gary and Gail for their faithfulness. They have dedicated themselves in following the Lord's call to bring the people together during this incredible ministry. We gave thanks to the Lord for all that He has done for us and spoke of what God has brought us out of.

I knew when the Lord spoke to me that morning that moving forward was about this book, and about future opportunities I may have to share my testimony. This book is about transformation. It's about living a transformed life every day. It's about recognizing who we are in Christ, our identity, and living out of a real understanding of who our Father is. He is love, and He first loved me even before I was aware of His love.

The Lord was directing me to move beyond the details of what He had brought

Introduction

Tonya and me out of. Moving forward for Tonya and me was about what were we going to do, and go from where He has taken us.

God is glorified by what we do after He intervenes, and we walk as disciples of Jesus. Jesus told his disciples in **John 15:8 – "By this My Father is glorified, that you bear much fruit, so you will by My disciples."**

Jesus also stated: **"Let your light so shine before men that they may see your good works and glorify your Father in heaven." Matthew 5:16**

I do believe there is power in testimony. A testimony of how God has transformed a person's life makes God more real to someone who may have a similar story. A person may be stuck in a dry place too long to see a way out. Often times I encounter people who do want their life to be different or better. A testimony creates a level of faith that brings hope. They may say: "Hey if God can do that for them, then it's possible for me too."

In this book you will see that scenario unfold in my life at the age of 20. The power of the testimony of Jesus is the spirit of prophecy (Revelation 19:10). It was the Spirit of prophecy that launched the testimony you are about to read.

For years, I strove to be what I read in the Bible and attempted to attain that standard. I wanted to be what I read. Unfortunately, no matter how sincere I was, it was a life lived based on performance; always trying to measure up. In a sense, I was treating the Bible as a self-help book, trying to follow the principles to a better and happier life; as if Christianity was nothing more than a sin management program.

I had completely missed it. It was love that met me at that altar. **"This is love, not that we loved God, but that He loved us…" 1 John 4:10.** Of course, because God is love (1 John 4:8). Since then, as a good Father, He has consistently shown me His love as He develops me spiritually. Despite who I am and my shortcomings, in His love, He chooses to work through me, and anyone who will surrender to Him.

Before God intervened in my life at GGG 2014 during an altar call, I allowed the circumstances of life, my experiences from childhood and adulthood to dictate my perspective on life and Christianity. My perspective was not in alignment with the Kingdom of Heaven.

My "theology" was based on the poor performance of someone who was trying to measure up. God seemed so distant in that cycle. I created even more distance from God in my hopelessness. I figured it didn't matter and that God wasn't really listening anyway.

God did an incredible work within me at the altar. He created in me a clean heart and renewed a right spirit. Then, there was a season of training that I needed to go through. After all, I had been in a dry place for 30 years! That's a lot of time to develop some very bad habits. So, God needed to retrain and equip me.

That training and equipping never ceases for a Christian. In John 15:1-2, Jesus explains that His Father is the vinedresser. Those branches that don't bear fruit needed to be taken away and those branches that bear fruit need to be pruned so they may bear more fruit. As the Lord continues to train and equip me there is fruit. He continues to prune. Sometimes that process is not pleasant, but necessary for further growth. It's a spiritual principle. The Christian life is one that bears fruit, and the pruning will bring better understanding to bear even more fruit from the same branch.

A clean heart and renewed spirit provided the clean slate I needed for new growth. Spiritually, the old ground had been plowed, the chaff removed, and a fertile field was ready for planting. Then a spiritual paradigm shift occurred when Tonya and I went to the Bethel healing conference in Redding California. We were immersed in a Kingdom culture every day. There was much breakthrough as the love of God finally sunk into my spirit. It's not what I can do for God but what He can do through me. I know that may not sound very earth-shattering to most. But I still functioned in the "task-oriented" mode.

We are called to love the Lord our God with all our heart, all our mind, and all our soul. But for me, Christianity was still what I was *supposed* to do. The shift came when I fully comprehended that God, who is love, loves me. And I only need to operate from that place, and everything else will fall into place. No wonder Paul wrote: "**...but if I have not love, I am nothing.**" 1 Corinthians 13:2

Once God moved me from a place of how I lived life, and taught me to operate out of His love, life became much less of a soulish struggle than it had been before. I turned a spiritual corner, and as the months ahead unfolded, I was being Spirit-led, and what a difference that makes in the walk of a believer!

The purpose of this book is not just an autobiography that seems to rehash in the deeds of the past. Rather, it reveals the possibilities of what God can do through anyone who is simply willing to surrender to Him. I will take you back to who I was, and where God has delivered me from so you will have an understanding, that if God can transform my life, He can transform anyone.

Although your circumstances and experiences may be different. Where we all

Introduction

stand is obvious. Jesus said: "He who is not with Me is against Me, and he who does not gather with Me scatters abroad." Matthew 12:30 As born again Christians, we have new identities, and we need to realize that, and live our lives as God sees us, through the finished work of our Lord and Savior, Jesus.

"And you, who once were alienated and enemies in your mind by wicked works, yet now He has reconciled, in the body of His flesh through death, to present you holy, and blameless, and above reproach in His sight…" Colossians 1-21-22

This book is about living the transformed life, as a new creation in Jesus. It is also about regaining what has been taken by deception in the garden. We were intended from the very beginning to live in right relationship with God (Genesis 1:26). It's time to stop doubting what God has made possible and live out what Jesus proclaimed to the Pharisees about the coming Kingdom of God.

Jesus told them that the Kingdom of God is within you (Luke 17:21).

Let's all move forward!

This is a New Season

"Create in me a clean heart O God, and renew a steadfast spirit within me" Psalm 51:10

Entering into a new season spiritually for me developed as unexpectedly as the seasons in the natural can change here near Chicago. One day it is 70 degrees and the next temperatures can drop 30 degrees. Although I was a believer, read my Bible, and went to church; I was walking as a mere man, as Paul had said to the Corinthians. I was carnal, defeated, and frustrated with every aspect of my life; which included what I called my Christian walk.

"For to be carnally minded is death, but to be spiritually minded is life and peace. Because the carnal mind is enmity against God; for it is not subject to the law of God (His ways), nor indeed can be." Romans 8:6-7

Looking back, I understand what this verse really means. I lived it. My life, my world, and my priorities were self-focused. Life was merely attempting to satisfy my carnal desires, and selfish pursuits. God fit in where it was convenient. Like many people in our western culture, we compartmentalize our beliefs to fit our schedules, and life styles, because we don't really want our beliefs to interfere with our daily pursuits. Such was I; but worse. I carried baggage and demons, wrapped tightly under the veneer of a knowledgeable Christian. Over time, I had become a professional church attendee.

However, the reality was that my carnal mind was actually death oriented, and at enmity with God. To be at enmity is a deep feeling of resentment or malice toward another. Strong words! I was angry. I was angry with how my life had turned out. Angry with the choices I had made. I was angry with God. I was at a breaking point once again. I knew it because I had been there before.

Looking back, it is amazing to comprehend that it truly is in His goodness, He leads us to repentance. My life is a living epistle of God's grace.

This is a New Season

Tonya and I had gone out for dinner on a Wednesday night in July of 2014. Nothing seemed to be going right in our marriage. By this time, we had been married for 7 years. However, during those 7 years, I had left once, and had moved into an apartment for six months. There was a consistent pattern of highs and lows, and the marriage was very strained. As we ate, I thought this was a waste of time, and just wanted to get back to the house. Tonya was distant, and it was evident that something wasn't right. I was in one of those, "I could care less" moods. As we drove home, we passed a bar, and Tonya suggested that we stop for a drink.

That sounded like a good idea to me. We sat at a table and Tonya could not decide on what to order. I was more than ready to get a beer headed my way. Not much of a decision for me. Tonya finally ordered a drink. That first beer went down quick, as they usually did. The atmosphere hadn't changed much and I was on beer number two. Tonya then announced that she wasn't happy about _anything_ in her life. I asked if that would include me, and the marriage. Tonya replied yep, I'm not happy with anything.

> *I would sit in the basement, and watch some old western, or cop movie, and drink beer.*

Well, that made two of us. I didn't know what to say. So, I just kept drinking my beer and staring off into the distance. With all of the fun sucked out of date night, we drove home in silence. Once there, Tonya went to bed, and I went to the basement to continue drinking more beer. At the time, this was my usual pattern. I would sit in the basement, and watch some old western, or cop movie, and drink beer. My movie selection when I was in a drinking mood was pretty much the same. The more violence, the better. My idea of a happy ending was when someone got shot.

The next morning, Tonya and I sat out on the deck drinking coffee. The atmosphere wasn't any different. Tonya again mentioned that she wasn't happy in the marriage. I agreed I wasn't either and said well I guess it's over, I can't keep living like this. I decided I would file the divorce papers on Monday. No sense trying to live through another failed marriage. This was the second marriage for both of us.

I took the day off of work because I didn't think I could handle any problems at work. Tonya took the liberty to arrange with her brother, Gary, for me to come and help set up for their annual tent-meeting – "GGG" (Give God Glory). I really didn't want to go out there and help set up for a tent meeting. But it was better than staying around the house and it gave me something to do. I had always been good at occupying my time. It seemed to keep my mind focused on anything but the problem at hand.

Friday evening arrived, and GGG (2014) was underway. Tonya wasn't feeling well and stayed home, so I went by myself. A missionary from India, Paramel Chummar Verghese, nicknamed PC was preaching. I sat there, listened, as he preached from John 15, how we cannot bear fruit unless we as Christians abide in Christ. I sat there and thought of all the rotten fruit I had brought to bear on my own. I prayed for my kids. I carried a tremendous amount of guilt that both of my children, now adults had walked away from the Lord. I really couldn't blame them. I wasn't much of an example of a Christian father and husband to their mother. When the altar call came, I left. I was told the next day that the kids who were there had been filled with the Spirit. I went home, drank beer, and watched what I usually watched – something where there was a lot of violence. By this time in my life, I had sat through 30 years of sermons and seemed pretty much immune from getting excited about an altar call. Besides, it was hot and humid, as summers are in Illinois, and there was cold beer waiting for me at the house. I sat in the basement, Tonya was in bed, I was miserable but at least I watched a movie with a "happy ending", and had plenty of beer.

Saturday morning, July 2014.

I left the house early to help set up for the day's event at GGG. Tonya and I drove separate, which was all right by me. I went about my business helping with some setup. Then as the service was about to start, Tonya called me. She was crying and told me she was leaving. Tonya then explained a situation that had arisen when she got there that it upset her so that she just wanted to leave. Great, another dilemma! I asked her to stay, and I walked up to the car, where she was still crying. I convinced her to stay for the day's events. I really didn't care about the meeting, but thought that if she left, it would just cause a family issue. Figuring we could at least stay for the morning service and see how it went.

It may seem odd to be concerned about a family drama given my decided course of action such as a divorce. But it was just crisis management. We just needed to get through this day without further incident. I had been a police officer for over 27 years. Cops think like that. Let me just get through this "cluster."

Men and woman have entirely different perspectives. For example, when Tonya and I sat on the deck Thursday morning, and I said that I was tired of living like this, she took it as a sign of hope that I would somehow make a change to improve the marriage. She didn't know with me it was a decision to file for divorce. So, when I arrived at the car, Tonya took it as I still cared, that I loved her, and wanted her to be with me. Tonya didn't know I just wasn't in the mood for any more family drama, I was hoping we could just get through the morning service, and then leave.

Tonya and I sat through the praise music and then the sermon. PC brought a message from Galatians 2:20. It is no longer the life I live, but Christ lives in me. At the time this was too abstract for me to grasp. Little did I know as I sat there with a defeated attitude, that this sermon would be prophetic for Tonya and I. At the end of the message, the invitation was given that if anyone wanted prayer, they could come forward. I grabbed Tonya's hand and we headed up to the altar. Tonya protested: "I feel like you are dragging me." I snarled back: "yeah, so what". Tonya will recount the event as a cop grabbing a suspect, and not a loving husband who wanted prayer for a failing marriage. Yeah, that was accurate. I was usually like a focused rhinoceros and people's feeling would often get trampled on. Mostly Tonya's. At the altar, people were clearing chairs and making room for everyone who had come forward.

As you may have assumed, I had not been motivated by an impressive sermon, although it may very well have been. I was not hyped up in anticipation of a miracle, or any mighty move of God. I honestly don't know why I was so eager to go forward other than the fact that I figured we needed prayer. My attitude was pretty much we could use some prayer – period. We were in a desperate place in our lives, and I knew it was on the verge of getting worse. Perhaps it was fear of where I may descend or crash. As I mentioned, I had been in that desperate place before and came very close to making a terminal choice. I will cover that later.

I didn't know then, but God was moving. His hand had been on my life all along. I just never really understood, nor acknowledged Him as I should have. That was about to change. Standing there was Apostle Charles Green from Milwaukee, and Solomon Kepkey of South Africa. What happened next was an encounter with God, at the hands these two servants of the Lord. One of the two anointed my head with oil, and Apostle Green asked if I was there with my wife. We were then directed to hold hands by Apostle Green.

Apostle Green began with the following: "I shall even make both of you sharpshooters. I will cause your aim to not be a misfire but a directional target."

What I didn't know at the time was that Apostle Green was given a prophetic word over us. I had never been exposed to the prophetic. I was assuming it would just be a prayer, asking God to help us with the mess of our life.

"Prophecy is a wonderful part of a healing process, and renewing process. Prophecy brings us, by direct verbal communication into contact with God's real perspectives on our lives and current situations."[1]

---

1   Developing your prophetic gifting by Graham Cooke pg. 29

MOVE FORWARD

Paul describes prophecy to us as one of the spiritual gifts that when spoken are for the strengthening, encouragement and comfort of men. 1 Corinthians 14:3 (NIV)

I like how John Eckhardt put it: "A prophetic word can change your life. Prophecy is powerful because it is the word of the Lord, and no word from God is without power.[2]

When the prophetic began to flow, I was overcome with the presence of something Holy. I had never encountered this before. I knew that I was in the presence of Holiness. It was not the two men of God, they were the servants of God. It was the very Presence of God that came upon me. All I could do was weep, and cry out: "Woe is me, for I am not worthy but only say the words and I shall be healed."

I had never encountered this before. I knew that I was in the presence of Holiness.

It was a scene similar to that of Isaiah chapter 6, as Isaiah the prophet stood in the Presence of God, he recognized his unworthiness and his sin before Holiness. I was not reciting a Bible verse. In my spirit, I recognized the presence of Holiness and could say nothing but the truth; there was holiness. Not wrath or judgment, which I deserved. Rather, in love and grace God met me there. I was not worthy. In my spirit, I knew He only needed to say the Word and I would be healed. Being in the Presence of God brought me into a level of faith I never had. In those moments, I experienced salvation (sozo), forgiveness, healing, and deliverance.

For the next seven minutes, both Apostle Green and Solomon gave a prophetic word from the Lord, and all I could do was stand there and weep. You must understand that at the time, I was a very hardhearted person, and had become very calloused. I didn't love God. I didn't love anyone. I certainly didn't love myself. I was a miserable person standing there. But God in His love met me where I was. When I look back at it, God in His righteousness could have look at me and said, "What do you want?" "You have caused more damage in the name of Christianity than most unsaved". Yet, in His great mercy, He expressed to me that He really is a God of love.

"No one can really understand God's love unless they understand the free gift of His mercy and His grace. And, paradoxically, no one can really understand God's

---
2   God Still Speaks by John Eckhardt pg. 8

grace without understanding what real love is all about – the nature of God's love toward us."³

In 1 John 4:10 we read: "This is love, not that we loved God but that He loved us and sent His Son as an atoning sacrifice for our sins." This was so true, this was love! God was intervening in a life that otherwise could not have been turned around in all my own efforts. As it was I had regulated the Bible to some sort of self-help manual; a book of principles to follow rather than the word of God. In essence, Christianity had become a sin management program. Needless to say, I wasn't having much success with that approach.

The prophetic word continued. "For there shall be a difference made concerning you, sayeth the Lord. For you have found favor with the Most High God, and out of the kindness of your heart I am going to extend kindness to many people through the words that you say. Have not I put counsel deep within your heart? Have I not put words within your heart to reach out to those who are weary and dwell in a land that is dry, and those who are tired and spinning their wheels, sayeth the Lord. I shall uproot things in lives of people that have caused them to become contained and out of balance."

I was so overwhelmed! How could I have found favor in the sight of the Most High God? As I stood there I was a mess. I didn't deserve His favor, His love, or His grace. Yet, that was exactly what I received. I surrendered to it. I received it, and it changed the course of not only my life but Tonya's life as well. "For I (God) put my hands upon you, and I'm now cradling you to a new season of divine comfort, and out of comfort, sayeth the Lord, you will establish every good word and every good work."

I was so overwhelmed! How could I have found favor in the sight of the Most High God?

Both Apostle Green and Solomon spoke prophetically over us as a couple, and over Tonya as well. Apostle Green continued: "God had called this woman beside you, and the two of you will walk together, and God is going to put a greater love between you, and you will be people who others will want to be around". Oh my, God you are a God of the impossible. He is, and we are thankful! Apostle Green also called out those who would desire to go to the divorce court. Only God could have been doing this. These two men didn't know us at all, and certainly had no idea what was going on in our lives. Apostle Green, speaking prophetically spoke out: "…I have

3   Grace & Forgiveness by John & Carol Arnott pg. 9

MOVE FORWARD

put abilities within your lips to cause the words to drop into your wife. Yeah, one will get and one shall confirm." Sounds like there will be a time ahead where we will actually be working together as a couple for His Kingdom.

Although Tonya later explained that she did not have the same type of God encounter experience that I had. Nevertheless, it changed and impacted her life as radically as it did mine. The prophetic flow continued for over seven minutes. When they moved on to someone else, I grabbed Tonya and hugged her as hard as I could. Tonya told me later that it was the first time she felt secure in my arms. Of course it did. Even though I didn't know it, but the man who hugged her was a changed man. I had just been touched, healed, delivered, and made clean by the Holiness of the Most High God. It was love that had just changed me, and it was *His* love that was now manifesting in the embrace Tonya was receiving. It was beyond our comprehension at the time but the secure feeling she was getting was the love of the Father. Something she had not received before; certainly not from me.

I did love Tonya but I only loved her as much as I was able to at the time in the natural. What I understood of love that is, which wasn't very much at the time. I had been drawing from a dry well all these years, so there wasn't much to offer. After we hugged, I had to sit down. I felt light. Something had been lifted off if me. All that tension was gone. I wasn't sure what had just happened. That wasn't like any "prayer" I had ever been involved in before. At the time I couldn't recall much of what had been spoken over us. I sat there on the stage trying to process what just occurred. My legs were too wobbly to stand.

As I sat there on the stage, I tried to recall all the words that had been spoken over us but I couldn't. It was like I had been off in another dimension. The prophetic word wasn't just an encouraging prayer, or words to make us feel better. It was the Presence of God. His Presence was ushered in through the prophetic ministry of two faithful men of God. I would later read:

"When the prophets begin to prophesy, thus says the Lord... it charges the atmosphere with faith and with power, the Glory, and the Spirit of God, preparing the way for miracles. It is the tangible manifestation of the glory and anointing of God that is going to bring forth miracles. You can feel it. You know God is in the house."[4]

The Presence of God is tangible. God's Presence brought forth a miracle. I felt lighter, something had been lifted. A deliverance had occurred. The demons I had been carrying were gone. The temple (my body/soul) had been cleared.

Then Solomon prophesied: "I see that the wind of the Holy Spirit blows away

---

4   God Still Speaks by John Eckhardt pg. 142

chaff. I see a field that is being completely cleared for new seed to fall within its belly, and for a new harvest to erupt and come forth." That was what exactly occurred. Jesus came in and cleared the temple of the debris that had defiled it. Each of us, whether we realize it or not, have been designed to be the temple of the Holy Spirit. As such, we are to glorify God in our bodies, and our spirits, which are God's, for we have been bought with a price (1 Corinthians 6:19-20).

Solomon continued: "The Lord says that He is taking you out of a season in which you felt trapped, in which you have experienced stagnation in which you have experienced depression, and He says as I have spoken through my servant (Apostle Green), so it shall be, this is a new day, it is a new season, it is a new beginning. " Yes, the prophetic ushered in a new season, it was truly a new beginning for Tonya and I.

As I drove home that night, for the first time in my life, I really knew what it was like to be a new creation in Christ. It was no longer just academic. I just encountered a Holy, loving God, who created in me a clean heart and renewed a right spirit within me. I felt clean for the first time in my life.

"Therefore, if anyone is in Christ, he is a new creation, old things have passed away, behold all things have become new." 2 Corinthians 5:17

The magnitude of the encounter with God at the altar was just beginning to sink in. I knew that I felt like a new creation. But in the weeks, and months to follow, God would reveal to Tonya and me that all things have become new. It was truly a new season for us, and those around us.

That encounter with the Lord, and being filled with His Spirit changed everything. In a matter of minutes, the power of the most High God (Luke 1:35) cleared out the temple. I have received the Spirit of God, as Paul writes in 1 Corinthians 2:12, I had "received not the spirit of the world, but the Spirit who is from God, that I might know the things that have been freely given to us by God".

The carnal had been cleaned, and cleared, like a farm field tilled, and ready for planting, the chaff had been blown away, the soil of my being was ready for God to sow in the Spiritual. I am not over dramatizing what occurred under the flow of a prophetic anointing when the Holy Spirit touched me. As you read on, you will discover more of the depths of despair I had been in. Although a veneer of Christianity covered the hurt, God demonstrated that it is His goodness that leads us to repentance. I encountered love, not condemnation. In His Presence repentance was the only option. Not that I didn't have free will, but His love was so overwhelming why would I refuse it. I surrendered. I was no longer going to fight with the Father who truly loves me.

Now, being transformed spiritually, into the same image from glory to glory, just

MOVE FORWARD

as by the Spirit of the Lord (2 Corinthians 3:18), God was about to take Tonya and I on a journey that would continue to amaze us, and still does. Rivers of living water were preparing to flow. The Lord would be taking us from the natural (man) to spiritually discerned (1 Corinthians 2:14), at an accelerated pace.

Although I had been a Christian for over 30 years, I had little experience in how the Spirit of God operated or moved upon His people. So, as the next few months unfolded the Holy Spirit began to teach us. It did take some time for me to allow the Holy Spirit to teach me, as He does (1 John 2:27). I had been an academic Christian and processed everything analytically. My discovery was that being academic hinders the Spirit at times. I also discovered that the Holy Spirit is a gentleman, but thankfully is also persistent

The carnal had been cleaned, and cleared, like a farm field tilled, and ready for planting ...

When Tonya and I stood at the altar during GGG 2014, I was a police sergeant with the Aurora, Illinois Police Department. Aurora is the second largest city in the State of Illinois, with Chicago being the largest. I had been in law enforcement for 27 years. Upon my return to work the following Monday after GGG 2014 I noticed something for the first time. When I entered the sergeant's office, I sensed a tension in the atmosphere. I never noticed that before. It was difficult to explain but the tension was tangible.

I didn't want to be in there. Apparently, my spirit, now immersed in the Holy Spirit was at odds with what I used to be so much a part of. I was fortunate however to have a private office nearby. I was a sergeant for the Community Policing Unit, and was able to escape there for much of my administrative duties.

One day, I had been assigned as the lead investigative supervisor involving a use of force situation with two officers from my unit. Such investigations are more common today than they used to be. In such cases, the actions of the officers are heavily scrutinized all of the way up the chain of command. The final results are then reviewed by a civilian review board for a recommendation on potential discipline. In addition, my investigation will be reviewed by the same command staff and review board. As a result, I had to be incredibly thorough. There I was at my desk typing everything up. I was completely focused on the task at hand. I was typing, proofreading, making sure everything was accurate. The focused rhinoceros at the keyboard.

This is a New Season

As I was typing, a vision came to me. I had never had a "vision". In the vision I was squatting down holding a black female toddler wearing a white dress. My sense was that I was not in the United States, the background was more tropical. I stopped typing, and literally pulled back – Whoa! "That was weird"! I wasn't sure what to make of it. I shook it off and went back to typing. Again, same vision! But this time Tonya was there with us. Then, the name "Kenisha" popped in my mind. Okay, this is really weird. It was like a snap shot that just appeared and disappeared. I was at a loss. My mind was entirely focused on this use of force report. I had already had difficult conversations with two lieutenants about the situation and knew this report would be a reflection on me as a supervisor as well as the officers. So, where this "vision" came from was beyond me. Oh, yeah, it certainly was beyond me.

I knew at the altar, God had done a mighty work in me. God had created in me a clean heart and a right spirit within me. He took my heart of stone, and gave me a heart of flesh, as Ezekiel wrote (Ezekiel 37:26). Perhaps God was showing me that I needed to embrace people of all races. Unfortunately, before God intervened in my life, I carried a lot of hatred, prejudice, and bigotry. I knew I had been delivered of everything at that altar. Perhaps the Lord was showing that He sees all races as precious as this toddler I was holding. But I still thought it was weird.

> *I knew at the altar, God had done a mighty work in me.*

Tonya and I would learn in due time what He was preparing us for and the reason for the vision. It was for an appointed time.

Even in my limited understanding, I knew this was not manufactured in my subconscious. An image such this was the furthest thing from my mind at that moment. I will cover dreams and visions in appendix B.

To be honest I was so freaked out by the vision I didn't tell Tonya for a long time. It wasn't until months later when we were considering going to South Africa on a mission trip that I related the vision to Tonya. She began to cry and felt perhaps it was confirmation that we were to go to South Africa. I wasn't so sure. Tonya and I decided to have Solomon over for dinner and I told him about the vision and my reaction to it. His response was: "That's not weird, that's the Holy Spirit." I was just beginning to experience what Peter would explain to the people in Jerusalem on the Day of Pentecost of Joel's prophetic word:

... "and it shall come to pass in the last days, says God, that I will pour out my Spirit on all flesh, your sons and your daughters shall prophesy, your young men shall see visions, your old men shall dream dreams..." Acts 2:17

MOVE FORWARD

That I had my first vision was awesome, but do I consider myself a young man? Perhaps in the Spirit, I was young. Ultimately, I would have more dreams than visions. But before we cover that, the Holy Spirit was about to introduce me to another portion of that scripture.

At this point, I wasn't sure if my encounter with God at the altar was simply the result of a prophetic anointing or had I been baptized in the Spirit. My early theology would suggest that I had not received the baptism in the Holy Spirit. When I first got saved, back in 1983, I belonged to a small Four Square Church. They were considered Pentecostal. However, the pastor at the time never preached or taught about a Holy Spirit lifestyle. My first Holy Spirit experiences were of someone standing up, giving a message in tongues, and then someone would interpret. Most of the messages given were of a general rebuke and anything but encouraging.

There was a period when I was searching other churches for more of the Holy Spirit, but I found it was pretty much a formula for them based out of Acts 2:38. If you were baptized in the Spirit, there was the evidence of speaking in tongues. During the prophetic word given over Tonya and me, it was prophesied that we would begin to hear tongues, and interpretations. Well, as of yet, neither Tonya nor I were speaking in tongues. So, based on what I understood of the scriptures I guess I had not been baptized in the Holy Spirit.

I had been at a local grocery store one day, and as I exited, I walked past a black female. We made eye contact, and in an instant, I felt as if I had just been given a "download" of information about this woman. I was to ask her about Demitrius. Tell her that the circumstances that he was currently facing, would ultimately be for his benefit. There was a brief picture of a young male black seated at a large wooden table. I sensed it was in a courtroom. I just looked up, and the woman walked right past me. I stood there, now wrestling as to what to do. Was that a prophetic word? I can't just go running after this woman. What if she looks at me like I'm crazy. What if this goes bad. I'm a police officer from another jurisdiction, how awkward would that be. I walked to my car. I sensed, with everything inside of me, I needed to share that with her. This can't be happening. Although it really bothered me, I just drove home. I was a wreck for a couple of days. I knew that I was to share that word with that woman. But the spirit of chicken took over.

The Spirit of God knew I would not deliver that word of knowledge. He was training me. At the time, I questioned who am I? I'm no prophet.

I had never given a word of prophecy before. I was beginning to discover exactly who I was in Christ. I had been filled with His Spirit and as a result, I was spiritually alive; able to hear the promptings of the Holy Spirit. This was something I would need to grow into. For about the last 27 years, I had become very mainstream in my theology. Somewhere along the way, between falling away and sneaking back into church, I guess I assumed people who moved in the Spirit were those super spiritual people. You know the ones that Jesus visits in the middle of the night, taps them on the shoulder and says, you are my beloved servant. Go therefore, and preach to the nations.

What I was beginning to learn is this fundamental truth. God seems to enjoy using ordinary people to do His work. Every believer has the same authority as sons and daughters of the King. We can serve Him as a personal representative of His Kingdom here on earth.

"Now when they saw the boldness of Peter, and John, and perceived that they were uneducated and untrained men, they marveled. And they realized that they had been with Jesus." Acts 4:31

Peter and John had been just ordinary fisherman of their day. They were uneducated, and untrained in the ways such as the Sadducees and scribes. But because they had been with Jesus, filled with the Spirit at Pentecost, they possessed a boldness. A miracle of a lame man healed and now walking because of the authority they operated out of could not be denied. They were ordinary men, filled with the Holy Spirit (Acts 4:8). So there I was, uneducated and untrained in the ways of the Holy Spirit. Nonetheless, a supernatural download of information had been given to me for someone who needed an encouraging word from the Lord. If only I had passed on what the Spirit of the Lord had given. It would have been encouraging, given comfort, and maybe even strengthened that woman (1 Corinthians 14:3).

Shortly after GGG 2014, Tonya and I attended a Sunday night meeting at a local church where Solomon Kepkey was speaking. After the service concluded there was an altar call. Tonya and I did not initially go forward, but as the ministering continued we did.

Once again, Solomon gave a prophetic word over me. This time, as he prophesied, I felt a tingling sensation all over my body. At first, I was wiping my arms, which were raised above my head. I thought something may have been crawling on me. I didn't see anything. I imagined as if dirt clods were being crumbled off of me. The sensation was all over me. Then I realized that something was breaking off of me. I wasn't sure what. Once again, I knew God was intervening in my life on a spiritual level.

Part of the prophetic word spoken that night was that a door will open before I even knock. There was something tangible that was going to be with that open door. I wasn't sure what that meant as far as having a "door open" for me. There are times that God speaks parabolically, and at other times he speaks more literally.

MOVE FORWARD

In this case, I had not yet made the connection.

Nonetheless, since my return to work at the police department, I did sense it was time for me to move on. It was time to retire from police work. I didn't have a clear sense of what I would do for a living if I retired. I had enough time vested to draw my pension. However, I had gone through a divorce in 2007, and would not receive the full pension amount. Therefore, I would need to be gainfully employed in addition to my pension. Also, as a result of the divorce, I had significant debt that I needed to pay off.

During my job searching online I had become very frustrated with the fact that I did not qualify for the better jobs. The jobs that I did qualify for didn't pay very much at all. The private sector did not pay as well as I had hoped. I finally focused in on the insurance industry, which seemed to always be in need of investigators. I had spent a considerable amount of my career as an investigator, so that appeared to be a logical choice. At work one day I retreated to my private office to do some Internet job searching. I typed in insurance investigator into a search engine. Before I could even click the mouse my cell phone rang. It was a former police officer, whom I had worked with previously. He was employed with a large, well known insurance company. He came right to the point. "Hey, we have an opening in our Chicago office. I just need to know, are you interested? Yes or no, I need to call my boss right back." I said yes.

That was so wild. Before I could even knock, or click the mouse, the phone rang, and I just committed to taking a new job. I sat at my desk stunned. I was stunned at what just happened, and apparently, after 27 years as a police officer, I just said I would be interested in taking a new job for an insurance company. God is so amazing. At the time I did wrestle with the direction I should go. I was now a new creation in Christ Jesus, and the PD sure needed the Presence of the Lord. If you have ever been around many police officers, you know that they are a great bunch of people. But they are also a unique breed. There was a definite need for ministry here at the department.

As God called Abram (Abraham) out of his home country, away from his family, and his father's house (Genesis 12), I would later learn that God needed to give me a fresh start. A new season really did mean, a new season. Don't misunderstand. I am not considering myself as an Abraham. I'm saying that for the restoration to be complete, or continue, God was taking me out of my familiar surroundings, and planting me somewhere brand new. For me, it was the best option, and I will

> *This time, as he prophesied, I felt a tingling sensation all over my body.*

unpack that later. For others, the work that the Lord has in store may need to be accomplished right where you are at.

It wasn't until the following day that I had a chance to talk with my buddy to get the details of what was going on. He filled me in on the job, and the potential timing of the actual opening. I learned that there were two investigators in the Chicago office, and the other guy took an opening in another state. So, my buddy said that he wanted to get my name to his boss right away, and suggested that I get a resume ready. His boss would be calling me very soon to set up an interview. Tonya was so excited that I would possibly have a "normal" job. At the time I was working afternoon shift. Tonya, unfortunately, spent her evenings home alone. As one can imagine, this was not the ideal situation for a marriage that needed restoration.

In the meantime, I went about my business at the police department. One night, I was sitting in my squad car reading, and approving reports that had been sent to me through the car's laptop.

> *... this was not the ideal situation for a marriage that needed restoration.*

I was sitting in one of my usual spots as a sergeant, which was behind our city parking lot along the Fox River. As I was reading, I had a strong urge to speak sounds… yes utterances. I spoke them out. As soon as I heard them I stopped. My mind started to process the sounds, and I thought it sounded like Hebrew. So, I decided to search the Internet for the meaning of the "words" I had just said. The search I came up with was of some Middle Eastern rock band. I figured that was not it. The Spirit had just given me the utterances to speak in tongues, and I let my natural mind run interference. I would later learn that this is a common problem with people who struggle with speaking in tongues.

What I didn't know then was that I had just quenched the Spirit. As you can see, the natural man does not receive the things of the Spirit of God, for they are foolishness to him 1 Corinthians 2:14. I had always been the type of person who had to analyze everything and had to figure it out. Unfortunately, over all of the years I had read the Bible, it was an academic pursuit. I knew so many verses. I knew the accounts of the Old and New Testaments. But I never took the time to get to the Author. It was really very sad. Now, the very Author of the Bible was speaking to me, and in my ignorance, I was missing it. This new season was going to be a season of training. Thankfully, God is patient. Well, I attempted to recreate the words but it didn't seem the same. I even went so far as to look up

MOVE FORWARD

Hebrew words so I could say those words during prayer hoping that would prime the pump and get the flow started again. That didn't work.

The regional manager for the insurance company called and we set up a day to meet for an interview. I met with the regional manager for the special investigative unit, or SIU, and we talked for over two hours. He was also a retired police sergeant who had an obvious passion for investigative work. I knew God had opened a door before I was even able to knock. In all the years of police work, I most enjoyed investigations. The regional manager didn't say much except that I was definitely the candidate for the open position. He explained that he did have several other interviews scheduled, and he would let me know. A couple weeks later, I was officially offered the job, I accepted, and that same day I typed up my letter of resignation/retirement from the Aurora Police Department.

My head was spinning with the speed at which God was working in my life. It was evident that He was coming alongside, in essence, and directing me into a whole new realm for my growth. Since I had languished 27 years in the wilderness, the Lord knew, I needed to begin a new season. A month later, I was retired and began my new career as an insurance investigator.

During the interim, I was off work the entire month of September, 2014. One evening Tonya and I attended a house meeting at Gary and Gail's. At the meeting were Owen Carey from New Hampshire and Donald Rumble from New York ministering. Don gave a message, and Owen then moved prophetically, giving prophetic words over various people in the meeting. Owen then prayed over a couple who had been sitting behind me. As Owen gave the prophetic word, he placed his hand on my shoulder. Throughout the word, I had an image of a very thick rope; the type that would be used to secure a cruise ship to a dock. The image of the rope coincided with the prophetic word given. I didn't say anything at the time. It was a few weeks later before I shared the image I had received with the couple. They confirmed that it did speak to them, and the situation they were dealing with. I was to discover, although through baby steps, that when I was in the company of the prophetic, I too would be given something. As it was when the messengers that Saul had sent to take David. When they came into the presence of a group of prophets, they too began to prophesy (1 Samuel 19:20).

The following Sunday Tonya and I attended a Fellowship, where Owen Carey was ministering. He gave us a prophetic word. In that word from the Lord, it was prophesied that "changes were coming. These changes will be difficult but as we make the adjustments, everything will get better. We haven't even begun to see what God has in store for us in His Kingdom." It didn't seem that there could possibly be any difficulties, everything appeared to be going extremely well. I was about to discover, that the prophetic is given as an encouragement. Prophetic words should always be recorded and written down so as time goes on, we can look back take comfort, and be encouraged that God really does care for every aspect of our lives.

When Jesus taught the disciples about the two sparrows sold for a copper coin, and that the very hairs on our heads are numbered the point was that we do not need to fear. We are more valuable than many sparrows, and God has even the smallest of details already figured out (Matthew 10: 29-31).

My first official day as an insurance investigator was October 6th of 2014. Those first two months were challenging for me. There was a tremendous period of adjustment. I did not expect the transition to be so difficult. For the first time in my life, I was now a virtual employee. Welcome to the 21st century. I was the guy who before taking this new job wanted to go back to having the one rotary phone in the house. Really! So, this was truly a leap into a new dimension for me.

Just prior to my starting the new job, a box, about the size of a washing machine was delivered. It contained a printer, monitors, a keyboard, and a host office gadgets I would need to set up my new home office. What was I supposed to do with this stuff? Then the laptop arrived. I had worked for a large city police department for over 22 years. I was accustomed to having IT people hook everything up, and if there was a problem, they would show up and fix it. I discovered that this was all up to me. No way! Those first two weeks were horrible. There were numerous difficulties in getting everything set up, password issues and just learning to navigate through a new system of programs to do my job. At some point during the frustration, it was finally figured out that I had not even had a profile set up on the network to access anything except company emails. This was after spending days on the phone with our IT service, which was overseas. That was painful.

I went out in the field with the new boss to work investigations. My first investigation was in Chicago, and I was driving all over the Chicagoland area. Meeting my boss in the morning, and driving home in the evening. I was learning patience in all of the Chicago traffic. Once I was home, I would spend hours trying to figure out how to enter notes, and otherwise do the job. There was also mandatory training that needed to be completed in the first 30 days.

Of course, it was online training. I felt as I if was going to buckle, come unglued, lose my mind. Perhaps I had made a mistake.

It is times like these that we need to review and pray over the prophetic words that have been spoken over our lives. Those words are Words from the Lord. As Christians, we can know the general will of God through reading His word. However, when a prophetic word is given, and it bears witness with our spirit, it reveals the will of the Lord for our lives more specifically. As I read the letters Paul wrote to Timothy, there was an encouragement given, from an Apostle, hand-picked by Jesus Himself. Timothy must have gone through his share of difficulties as he began his ministry.

"Do not neglect the gift that is in you, which was given to you by prophecy, with the laying on of hand of the eldership. Meditate on these, give yourself entirely to them, that your progress may be evident to all." 1 Timothy 4:14-15

There is a lot in these two verses but for now, Paul was encouraging Timothy to not neglect that which was given to him through the prophecies spoken over him by the eldership. Timothy was to also meditate on them, and give himself entirely to them. In other words, those prophecies are to remain at the forefront of our lives, and we are to give ourselves to them completely so that they may direct our lives as God intended them. After all, a true prophetic word is the word of the Lord.

For me this was difficult. I had been prone to just giving up. This was a new season, and I did have a new attitude. These trying days were a test of my faith. Would I remain faithful or faultier? There were battles with my old self through these days. It reminded me of the training from police work. Many officers would presume that they would rise to the occasion when they were confronted with that life or death situation. However, the reality is that we, even police officers will fall back to our level of training. So the officer who doesn't spend much time training on his tactical skills can't expect much under enormous pressure where a decision needs to be made in a moment of time.

There were battles with my old self through these days.

To my credit, over the years I did read, and study the Bible, so I would retreat into the word. I found myself praying over the following verse, on my knees.

"We are hard pressed on every side, yet not crushed, we are perplexed but not in despair, persecuted but not forsaken, struck down but not destroyed." 2 Corinthians 4:8-9

This was definitely a pruning process that the Lord was taking me through. In the past, I would have drowned my frustrations with plenty of beer. Though I did struggle through the process, eventually I was able to see through it. Pruning is done to bring forth new growth. John 15:2. Every branch that bears fruit God prunes so it can bring forth more fruit. Bearing fruit is not instantaneous, it takes a season to produce fruit ready for harvest. This season was yielding fruit, so I was in a continual growth process. I heard Pastor Bill Johnson says that God is always positioning His people for increase. I would later be able to look back, and realize that the pruning was for fruit that would be needed in the future.

The retirement from the police department and the new job was a tangible blessing. As I mentioned, I had been in significant debt prior to retiring. Since I had worked for the city of 22 years, I was given a severance package based on the years of service. Virtually every bit of it went to pay off the debt. Most guys get the chance to buy that new truck, or other prized item for themselves once they retire. I paid off the debt. It was a blessing. If anyone has been in debt knows it is easy to add to (debt) but almost impossible to get out of. So, the Lord did bless us. There was also a company car that came with the new job. At the time, I was driving Tonya's 1999 Ford Taurus, which had over 220,000 miles on it. It was so rusted out that the oil change place that I took it to refused to put it on the lift. They were afraid it would crumble. The poor guys had to jack it up with a roll under hydraulic lift and use jackstands. Praise God for the company car.

The new job brought a new focus. It was a part of the pruning. My entire life I had been one who was more concerned with my own agenda, or self-interest. Now I was learning to make changes, and look at the big picture so to speak. The job became a priority, yet walking in a manner that was worthy of the Lord was always present. My new job began in October. Being from Illinois means that October is the start of bow season. That's deer hunting if you didn't know. The year before, I had arrowed a 12 point buck in a lot near the house. I was eager to get out there for a repeat. The new season the Lord had brought me into didn't leave much time for bow hunting. I knew the Lord was pruning me from my old pursuits. I'm not suggesting that there is anything wrong with bow hunting, or almost any hobby.

> *The new job brought a new focus. It was a part of the pruning.*

However, if that hobby or pursuit becomes such a focus in your life, it may be grieving the Lord. It's possible that it may be hindering you from seeing breakthrough in your life spiritually. For me, there was a need for a season to let bow hunting rest.

During my daily times of prayer, I would continue to press Holy Spirit for the utterance as I begin to speak, that a new tongue would come forth. My traditional Pentecostal understanding of being filled with the Spirit and speaking in tongues as the only evidence of such was confusing. The Holy Spirit had been moving, and giving me a glimpse of what was to come. But where were the rivers of living water? Then one Saturday morning during prayer, in a very soft voice, as I began to speak, Holy Spirit gave me an utterance. I was speaking in an unknown tongue. It seemed like a complete sentence of an unknown dialect. Then I simply followed that with the words in English. There was a clear, and direct word from the Lord. "That was a tongue and that was the interpretation". Whoa! I was so excited. I usually prayed in my home office. So, I must have gone back into the office a dozen times during the day to make sure the "tongues" still worked. It did every time. Tonya had also been struggling with speaking in tongues. She was to the point that if she heard one more person tell her…" just begin to speak, the Spirit will give you the utterance", she would scream. So, being the brave soul that I am, I didn't tell Tonya for three days that I had been speaking in tongues. Tonya wasn't happy with me that I had kept that from her.

The following Saturday there was a Holy Spirit conference at the York's house, and Solomon was teaching. The conference taught on the operation and work of the Holy Spirit.

At the conclusion of the teaching portion, there was an invitation to come forward for anyone who wanted the baptism in the Spirit. Several people forward to receive the baptism in the Spirit. I decided to get a cup of coffee in the kitchen. When I returned, there was a small group of high school girls and one of the girls was frustrated that she had not received her prayer language. She was even more frustrated because one of the girls there had only been a believer for 2 weeks, and had just been baptized in the Spirit. The new believer was standing there speaking in tongues. Tonya recruited me to help pray for the frustrated girl. I didn't want to get involved. I could plainly see the girl was upset.

Reluctantly I set my coffee down, and a group of us prayed over the girl to be filled with the Spirit. As we prayed, I was praying in the Spirit. But at some point, I stepped away because there was so much commotion that I wasn't even sure if I could pray in tongues. Nothing seemed to be happening as we prayed. The girl, Andrea seemed to be getting even more frustrated. I noticed Solomon sitting on a nearby sofa, and requested him to come over and help. I quickly explained to Solomon that Andrea wanted to be filled with the Spirit. Solomon responded sure, let's pray. He then took my right hand and placed it on Andrea's forehead, and Solomon, Tonya, and I began to pray.

An anointing came upon me, and I began to speak in tongues, very boldly. There was a tremendous flow of the Spirit. It was a completely different dialect from the week before. The living waters just kept flowing. I was astonished. Then I began to get louder and the tongues were flowing from me. This had never happened before. I heard Tonya speaking in tongues. This was her first time speaking in tongues. Then Andrea began speaking in tongues. It was incredible. The flow continued for several minutes, until there seemed to be a release from the intensity of the Spirit. There were hugs and rejoicing when we stopped. My legs felt wobbly and I needed to sit down. I hadn't felt like that since GGG just a few months before. Then I realized that everyone in the house seemed to be staring at us. Oh my. What just happened? Was I really that loud? Now, I really needed to sit down. Where was my coffee?

What had happened was an anointing of the Holy Spirit that came upon me, to do the work the Lord wanted in Andrea's life. Remember, I had only been speaking in tongues for a week, and it was nothing like this. An anointing is a tangible measure or presence of the Holy Spirit imparted upon those whom God chooses. This anointing gives the person the supernatural ability to fulfill God's call, either in a situation, or a call in their life. When the anointing comes, there is power. It is this power that Jesus referred to when he told the disciples that they would receive power when the Holy Spirit comes upon them in Acts 1:8. They would need such an anointing as they began to spread the gospel throughout the land.

The anointing may have been upon me as an individual or God may have taken the same anointing that Solomon had and put it upon me. We see in Numbers 11:17, & 25, that was exactly what the Lord did with Moses and the seventy others. Regardless, the anointing was for the purposes of God to achieve a breakthrough in Andrea's life. I did not realize it then but the blessing I received as a result of Andrea's breakthrough was overwhelming. It was through the prophetic anointing of two men of God at an altar only a few months before that Tonya and I received a breakthrough. Andrea's breakthrough was something that we could not have managed in our own efforts. It was a moving of the Holy Spirit. The anointing for speaking in tongues was upon me for several days.

Andrea explained afterward that when my hand was on her forehead it was like flaming arrows, or electricity, were shooting through her. Andrea also said that she felt weak in the knees afterward. I would later learn that this manifestation of the Spirit is common. Although not everyone will receive a tangible manifestation such as Andrea had. I will cover the various manifestations and their purpose in more detail later in chapter seven.

God was doing a quick work in Tonya and me. The past five months had been incredible. Yet, the journey was only just beginning.

2

The Early Years

The reality is that we are spiritual beings living a temporary human existence. We are not merely human beings living to have a spiritual experience. Although many people live their lives in the natural as "mere humans," as Paul says in 1 Corinthians 3:3. When living exclusively in the natural, we tend to seek to have a significant spiritual experience that will validate ourselves as "spiritual" people. We were ALL created in the very image, likeness, or similitude of the Triune God; Father, Son, and Holy Spirit (Genesis 1:26). Since we were created in the image of God, who is Spirit, we are spiritual beings.

We were not created at the time of our natural conception. I cannot explain it entirely. Paul writes to the Christians at the Church of Ephesus that we were chosen, before the foundations of the world that we should be holy and without blame before Him in love (Ephesians 1:4). Further, we are His workmanship created in Christ Jesus for good works, which God had prepared beforehand (before the foundations of the world) Ephesians 2:10. Don't get hung up on predestination, just know that everyone who lives, God has created in the spiritual. Further, before the foundations of the world were formed, God provided a Lamb, a way of salvation for each of us. However, God will not violate our free will; just as He did not violate the free will of Adam and Eve. Although God set everything into motion before He spoke the natural world into creation, including each of us, we each still have an ultimate choice. That choice is to accept the provisions for our salvation and come to an understanding that each of has been made in the image of the Creator of it all, or not.

As spiritual beings, this is the reason we each must be born again spiritually (John 3:3-6). I started this chapter with this exhortation to establish a basic principle. What occurs in the natural effects the spiritual, and what takes place in the spiritual effects the natural. The two are intertwined whether we realize it or not. The spiritual realm is very real. That is why Paul also writes to the Ephesians:

"For we do not wrestle against flesh and blood but against principalities, against

The Early Years

powers, against the rules of the darkness of this age, against spiritual host of wickedness in the heavenly places." Ephesians 6:12

As I recount my childhood experiences, you will see the many spiritual doors that had been opened, and the enemy exploited every one. It would be many years of struggling before I would be set free (delivered) of the many demons that plagued my life.

My earliest childhood memories were of my dad coming home drunk, and fighting with our mom. I would run down to the basement and stand on the landing crying. On one occasion, my brother Jeff, who was 12 years older than me, came downstairs, and we left in the car. I remember that the fight was so bad that there was bouncing around upstairs. I believed then, and still do, that the argument turned physical. Many years later, I asked my mom about it, but she denied that it had turned physical. In any event, I never really had much of a relationship with my dad.

On Sunday mornings my dad would take me to a café that was on the first floor of the city of Aurora city hall building back then. I would sit on the old diner stool drink my chocolate milk while dad nursed a hangover with his coffee. He never spoke much except to tell me to be quiet while he would thumb through a newspaper. We would sit in that café while my mom went to church. She was an Irish Catholic and faithfully attended mass every Sunday.

> *Getting my mouth washed out with soap was a routine practice. But it was not very effective.*

The impact of the dysfunctional home that I was being raised in manifested early. I recalled my first fistfight. It was in kindergarten. I began punching a classmate who was either trying to take the truck I was playing with or wanting to play with. At about the same age I had been at a friend's house playing in the backyard. I apparently was using the "f" word but wasn't aware of it. That is until the boy's mother grabbed me by the shirt, and pinned me up against a swing set pole. I recall that she was in my face, yelling "we don't use that word around here." I didn't have the faintest idea what she was talking about. She told me to go home. When I arrived home, I got my mouth washed out with soap. This was back in the late 60's when neighbors would call other parents and fill them in regarding their child's misbehavior.

Getting my mouth washed out with soap was a routine practice. But it was not very effective. I continued to swear as routinely throughout most of my life.

MOVE FORWARD

Apparently, I had picked that up from my environment.

By the time I was eight years old, our parents had separated and then divorced. I vividly recall when my mother sat me down on the side of her bed to tell me that my dad would no longer be living with us. I had already noticed that one of the pillows was missing from the bed. Although I don't remember what my mom said at the time, I do remember blaming myself for the divorce. Not an uncommon reaction for a child. Rejection set in. When I was older, I learn that my birth was not planned. Going through junior high and high school, I often believed that I was a mistake and should have never been born. Living life through that lens, nothing seems to matter really. There was a sense of recklessness to my life, because, after all, nothing really matters. I should have never been born, or so I thought.

My brother Jeff had already been off to college when the divorce became final. Unfortunately, once our parents divorced, our dad pulled the funding for Jeff's college education. Jeff came home briefly. He then elected to move away with some friends in another state. Jeff would become very transient for the remainder of his life. I didn't understand it at the time, but Jeff's world had been shattered as well. I would later learn that he had lived a pretty normal childhood. Jeff was the bright, outgoing kid who excelled in school, and sports. He had been at the University of Dayton, in Ohio when the divorce was final. I'm sure the hopes and dreams he had of a career crumbled when he was not able to register for the next semester at school.

The divorce had little noticeable effect on the household initially. My dad wasn't home very much, even before the divorce. Before the divorce, my dad had little or no interaction with me. He was rather stoic and usually just grunted when I would ask him questions. After the divorce, weekend visitations were arranged. At first, I was to spend every other weekend with my dad. He had moved to Joliet Illinois, where he was managing a Montgomery Ward store. The visitation weekends were usually the same. My dad would pick me up on a Friday evening then we would go to some bar.

There he would sit at the bar drinking, while I played with some bowling machine by myself. One weekend we went out to dinner, and my dad got so drunk he began swearing at the waitress and making inappropriate comments to her. These were suggestive comments that should have never been made, let alone in front of a ten-year-old boy. The manager threw us out. This was in the early 70's, and I don't think drunk driving was as much of a concern then. We got back to my dad's apartment where he went to bed, and I just sat in the living room alone. I hated those weekend "visitations."

Anger, hatred, and a quick temper were evident at an early age. I recall one evening my mom tried to help me with homework. I was so frustrated about something that I actually had a compulsion to just jump up and run right through the upstairs window. There was a rage inside of me that would surface at times. For some reason, when that anger started, I had a nearly uncontrollable desire to do something crazy, like jump right through a window. Years later I would come to understand of the source of that anger.

As a result of the divorce, my mom had to get a full-time job. She had been a stay at home mom ever since Jeff was born, so she was new to the job market. Mom got a job at a local Carson's Department store. A problem arose when the store hours went into the evening. It would mean that I would need somewhere to go after school for a few hours Monday through Friday. It worked out while that there was a classmate of mine whose mother agreed to watch me. For the most part, it was great. We spent our after school hours doing what kids did back then. We played with other neighbor kids, played a lot of baseball and otherwise were outdoors whenever we could be.

My classmate, however, had an older brother, who was very twisted. There were occasions he would take me into a bedroom and beat me. Usually, he would throw me on the bed, pin me down, and punch me in the head. I didn't realize it then, but he was smart enough to punch somewhere that wouldn't leave a mark. I recall that as he had me pinned down, there was such anger in his face. There was a real sense of hatred. No matter what I would say, he seemed to just get madder and keep punching me. I would lay pinned under his leg, and wonder: "why are you doing this to me?" I have no recollection of being sexually assaulted, but looking back, as an adult, I often suspected I had been. My assumption is that I had blocked the memory. Nonetheless, the trauma of the abuse would leave a lasting effect on me. As a result of the situation, I hated my dad. It was his fault I was being beaten up by someone's older brother. Tremendous anger and a hatred billowed inside of me and it would soon manifest even more.

I would not be released from that stronghold until the Lord intervened, at a very unpredictable moment, which serves the purposes of His Kingdom. I never spoke about the abuse to anyone. Ever! I never even told my first wife. This was a part of my past that was on lockdown deep within me. When I married Tonya, 40 years after the abuse, I only mentioned it occurred but never shared with her any of the circumstances. It wasn't until Tonya and I were in South Africa on the mission field that the Holy Spirit had prompted and prepared me to share that part of my life at a men's prison during a scheduled ministry. I will cover that later in the book.

By the time I was in the sixth grade, I had become unruly. I was full of anger and very quick-tempered. For reasons I could not explain then, I was the kid who was looking for a fight. I enjoyed it when a fight would start, and the other kids would

MOVE FORWARD

gather around and yell "fight, fight, fight!" At that age, I didn't honestly care how the fight turned out - win, lose or get separated by a teacher. I just wanted to punch someone. I enjoyed it. There was a school bully in the sixth grade. He intimated everyone. One day, I said something to him; he pointed at me and ordered me to meet him after school for my beating. I was pretty nervous but I met him and his friends between the church and rectory next to the Catholic school we attended. He started off by telling me about the beating I was going to get, and just running his mouth. I had had enough of his babble, so I just punched him in the face. He didn't expect that and I just kept hitting him. He never bothered me or anyone after that. Depending on how you look at it, I learned a valuable lesson that day. It became my MO from then on; punch first and keep punching until there is no fight left in the other person.

A time came when my mother could no longer afford to send to me to the private Catholic school. Also, my behavior had taken a toll on the mother who had been watching me after school. We were staying out too late on some evenings. Then I got my classmate in trouble with the police for damaging a pond in someone's backyard. I would even wander around alone sometimes. I broke into a garage once because I knew the family was gone on vacation. I stole all the tools I could carry. I had been stealing cigarettes and smoking in a nearby park. I knew word got around and I suspected my "babysitter" had had enough of me.

> *I didn't honestly care how the fight turned out ... I just wanted to punch someone. I enjoyed it.*

For 7th grade, I went to Franklin Junior High, a public school. There I took a turn for the worst. I was in the seventh grade, smoking cigarettes, getting high, drinking, and was experimenting sexually with promiscuous girls. And I got into a lot of fistfights. I still had such a desire to punch someone. I knew my mom had no idea what to do with me. I was pulling straight F's in every class. I was absolutely out of control and didn't care. For the most part, I was left to my own devices. I would walk to school in the mornings so I would sit on someone's porch before school, get high, then go to class. As a latchkey kid, after school, I was free to hang out at some girl's house, who was pretty much in the situation as me.

My getting high came to an abrupt end one night when a friend and I decided that since we were out of weed, we would break into his older brother's stash. We didn't even make it through the first bowl when we knew something wasn't right. We both started to freak out. This wasn't like any high I had experienced before. Things were moving, I was hallucinating, and I was afraid that I might die. I managed to run home and jumped in the shower, hoping that would stop the high. It didn't work. I recall lying on my bedroom floor for the rest of the night freaking out waiting for the high to pass.

I woke up the next day and met up with my buddy. He had the same experience. We later discovered that the weed we smoked had been soaked in LSD. I would then learn what flashbacks were. For the next year, for what seemed like no particular reason, I would get hit with a flashback. In an instant, I would be stoned out of my mind. One of the worst flashbacks I had, hit me in the car when I was going shopping with my mother. I was wasted while trying to find a pair of jeans at a department store. Although I was young, I was concerned that I would have these flashbacks for the rest of my life. How would I ever be able to function?

> *Things were moving, I was hallucinating, and I was afraid that I might die.*

During the 8th grade, I decided to stop smoking weed and begin playing football. I briefly attempted to get decent grades so I could stay on the football team. But it was temporary. I enjoyed football practice but soon realized that I wasn't big enough to play my position of inside linebacker. Since I was so skinny and needed muscle mass, I turned my attention to weightlifting. By the time I was fourteen, weightlifting had consumed me. It was perfect for me. I was lifting six days a week. Full of anger and hatred, I took it out on the weights. Lifting was therapeutic. But in time it would give me a false sense of being indestructible. By the time I entered high school, I was carrying some muscle and strength, which made getting into fistfights even more violent. On two occasions in high school, I got my butt handed to be me during fights. I discovered that I wasn't invincible, even with a little extra muscle. Unfortunately, it only made me more determined to be more aggressive, and not allow that to happen again.

I only modified my behavior in that I stopped getting high, and I turned my attention to bodybuilding. I did not care about school and was failing almost every class. I was continually in trouble for some type of aberrant behavior in school. I had been suspended for everything from throwing a glass beaker against a wall during class to cussing out teachers and sleeping in class. I spent more time sitting outside of the school with the "stoners" than in class.

Even though I didn't get high anymore, I still enjoyed hanging with the stoners. Mostly, I liked the stoner girls. I really didn't feel like I fit in with any of the cliques in high school. I knew I was unique and I never felt as if I was a part of any particular group. I preferred to just be by myself. I had an orphan spirit, among others but didn't realize it back then.

My propensity for fist fighting did get curbed to a great extent during one of my last high school fights. The other guy was a senior, and much quicker than me. He punched me in the face so hard I was out on my feet with the first punch. Everything was foggy. I knew I was still punching back and he was hitting me in the face. However, I could no longer feel the punches landing. When a teacher separated us, I was ready to be dragged to the office. Of course, I was suspended from school and that was all right with me. The next day my entire face hurt. For the second time in my life, I believed that my nose had been broken.

In my rebellion, I refused to conform to any kind of authority. I was determined to do everything either my way or on my own. In my mind, I was on my own, so I would do everything my way whether it made sense to anyone else or not. Even though I was skipping classes, I would sit in my car somewhere, listen to "Kansas" or "Rush," and still complete my homework. I just refused to turn it in. I especially enjoyed accounting. Odd perhaps, but there was a sense of order to it that I could follow. I was an avid reader but I would not apply myself read to anything that would benefit my grades. I eventually dropped out of high school. I was able to do the class work but simply refused. Eventually, I isolated myself from everyone and focused exclusively on working out. Bodybuilding consumed me. I was so focused with my workouts that I refused to even hang around girls since their drama was too much of a distraction.

I got a part-time job delivering furniture at a local department store. The guy I worked with was a year older than me and was the owner's son. He too was a bodybuilder. We became workout partners. He had a personality similar to mine. We were full of testosterone, and always angry about something or with someone.

During the next two years, I entered two competitive bodybuilding contests. Although I did place, I was learning that I wasn't quite as bulky as the guys who were winning the contests. My body type is an ectomorph, the small frame, slight build with small joints and lean muscle. This was not the ideal structure to have for a bodybuilder in the late 70's. Bulk was the favorite presentation for a bodybuilder. Arnold Schwarzenegger was the king of the bodybuilding world at the time. Then, bulk and muscle mass were the only way to win competitions. I kept working out for another year until I decided to take a complete break from bodybuilding.

Until then, my entire world had revolved around my diet, working out six days a week, and work. Compared to most eighteen-year-olds at the time, I was very muscular, 180 pounds with a low body fat percentage. But I knew my physique was not going to propel me into the spotlight of teenage Mr. America let alone

The Early Years

have a bodybuilding career. I elected to take up Hapkido, the art of Korean street fighting. As I matured, I realized the need to harness this anger, and energy that I possessed. My intent for taking Hapkido was as an alternative workout, with the by-product of learning to become a more efficient fighter. I continued to work out with weights but kept it basic, since I was doing so much cardio with the martial arts.

Hapkido is not only a complete system of martial skills but has a strong influence in "KI" meditation. This "KI" as it is called, is identified as the power of the universe, the vital energy and life force that is an individual's inner strength. It wasn't long before I began exploring the spiritual aspects of other martial arts practices. However, I was particularly interested in understanding this "KI." This "KI" is described as an energy that needed to be harnessed and used as a practitioner of Hapkido. My thought at the time was if I could develop my KI, as an essential element of my life, it would not only help in my physical skills but also in my life in general. I didn't realize it then, but I was searching to satisfy my spiritual nature.

Inherently we are all designed to be alive spiritually. I was seeking to understand or come to terms with a deeper meaning to life. All of the fighting techniques were great but deep down I wanted more. There was a spiritual desire inside me that yearned for understanding and meaning. I was searching.

That was why Jesus explained to Nicodemus, that each of us needs to be born again. This was a profound teaching given to this Pharisee. Jesus addressed him: **"You are a teacher of Israel, and you do not know these things?"** In other words, as profound as this may sound, it is the essence of life. Being born again spiritually is not just a means to go to heaven after we die, it is a fundamental truth for living life here on earth. I believe that Jesus made a clear distinction as He explained this to Nicodemus in John 3:3-10.

Nicodemus, a ruler of the Jews (verse 1) no doubt followed a strict observance of the Jewish traditions and the written law; the outward acts of obedience. But Jesus broke through the outward acts and said that unless a person is born again, one cannot "see" (verse 3) the Kingdom of God. Then in verse 5, Jesus said that one cannot "enter" the Kingdom of God unless one is born again. The original language of the word "see," means "to perceive not only with our eyes but to perceive with any of our senses." To perceive, notice and even discern. This is spiritual in nature. One born merely of flesh and blood cannot discern things of the Kingdom of heaven or the Holy Spirit. Then in verse 5, one must be born again to "enter" the Kingdom of heaven. The original language for "enter" is "to come into," as one would enter a house (heaven). Therefore, to enter the Kingdom of heaven, one must be born again. The distinction is, we each need a re-birth, in the Spirit, in order to perceive and discern the Spirit of God and

MOVE FORWARD

His Kingdom here on earth. It is inherent in our nature to have this spiritual rebirth. As I mentioned at the beginning of this chapter, we were created as spiritual beings, not just flesh and blood. Unfortunately, many people, myself included, seek "spiritual enlightenment" in a variety of ways that do not lead to spiritual rebirth and eternal life.

Back to this "KI." The idea was also to use your opponents KI (energy) against them with the various Judo type throws. Aikido and Hapkido use the term "KI" whereas Chinese martial arts refer to this energy as "Chi."

For the student of either Hapkido or Aikido, you were to master your KI to better control your emotions, your breathing, and your inner strength. I was aware that I needed an inner strength.

> *The idea was also to use your opponents KI (energy) against them with the various Judo type throws.*

As a child I was asthmatic. My asthma was so bad when I was in grade school, that my mom would have to frequently take me to the ER. Little did my mother or I know at the time the real source of my asthma. I have since learned that asthma is not necessarily caused by something obstructing one's breathing, such as dust, dander or pollen. Asthma is also caused by fear, anxiety, and stress. I would later read: "Usually the type of fear and anxiety which produces asthma has to do with great fear concerning relationships… it is a spirit of fear."[1] It was little wonder I had been an asthmatic child.

At this time, I was doing the deep breathing exercises almost daily, not only harness my "KI" but to also exercise my lungs and help with my breathing, and my asthma had subsided to a large extent. Because of this, I was told that I had grown out of it. However, on occasion, I would still battle with it. The deep breathing exercises seemed to help some but I was not free of asthma, at least not yet.

As my confidence and skill level grew, I progressed through the ranks in Hapkido. My desire to fight with someone waned, partly because I was maturing. But I had also become focused on learning self-control. Throughout my childhood, and adolescent years I had very little self-control. Being able to exercise self-control was a large part of my martial arts training.

---

1   A More Excellent Way by Dr. Henry W. Wright pg. 242

The Early Years

By June of 1982, I managed to get a full-time job as a security guard working the midnight shift. This worked well for me as I was able to maintain my workouts and martial arts schedule. I had been assigned to an office building in Lisle, Illinois. Since I had an abundance of free time during my shift, I began studying for my GED. Within a couple of months, I took and passed the GED test. Once I had accomplished that I decided to enroll in some night classes at the local junior college, Waubonsee Community College. I started off with computer science as my major. In time, sticking with the workout and martial arts regimen, and classes became too much. I drifted away from the workouts and Hapkido.

There was a young receptionist named Brenda who began bringing me cookies when she arrived for work in the morning. Soon we were dating, and I was completely enamored by her. Although we had only dated for a couple of months, I knew I was in love with Brenda. When I told her over the phone that I loved her, there was a pause, and I knew I was rushing things. She too was attending a community college, College of DuPage, taking classes at night, and wanted to finish her degree before getting serious. Eventually, Brenda told me that she wanted to take a break for a while. Although I knew I had rushed the relationship, I also knew I would give her some time then ask her if we could start over.

In the meantime, unrelated to my relationship with Brenda, I was re-assigned to a larger facility nearby that was under construction. A co-worker, "Shawn," showed me around the new facility and we became fast friends. He was re-assigned to a nearby employee training facility. This training facility was used to host corporate seminars and classes for the contract company that hired our security service. Shawn would gather left-over beer around the training center. He would usually fill a garbage can full of ice for the acquired beer. We would meet after work, at 8 in the morning. It became a regular, almost daily routine for us to carpool home, grab a pizza, and drink that free beer until noon, get some sleep, then get up and go to work for the midnight shift. It wasn't long afterward that I began getting high again. If I wasn't drinking beer at 8 in the morning, I was smoking weed before going to bed for the day. I had stopped working out, and taking Hapkido. I was getting either stoned or drunk every day, working, and doing homework.

Although we had only dated for a couple of months, I knew I was in love with Brenda.

Early in 1983, another buddy of mine from work, who worked at the office building I had been assigned to previously called me to ask how I had been doing,

MOVE FORWARD

with what happened to Brenda. I wasn't sure what he was talking about. He asked me if the police had contacted me since they had questioned some people at the office building. I still had no idea what he was talking about. He told me that Brenda had been murdered. I was devastated! Apparently, I was too out of touch, working the midnight shift at a different facility and getting wasted every day.

I would later learn that some guy had been stalking Brenda at school. One night after class he accosted her at gunpoint, got her into her car, shot her five times, and put her body in the trunk. He then drove Brenda's car to an apartment building across the street from the college. Brenda was reported missing when she did not come home that night. Residents of the apartment complex called to complain about Brenda's car in the parking lot. The passenger side window of her Camaro Z28 had been shattered. When the police arrived, they discovered Brenda in the trunk.[2]

I had no idea this had happened. I missed Brenda's funeral and was beside myself with grief and anger. I couldn't believe something like this could happen. This was my first exposure to mortality. Brenda was only 21 years old. The thought of what she may have gone through in those moments overwhelmed me. Looking back, I wondered, what if we still had been dating? If I knew about this guy stalking her, I would have insisted on picking her up from class. Perhaps even taking classes at College of DuPage rather than Waubonsee so I would be near Brenda. Most likely there would have been a confrontation. This guy was carrying a gun and obviously had no reservations using it. All I could do was speculate as to what could have unfolded.

For the first time in my life, I began to consider life after death. Brenda was the closest person who I had ever known to have died, let alone be murdered. Although I wasn't sure how I would continue to deal with the aftermath of such an event, I sensed I needed to make some personal changes of my own. I just didn't know how ... yet.

For the most part, my life resumed. The routine of drinking and getting high almost every morning, sleeping it off, and going to work, continued. However, on my one year anniversary at the security company, I was fired with no explanation. Shawn and I had not carpooled that day. I then learned that he too had been fired the same night. Apparently, someone had noticed our friendship, and perhaps even suspected our partaking in helping ourselves to the "free" beer from the training facility. Regardless of the reasons, there I was, out of a job with only a GED. I knew I needed to make some changes in my life.

I didn't have a lot of options, so I seriously considered joining the Marine Corps. I knew I could get back into shape physically and believed the structure would

---

2   People vs Chris Rogers DuPage County Illinois April 1983

be helpful. I also thought that learning a trade through the Marine Corps (MOS) would be my best option. However, when I told my mom my plans, she came unglued. She didn't seem to think that was a good choice, and for some reason, I shelved the idea. I've often looked back at that decision and wondered if God had his hand on my life, and I didn't even know it. On October 23rd, 1983 the Marine barracks in Beirut, Lebanon was attacked, and 241 US Marines died. Given my lack of education, if I had entered the Corps, I would have most likely been assigned to infantry. There was a possibility, based on the timing, I would have completed basic, and been deployed to Beirut as a part of the peacekeepers. Perhaps there was a measure of protection there keeping me from that possibility. It was just speculation. But now there were two events in my young life, that I had to wonder, even then, if God had been steering me away from potentially deadly encounters before my appointed time.

About a month later, I got a job as a cook at a local McDonalds. I didn't care for the work but it was a job and they offered flexible hours. At the time it was great, everyone was my age, and there were always parties to go to. I wasn't very social, and I thought I needed to try to change that. I also enrolled in Waubonsee full time to accelerate getting my associate's degree.

Since I had classes Monday through Thursday, Thursday evenings were mine to sit in front of the TV. The Thursday night line-up in 1983 for me was Cheers, Hill Street Blues, Johnny Carson, and beer. By the time Late Night with Tom Synder came on, I had smoked a couple of bowls of weed. That was pretty much my life; it was very solitary. I was a loner and I was just fine with that. Not long after Shawn and I were fired as security guards, Shawn and his girlfriend had moved to Florida anyway.

A few months later Shawn and his wife and baby returned to Illinois. When he arrived at my house, I assumed we would go grab some beers and celebrate his return. However, Shawn informed me that he no longer drank. He told me that he had become a born-again Christian. A what? You have got to be kidding me! Shawn managed to get a job at a local Christian bookstore. Initially, we did not spend much time together, since now we seemed to have very little in common. One day he gave me a book called the Satan Seller by Mike Warnke. The title was interesting enough to me, so I read it. Looking back, it is obvious that God was grooming me for an introduction to Christianity.

I was a very independent as a person. I trusted no one and had little genuine interest in others. Little did I realize how much my childhood had impacted me, and the outlook I had on life. I had become very self-focused, interested only in how to improve myself. Since my attitude was that I needed to be self-made, I was drawn to the "self-help" section of the bookstores. There I discovered books by Norman Vincent Peale, best known for writing the Power of Positive Thinking,

MOVE FORWARD

and Enthusiasm Makes a Difference. He had been an ordained Methodist minister but was better known as the pastor of Marble Collegiate Church in New York City. As a result, his books were filled with Bible references which on occasion I looked up in a Living Bible that I found in the house.

I found myself caught between two worlds. One world of self-destruction, and the other of self-improvement. It was a battle that I did not understand and would continue to fight in the years to come. I enjoyed sitting around on those Thursday nights of 1982 through 1983 getting buzzed as I watched several hours of mindless entertainment. But when Friday came, I had a desire to push into something more productive, such as my homework, or finding a nugget in one of the books I was reading that would help me to make something out of my life. I was twenty years old and wasn't proud of dropping out of high school. I had vowed that I would never be like my dad. Yet, there I was struggling between two worlds. When I was tired of the fight, there was the escape of TV, beer, and weed.

I found the Satan Seller to be intriguing and read the book nearly in one sitting. Author Mike Warnke claimed to have been a satanic high priest. Throughout the book, he wrote of the exploits that he and the members of his coven had been involved in as Satanist in California during the 70's. Warnke also wrote of the circumstances that lead to his conversion to Christianity. At the end of the book, there was an invitation to receive the Lord, which I prayed. I figured that if God could have grace and mercy enough to forgive a Satanist high priest, then He could forgive me. Right there in my bedroom, I prayed the prayer, and become a born-again Christian. It was an authentic conversion. I was born-again, and made brand new. I quit drinking, getting high, and destroyed all of my secular albums.

I found myself caught between two worlds. One world of self-destruction, and the other of self-improvement.

Although Mike Warnke would later come under scrutiny for many of the claims in his book, some of which he acknowledged later had been exaggerated. Nonetheless, God, in His purpose used the book as a vehicle to lead me to Him.

"Many are the plans in a man's heart, but it is the Lord's purpose that prevails." Proverbs 19:21 NIV

I don't know Mike Warnke's intent for writing the book. But I take it that he

The Early Years

wanted to share his testimony of how God intervened in his hellish lifestyle, and he became a Christian. For Mike Warnke, his ministry and personal life did seem to unravel. If you research Mike Warnke, you will find writings that refer to him from a fake, charlatan, a deceiver, and worse. I mention this only because God will often use even the most unconventional methods to get our attention.

There are schools of thought that suggest that someone who has had a genuine conversion would not find themselves back in sin, let alone stooping to such moral lows that may have even been worse than the state before their conversion. However, as you continue to read, you will discover that my life, unfortunately, tumbles down just such a path. In the summer of 1983, I made a genuine commitment to Jesus Christ, to be my Savior and Lord of my life. As in any conversion, there was a spiritual transaction. I had the faith to believe that Jesus would forgive me of my sins. I confessed with my mouth that Jesus was Lord, believed in my heart that God had raised Him from the dead, and in doing so, new life was possible for me. I then began to walk out my new life in Christ. Like any new Christian, I was excited to follow the Lord. As an avid reader, I eagerly read my Bible. My buddy Shawn gave me as a gift a Ryrie study Bible. I also began reading books by popular Christian authors. I had such a desire to please the Lord; to live for Him. The desire of my heart was to walk in a manner that was worthy of the Lord and to fully please Him.

There are schools of thought that suggest that someone who has had a genuine conversion would not find themselves back in sin ...

The 1980's was a time when Christians were convinced that the rapture was imminent, and the tribulation would follow at any moment. There was an air of urgency among the evangelical community of the day. At least among the Christians I had been associated with at the time. So, I was consuming the popular books on end times Bible prophecy. Being raised Catholic, I knew the basic tenants of Catholicism. However, I did not know the basic differences between Evangelical Protestantism. When I announced to my mother that I was born again, she was not happy. To her, an Irish Catholic, it was as if I had not only insulted her but now was jeopardizing my own eternal destiny. To my mother, as with many devout Catholics, attending mass and following the sacraments was the only way to ensure heaven upon one's death. So to leave the Catholic faith,

MOVE FORWARD

you were committing a mortal sin, and in danger of going to hell.

As I read and studied the Bible, I was discovering an entirely different view of God, Jesus, and doctrine. I then began church shopping.

I visited a couple of churches in the area, but that was too awkward. People seemed too eager to get to know the new person who showed up at a service and to have the visitor card filled out to schedule a follow-up visit. I elected to skip the church shopping for a while. I was still attending the local community college, which is where I met my first wife, Stacy. She was not a Christian when we met. We began dating, and initially, I did not proselytize much to her even though we began attending Christian concerts. Once, at a DeGarmo and Key concert, there was an invitation to come forward to accept the Lord. For some reason, I was resistant and didn't offer any encouragement to Stacy to go forward. She later told me that she felt inclined to go forward. Despite my lack of support, Stacy accepted the Lord as her personal Savior on her own. The relationship blossomed between the two of us. We were engaged in February of 1984, then married in September of 1984. Just before getting married, I managed to land a job with a large office furniture manufacturer in the area. I started out as a payroll clerk working the night shift. It paid well and had full benefits.

Stacy and I began attending Open Bible Church and were married in that church. The Open Bible Church was a part of the Four Square Evangelical Pentecostal denomination. Although this was not my first exposure to a Pentecostal church, it was more mainstream Evangelical than the other Pentecostal churches I had visited during my brief church shopping experiences. Life as two young, born again, Christian newlyweds was pretty good. We were involved in various ministries. Stacy and I volunteered at a local food pantry and a local homeless shelter. Stacy taught sewing classes at a woman's ministry for young expectant mothers, and I became a part of the jail ministry through the homeless shelter.

In less than a year of marriage, we would be blessed with the birth of our first child, Sarah. Stacy and I adapted to parenthood as most young couples do. During the same time, I had been promoted to assistant foreman at the factory. Although life was good, I did find it to be stressful. I was running a production line, managing a stockroom and supervising guys who were old enough to be my dad. I was fortunate to be associated with a group of believers at work. But I found that over time, I was just going through the motions in my faith.

I had lost sight of my first love; the Lord. I had allowed the stresses of life to weigh me down. Even at a young age, I was frustrated with the grind of life. I found myself agitated most of the time.

Jesus warned His disciples:

The Early Years

> **Be careful, or your hearts will be weighed down with carousing, drunkenness and the anxieties of life, and that day will close on you suddenly like a trap. For it will come on all those who live on the face of the whole earth. Be always on the watch, and pray that you may be able to escape all that is about to happen, and that you may be able to stand before the Son of Man. Luke 21:34-36 NIV**

Although the context of the passage is a warning to the disciples of the signs of the end times, the principle is on guarding one's heart. We should always guard our hearts. For out of our hearts will either flow living water or evil desires. To "guard" one's heart means to protect it. Protecting our hearts is protecting our spiritual lives from anything that may hinder or interfere with our relationship with the Lord.

I was on that slippery spiritual slope of decline but did not recognize it. Unfortunately, I was so academically inclined, that I was more interested in doctrine than in relationship with the Author of my faith. Please don't misunderstand, having sound doctrine is essential in our walk as Christians. But if Christianity is nothing more than an academic pursuit, we have missed it. In the Gospels, Jesus called His disciples to be with Him first, then He taught them, and then they were sent out into ministry. We have to know Jesus, not just know about Him. This takes having an intimate relationship with Jesus. My understanding of closeness in relationships wasn't one of real intimacy. It was more self-centered and superficial. I desired more but seemed to struggle.

In any event, I had grown uneasy with the manufacturing cycle of the company I worked for. Since we manufactured office furniture, the incoming orders cycled around the construction industry. This meant that every fall layoffs would come. The union workers in the shop would get laid off, and foreman would be fired. I had been promoted to foreman, and I was a part of management.

There was no union protection for us in management. I decided, after watching an older foreman get fired, that it was time for a career change. I needed to find a vocation that was pretty much recession proof.

Ever since I was a kid, I wanted to be a policeman. I changed my major to law enforcement and began taking some classes during the day. I also began testing at any police agency that was testing. At about the same time, the company I was working for had been sold, and it was clear that big changes were in store. Production lines were being moved out, and there were a lot of layoffs. The day came when the general foreman approached me and advised that the company was moving to Mississippi. I was welcome to relocate if I was interested. But I had no desire to relocate to Mississippi. I took the first police job that was offered to me. Just before my company officially shut the doors of the plant, I had been hired as a police officer with the Warrenville, Illinois police department. In 1987 I began my career in law enforcement.

As a part of my basic training, I spent ten weeks at the Illinois State Police academy. Although I thoroughly enjoyed the academy, it was there that I made the first major compromise of my Christian walk. In my heart, I had already compromised my first love. It may not seem like much, but once we, as believers, begin to compromise, the next one becomes even easier. I had been a Christian for over four years. My wife and I had been attending a solid Bible-based, Pentecostal Church, and I had studied so much of the Word. Yet, I was ignorant or blinded to a common scheme of the devil, compromise.

Illinois State Police training academy is ten-weeks of basic training for police officers open to Illinois municipalities. It was structured after the Marine Corps basic training. I thoroughly enjoyed the structure, the PT, and entire atmosphere. I excelled in the academy as I knew I would. I even enjoyed the morning two-mile runs with Master Sergeant Parnell, a Marine from a previous era. Master Sgt. Parnell was our very own "Gunnery Sergeant Hartman." Interestingly enough, the movie "Full Metal Jacket" was also released in 1987. I even relished being referred to a "maggot." That would only be humorous to those who are familiar with Full Metal Jacket or being in the Corps.

> *...once we, as believers, begin to compromise, the next one becomes even easier.*

I was either so caught up with my desire to excel at something, or ashamed that any expression or indication of faith would be a sign of weakness, that I never even open my Bible, prayed, or spoke with anyone about the Lord the entire ten weeks. I was more focused on fitting in and excelling at being the model cadet.

Perhaps I wasn't involved in any particular "gross sin" so to speak. But I did deliberately set aside any effort to seek the Lord during my time in the academy. It was as if I put the Lord, and my spiritual life, on a furlough. I had a "No thanks God, I've got this handled" mentality. Being a born-again Christian is not something we do when it is convenient. Unfortunately, far too many Christians compartmentalize their faith, going to church on Sunday, but living their life the remainder of the week whatever way that best suits them. Being a "convenient" Christian is self-serving. It can be nothing more than "fire insurance."

Paul wrote:

> I have been crucified with Christ, it is no longer I who live, but Christ lives in me, and the life which I now live in the flesh I live by faith in the Son of God, who loved me and gave himself for me. Galatians 2:20.

Paul also wrote: "…He (Jesus) died for all, that those who live should no longer live for themselves, but for Him who died for them and rose again." 2 Corinthians 5:15

Jesus gave His life for us that we may live. Therefore, we are to live our lives for Him, every day, every place, and under any circumstance. It is about Jesus in us, the hope of Glory, and it really is no longer just about ourselves. The Jesus in us should be evident to everybody around us. Christianity is a lifestyle, not a set of beliefs we unpack during special occasions. Then pack away until the next convenient time. Ministry is not something that we do; it's the life that we live.

The Jesus in us should be evident to everybody around us.

At this time in 1987, I obviously was not in a boldness in my walk with the Lord.

There is a spiritual principle that reflects a natural principle. You reap what you sow. If nothing is sown, there is nothing to reap. At the end of the season, you have no harvest.

Paul explained to the Galatians:

> Do not be deceived, God is not mocked, for whatever a man sows that he will reap. For he who sows to his flesh will of the flesh reap corruption but he who sows to the Spirit will of the Spirit reap everlasting life. Galatians 6:7-8

This was a new career for me, and I should have been thankful for the job opportunity. The factory that I had been working at was about the close its doors for good, and the Lord opened a new door for my family and me. I had little idea at the time just how challenging police work was going to be. Police work would demand a lot from my family and me. I was at a crossroads and should have been relying on the Lord for strength, wisdom, and protection. However, I chose to think that I could handle everything on my own.

Paul wrote of people who know God but choose to not recognize Him, or give Him the glory or be thankful. Ultimately, such people, including myself become futile (worthless) in their thinking, and then their foolish hearts become darkened (Romans 1:21). In reading the first chapter of Romans, we see that those who fail to acknowledge the God they claim to know can then fall into all sorts of sin. I had turned my back on God and deliberately chose to do things my own way. This was not a new phenomenon for God's chosen people.

God heard the groaning of His people because of the bondage that they were in. God remembered His covenant with Abraham, and God looked upon His people and acknowledged them (Exodus 2:23-25). God delivered His chosen people from the bondage that they had been in. He made a way where there was no way. Even as Pharaoh, a type of devil, came after God's people with his army, God performed a miracle parting the Red Sea, allowing His people to escape certain death and He utterly destroyed the enemy.

However, it wasn't long before God's chosen people complained, murmured, became an idolatrous people, involving themselves in a sinful lifestyle. They opted to live their lives as they saw fit. They seemed to forget all that He had done for them. In the end, God's chosen people wandered the wilderness for 40 years before entering the land that they already possessed. They did not seem to understand God's promise to them.

They simply needed to occupy what had been promised. Although they had been delivered physically from the land that held them in bondage, their hearts, and minds remained enslaved to the practices that once held them.

As a result of my own stubbornness, selfishness, and being stiff-necked (Exodus 32:9 & Acts 7:51), I too was about to wander a (spiritual) wilderness for the next 27 years. Once again, I was determined to do things my own way. As I entered this wilderness, I would carry baggage that had been collected over the years. This baggage had never been properly dealt with. The traumas and wounds of life that are often termed "baggage." A more accurate term would be "garbage." This spiritual garbage, if not disposed of, will rot and attract spiritual flies. Flies are drawn to that which is decomposing. It is no coincidence that the natural parallels the spiritual.

The Pharisees accused Jesus of casting out demons by the authority of Beelzebub, the ruler of demons (Matthew 12:27). Beelzebub, the god of Ekron (2 Kings 1:2-3), also means, lord of the flies. Think about that the next time you see flies in the natural swarming around the house, the yard, or stuck in your car. They feed off that which is about to spoil. This spiritual garbage needs to be dealt with if we are to be completely free.

Dr. Charles Kraft, of Deep Healing Ministries, uses the analogy of rats being attracted to garbage.

The Early Years

He writes:

> Demons are like rats, and rats go for garbage. With certain exceptions, then, it is the presence of spiritual and emotional garbage that allows demons to enter if they have not come by way of inheritance...[3]

That is not to say that everyone who has suffered life's traumas or been wounded during their life has demons. Rather, there does need to be an understanding that these traumas, wounds, and even deliberate acts of disobedience, can be open doors that the enemy will exploit to destroy that which God loves, which is us.

> ...the human problem is primary and the demon problem is secondary. Demons piggyback on human problems. It is never either a demon or an emotional or spiritual problem; it is both a demon and an emotional or spiritual problem.[4]

Remember, the devil has only one purpose; to steal, to kill, and destroy. His primary targets are the Good Shepherd's sheep (John 10:10). Unfortunately, there are those that are so proficient at self-destruction that the devil doesn't need to do much to interfere. They are doing his work for him and don't even realize it. They have had their senses dulled to such an extent they can no longer escape the snare of the devil. The devil can reinforce his stronghold with his minions, and the person has become a captive (2 Timothy 2:24-26).

I had deliberately taken the first steps down the wrong path in my Christian walk. I invited a "foothold" for the devil. Which the devil would exploit, and develop into a stronghold.

"In all your ways acknowledge Him, and He shall direct your paths." Proverbs 3:6

My refusing to acknowledge the Lord in all my ways and deciding to walk without Him, doing everything my own way, was an open invitation to a tremendous fall. As a police officer, I was embarking on a career where the job is to be in the mist of all that is wrong with our society. It was a time where I needed to have a relationship with the Lord. But I was about to enter the world of police work on my own.

---

[3]   I Give You Authority by Charles H. Kraft pg. 258
[4]   Ibid pg 259

3

My Own Way

"There is a way that seems right to a man, but in its end is the way of death." Proverbs 16:25

My two and a half years with the Warrenville Police Department provided an introduction into the world of police work and the police subculture. Warrenville, Illinois was not noted for its violence or high crime rate. It is a small bedroom community just 30 miles west of Chicago. I discovered that the life of a police officer is pretty much the same regardless of the jurisdiction they work in. Of course, the threat levels in more violent communities raises the physical risk officers faces during their shift. However, the hypervigilance, the biological and psychological roller coaster that an officer endures is much the same. It affects not only individual officers but also their families in many different ways. Police officers are exposed to a perverse and a tragic side of life most people never witness first hand. Police officers can suffer collateral damage and not even realize the psychological effects until significant problems surface in their lives.

In 1987, Warrenville PD did not have a structured field training program, so I rode with the senior officers who were available for three weeks. I had been assigned to work the three shifts to get a feel for the different activity on each shift. On the first night of the midnight shift, the senior officer, "Pat" and I were driving on Route 59 when we observed a vehicle in front of us weaving between the lanes. We initiated a traffic stop and approached the driver. It was December, cold, and windy, so I was not able to smell the odor of alcohol as we spoke with the driver. Nonetheless, "Pat" requested the driver to step out of the car to perform field sobriety test. We administered the field test as best we could with the weather conditions. I honestly wasn't sure if the driver was DUI. However, "Pat" gave me the nod for me to make the arrest. It's difficult to articulate exactly how I felt at that moment. I had never arrested anyone before. Although I told the driver he was under arrest for DUI, there was a complete lack of confidence in what I was doing. Once the driver was handcuffed and placed into the back of the squad car,

My Own Way

we finished up with the tow of the driver's car and drove to the PD for a breath test. Once we were in the confines of the squad car I could really smell the odor of alcohol on the driver's breath, but I still wasn't convinced that he would blow over the legal limit.

At the police station, I read him the Illinois warning to motorist, which is his warning as a driver of the legal consequences of driving at a time when his blood alcohol tested over the legal limit of .08. Then I was required to ask him if he was willing to submit to a breath test. His response was: "you're the one with the badge and the gun." He consented. To my surprise, the driver blew almost double the legal limit. The driver was charged with DUI, posted bond and was released with a court date issued. I had successfully completed my first arrest as a young police officer.

Years later, I would look back at the parallels in that first arrest, and compare it to the power and authority we as Christians have been given. At that time when I exercised my lawful authority to make that arrest for DUI, I did not recognize, as quickly as the senior officer had, that all of the elements of the offense were present. It wasn't until I had the results of the breath test that I gained the confidence that we had made a good arrest. Although I did not have the confidence when making the arrest, I continued to step through the arrest, as the senior officer nodded in agreement that it was okay.

> *The badge and the gun represented the authority and power we carried as police officers.*

The driver we arrested recognized that we, as the police carried the power and the authority over him in that situation. When I asked him if he was willing to submit to the breath test, his response was a recognition of that authority. The badge and the gun represented the authority and power we carried as police officers. At that time, I had no idea I would look back and reflect on the spiritual parallels of that first arrest. Later, I will cover more specifically what authority we do have as born-again believers. As a brand new police officer, I had graduated from the police academy but did not fully recognize my identity as a police officer. I did not have a full understanding that I represented a judicial system that was much larger than myself. When I made a lawful arrest, I had the support of that entire system but didn't realize it as a rookie officer.

Many Christians do not have a full understanding that they are the representative of their Father's Kingdom on earth. Unlike the centurion of Jesus' day who understood, (Matthew 8:8-9) I did not fully comprehend the authority at my

MOVE FORWARD

disposal, nor how to operate under such a command structure.

We read in Matthew chapter 8 where a Centurion came to Jesus and pleaded with Him to heal his servant who was "paralyzed, and dreadfully tormented." Jesus agreed to go with the Centurion. The centurion answered that he wasn't worthy for Jesus come under his own roof. Since he was one who operated under the rule of authority, he understood how authority worked. Therefore, just say the word, Jesus, and my servant will be healed. Jesus marveled at such understanding of spiritual authority and faith. "Our ability to walk in authority hinges on our ability to recognize and walk under the Father's authority."[1] In other words, the power and authority believers walk in is not in and of themselves. Rather it is of Him who lives in us (Romans 8:11). Later, we will revisit the authority we as believers have, and what that looks like in our daily walk. At this time of my life, however, I was not making any effort to understand spiritual principles.

As I began my police career, I quickly acclimated to the police culture. My on-duty hours during the midnight shift were saturated with various forms of human misery. I was exposed to my first two fatal crashes, one being a motorcycle crash. The morning after the crash I wasn't able to sleep. Every time I closed my eyes I saw the image of the motorcyclist who wasn't wearing a helmet. In this bedroom community, we responded to a lot of domestic disputes. Many of these domestics were physical. I found it surprising, as I would listen to the people fight as we intervened, how depraved their lives had become. It was during one of these violent domestics that I was involved in the most hard-fought fight with a suspect of my police career. It eventually took two officers to subdue a 150-pound young man who was high on cocaine. Initially, when I attempted to arrest him for domestic battery, although I outweighed him by 50 pounds, I was not able to get him handcuffed. He displayed superhuman strength and had no adverse reaction to pain. It took a second officer to repeatedly slam this guy's head on the tile floor to knock him out before we were able to handcuff him.

I also found myself in situations at calls where I was offered invitations by females that were difficult to resist. I managed at the time to resist the mire of the sexual temptations that were offered. However, the erosion of my moral foundation had begun. In time I was back to drinking after work. Usually once a week a group of us would stop at another officer's apartment after the midnight shift and have a few beers. For me, this opened a door for me drinking periodically alone at home as well.

There is a level of cynicism among police officers that it not usually understood outside of the profession. Many police officers tend to simply carry a contemptuous distrust for all humans and their motives. When most people see a young male walking through a parking lot, they see a person looking for their car. Most

---

1   Emotional Survival for Law Enforcement by Kevin M Gilmartin pg. 27

My Own Way

cops see the same person and see a car burglar. These changes were becoming evident in my life as a young police officer. Even for the most well-grounded person entering the police profession, change in personality and outlook on life are inevitable. These changes will affect not only the officer but also their family and will challenge their core beliefs.

"What happens to young enthusiastic and idealistic men and women when they begin thinking everything is 'crap'? How long before the core values and idealism they brought to the job, begin eroding and start seeming like a meaningless, useless and extremely naïve way of viewing the world that police officers see every day? And how long before this belief spreads to the remaining areas of an officer's life?" [2]

As I was transitioning into this cynical young police officer, it was convenient for me not go to church since I was working the midnight shift on the weekends. By this point, I was not being fed spiritually. I was not reading my Bible, praying or going to church. I spent what quiet time I had reading "true crime" books. I was completely immersed in the police culture, and nothing else really seemed to matter.

I was not blind to my spiritual condition, but I was living in open rebellion against the Lord. I was in a season of enjoying a carnal lifestyle. I relished the attention and possibilities I was receiving from the females I was encountering on the job. As a "Christian," I should have been evaluating the path that I was on. My heart was just beginning to harden. I was also too caught up in myself to consider how my lifestyle may eventually significantly impact my wife, our children and even those around us who knew we were a Christian couple. At about the same time, a scandal erupted with televangelist Jim Bakker, who had an affair with his secretary. I recall ridiculing him for such a moral failure. Although I had not committed the act of adultery, I had laid the foundation for the same moral failure.

In **Colossians 1:13: "He (God) has delivered us from the power of darkness and conveyed us into the kingdom of the Son of His love."** Once again, God has delivered His people from the power of darkness (evil) and transported us into the kingdom of His beloved Son. Although all of the resources of His Kingdom are truly available to us, we have to make a choice whether or not we are going to access what is available for us. We also have to make a decision to exercise the authority we possess as believers.

"It is the will that ultimately makes each individual choice of whether we will sin, or obey. It is the will that chooses to yield to temptation or to say no. Our wills then, ultimately determine our moral destiny, whether we will be holy or unholy

---

2   When Heaven Invades Earth by Bill Johnson pg. 83-84

in our character and conduct."[3]

In understanding the operation of our will, we need to understand that what our heart desires our wills, will follow. Therefore, we must be ever careful to guard what thoughts we entertain and what influences our emotions.

I was guarding neither, and setting myself up to be entangled in the sin that can easily trap the unguarded heart of a man (Hebrews 12:1).

That was precisely why Solomon wrote:

"**Above all else, guard your heart, for it is the wellspring of life.**" **Proverbs 4:23 (NIV)**

The word heart, in Hebrew, "leb" is used widely for the feelings, the will, and even our minds; it is the center of us, our inner man, or soul and understanding. It stands to reason that the best defense is an aggressive offense. Paul writes in **Colossians 3:1-2 "If then you were raised with Christ, seek those things which are above where Christ is seated at the right hand of God. Set your minds on things above, not on earthly things."** This is to be an active pursuit of the heart (inner man). Then in verse 5, we are told to again be proactive:

"**Put to death, therefore, whatever belongs to your earthly (carnal) nature, sexual immorality, impurity, lust, evil desires and greed, which is idolatry.**"

Yet there I was becoming too comfortable with my carnal nature and doing nothing to prevent a potentially serious moral failure. Still, there was a faint spiritual heartbeat. I was once again caught between two worlds. One world of self-destruction, and one of self-preservation. There was a battle for my soul, but I didn't recognize the conflict beyond my desire for sin, and not wanting to suffer eternal consequences. My struggle was only in quiet moments when I was alone.

> *I was becoming too comfortable with my carnal nature and doing nothing to prevent a potentially serious moral failure.*

I had been offered a job with the Geneva Police Department which offered more pay and appeared to have a better long-term future. I took the position as a

---

[3] Do What Jesus Did by Robby Dawkins pg. 167

patrolman but soon discovered that as far as a law enforcement career, this was most likely not the police department for me. Geneva, Illinois is what I would consider more of an upper-class jurisdiction. The city was not plagued with crime. Once again, I was assigned to the midnight shift. Patrol work on that shift was mostly boring. Unless I made a DUI arrest early in the shift, I would drive around conducting business checks. My time with Geneva PD became a transition period of sorts.

There were no moral challenges in my encounters as a patrolman. The long midnight shifts gave me a chance to listen to a host of preachers on Moody radio. Although I was not going to church much, I was back to reading my Bible some. But I was still allowing a lot of worldly influences such as secular radio, TV, and reading a lot of crime novels to diminish what spiritual advances I might have potentially made. I was not addressing the source of the problem. I was only allowing God into my life when it was convenient for me, listening to sermons as I drove around at night. This was having little impact on my spiritual development. My heart was not willing to change. I did stop drinking, but these were superficial changes. The behavior modifications were not going to produce any lasting effects or life changes that I truly needed. Although I was listening to sermons on the radio, I was not acting on much of anything I was listening to. I was a classic example of what James wrote about.

The long midnight shifts gave me a chance to listen to a host of preachers on Moody radio.

> Do not merely listen to the word, and so deceive yourselves. Do what it says. Anyone who listens to the word but does not do what it says is like a man who looks at his face in a mirror and after he looking at himself goes away and immediately forgets what he looks like. James 1:22-24

After a year in patrol, I was offered an opportunity to work in investigations. I knew from my time in the police academy that I wanted to work as a detective. Working investigations in Geneva wasn't very dynamic, but it was a great opportunity to work on something that interested me. I was also able to work the day shift with weekends off. I was attending church again on Sundays. However, I was merely going through the motions; reading my Bible and going to church occupying a church pew. There was no commitment to my Christian life. I was just floating along, doing what I pleased, no longer honoring Jesus as Lord, nor as the Savior,

MOVE FORWARD

as I had once confessed Him to be.

As Christians, we need to understand that we have been bought with a price (1 Corinthians 6:20), and as such we are to honor and glorify the Lord with our bodies, and our spirits. I was on the verge of spiritual bankruptcy, and I was unaware of what that really meant. I completely lacked a fundamental understanding of the potential impact this spiritual bankruptcy would have. I was only willing to make slight modifications in my behavior but those "changes" lacked any real spiritual depth.

I still believed in the basic tenants of Christianity, but I was no longer living out those beliefs in the real world. Unfortunately, I had succumbed to a compartmentalized version of Christianity. As if Christianity can be considered a belief system of convenience. Go to church on Sunday live life my own way the remainder of the week. Tragically, I would eventually regulate what I believed to an academic understanding of Christianity.

> If our study of the Bible doesn't lead us to a deeper relationship, (an encounter), with God, then it just is adding to our tendency towards spiritual pride. We increase our knowledge of the Bible to feel good about our standing with God, and to better equip us to argue with those who disagree with us. Jesus did not say, "My sheep will know my book." "It is His voice that we are to know. Why the distinction? Because anyone can know the Bible as a book, the devil himself knows and quotes the Scriptures. But only those whose lives are dependent on the person of the Holy Spirit will consistently recognize His voice.[4]

After a year being assigned to investigation at Geneva PD, I was hired by the Aurora Illinois Police Department. Aurora, Illinois is the second largest city in the state of Illinois, with Chicago being the largest. During the early 90's, Aurora was notorious for the amount of gang violence. Working patrol on the night shift with APD was a complete contrast from my time in Geneva. We were running from call to call every night. I was initially assigned to the midnight shift. We were responding to shootings, violent domestics, burglaries in progress, getting into foot chases with suspects. It was what a young police officer would call "real" police work.

Being a city police officer is a unique life. These officers are literally putting their lives on the line every day when they hit the streets. Not only with the obvious dangers of the street but the risk of losing everything they may have worked for if something were to go wrong. Their family life also suffers tremendously. As you continue to read my story, understand that is not unique in the sense of the perils and negative impact that the police profession has on officers and their families.

---

[4]   The Pursuit of Holiness by Jerry Bridges pg. 124

My Own Way

As a new hire, I was to be assigned to the midnight shift and had to work weekends. This meant once again that I was not going to be attending church. With my heart not into following the Lord in any meaningful way, occupying a church pew every Sunday was not likely to benefit my spiritual life anyway. Back then, my attitude toward attending church was more of what's in it for me? What bullet points could I get out of listening to the sermon? Since then, I have discovered that our local assembly of believers is to be an equipping center for everyone who attends. A place where believers can join together as one body, the body of Christ. Then, as the body is joined together in unity, each has something to give, and there is an expectation of His Kingdom manifesting because His people are there together. These days, I so look forward to attending a gathering of like-minded believers. A place where the worship team understands they are not just singing songs, but ushering in the very Presence of the Lord. The atmosphere is charged with the expectation of what the Lord may do in the midst of His people. The local church is also to be a source of love and encouragement for believers as they gather, and share life together.

> Consistent love for other Christians is key to a healthy spiritual life because having loving fellowship is God's prescribed environment for growth. The kind of love is based on commitment to God Himself. To be committed to God is to be committed to His community, the Church. This is not a commitment to the theory of the Church, but to an actual body of other infallible, imperfect people.[5]

Unfortunately, I had chosen to live my life independent of God, and not in response to Him or His Word. I had elected to live a life independent of authentic relationships with His people. Although I had attended church more than I had been, I had no desire for His people or His community. I was just a "church attender." The carnal life is easier to camouflage when you are not exposed to people who are living a surrendered life to the Lord. When a Christian refuses to surrender their life to the Lord, they, in essence, live out of the natural, which is contrary to a life in the Spirit. Therefore, a Christian, such as myself, is set up to fulfill their carnal desires. Such a Christian is refusing to acknowledge a need for God, refusing to recognize what has been accomplished for him (Colossians 1:19-23), and denying for himself the resources available to him through Jesus, and His Kingdom. It's a refusal to surrender, which would mean trusting in Him.

Choosing to live a life independent of God must be very grievous to God. For it was God, who, in His love, who chose us. "…just as He chose us in Him before the foundations of the world that we should be holy, and without blame before Him in love." Ephesians 1:4

However, at this time in my life, I was more excited about what I may be involved

---

5   Everyone Gets to Play by John Wimber pgs. 34-35

MOVE FORWARD

with on the street as a patrolman. I hadn't even made it out of the training program before my field training officer (FTO) and I had been shot at. On a quiet Sunday morning, as we drove past a park in a black and white squad car, some guy shot at another person in the park. Neither of us could believe what we just saw. The person who had been shot at ran, and we drove into the park. I had been driving and my FTO was in the front passenger seat. When the shooter saw the squad coming towards him, he ran. And as we got closer, he turned and fired a round at the car. My FTO, hanging out of the window was about to shoot the guy but he dropped his gun and stopped running. The guy, a gang member, was drunk and was walking through a park carrying a .44 magnum. It was evident that this was not going to be a boring place to work. Once I had completed my field training, I went to the midnight shift.

One night as I was driving near the downtown, a general dispatch went out of a subject with a gun, driving a dark colored pickup truck. The dispatcher gave out the location where the truck was last seen, and there I was at that very intersection; the truck passed right in front of me. I knew when the driver looked over at me it was the suspect. I wasn't able to get on the radio right away, a common occurrence back then because of all of the radio activity. I activated my emergency lights the driver accelerated, turned off his lights, and drove down an alley. I was now in pursuit but still couldn't get on the radio with all of the other radio traffic.

> *When the shooter saw the squad coming towards him, he ran.*

By the time I was able to call it out, the driver had ditched the truck and was running on foot. I probably sounded like Mickey Mouse calling out my location on the radio as I ran after him. The subject ran around an apartment building and without giving any thought to what I was about to do, I ran around the same corner. When I came around the corner, all I saw was a silhouette, then I heard the gun shot. We were between two buildings and I heard the sound of a bullet whizzing by me, like in an old western movie.

I fell face first to the ground, pulled my gun, looked up, and the subject was gone. I ran up the hill between the two buildings. The subject was gone but there was a .25 caliber pistol lying there on the sidewalk. I was surprised it was only a .25. To me, at that moment, the gunshot was so loud I would have expected a .357. I called it out that I had been shot at and the subject was last seen running from the scene. I didn't have a clue where he ran. Nor, did I care at that moment.

The magnitude of what just occurred hit me and adrenaline dumped into my system. I was shaking as my body began to process all of the adrenaline pumping through me. We were so busy that night that only the shift Lieutenant showed up to make sure I was okay. I said I was fine, and he drove off to the next cluster (that was the term we used to describe the crazy situations at hand). So, there I was, with a discharged gun and an abandoned truck. I had just been shot at. Perhaps this should have been a "come back to Jesus" moment for me, but it seemed to just reinforce a sense of bravado and an embrace of a lifestyle in the police culture.

My home life was initially relatively normal. As normal as a home life can be with a type A personality police officer, who preferred to occupy his off-duty time weightlifting, and reading crime novels. I was not investing in my marriage or kids. Looking back, it is easy to see the self-centered lifestyle I developed by the time my daughter was 8 years old, and my son was 3 years old. A few months after getting hired by APD, my mom was diagnosed with stage 4 non-Hodgkins Lymphoma cancer. The surgeon removed a large tumor from her abdomen but told us that she was full of cancer, and it was only a matter of time. Jeff had moved back home from Utah and was living with our mom. He agreed to help her since he wasn't working. However, in the years that Jeff had lived out of state, he had become an alcoholic. It was clear that his drinking wasn't going to allow him to be much help. As a matter of fact, when I would arrive at my mom's house to check on her in the morning, Jeff would either be already drunk or passed out. He was becoming more of a hindrance than any sort of help. I clearly was not going to be able to count on him to take care of mom at this stage of her life as I had hoped.

I had just been shot at. Perhaps this should have been a "come back to Jesus" moment for me ...

As a result, I had to take her to all of the doctor appointments, usually bringing my son with us. Anyone who has had to watch a loved one suffer through cancer knows that these are difficult times. My mother, once an active and happy grandma, was now struggling with the routine of getting through the day. She was on an aggressive chemotherapy which seemed to do more harm than good. It is hard to tell which was worse, the cancer, the chemo or the side effects from the chemo. Mom was either going to the doctor's office or the hospital a couple times a week. I would stop by on Thursday, since she would have chemo on a Monday, and find mom slumped in the chair. Her white blood cell count would drop so low that I would have to pick her up, put her in the car, and taken her to the ER for blood. This was becoming a weekly occurrence. Jeff was either too drunk to notice, or not at the house.

I left the midnight shift for the afternoon shift, which was very busy in Aurora. On top of the gang shootings, there were car crashes, domestics, and an assortment of in-progress calls. There were periods during the shift that we were able to patrol the neighborhoods. One day, as I drove through a westside neighborhood, I saw a woman washing her car in her driveway. She attended the same church that my wife and I did. After a brief wrestling match with my conscience, or more like my courage, I decided to pull in the driveway and ask her, jokingly if she would wash my squad car next. She laughed and responded: "Sure." We spent the next hour standing in her driveway talking. The fact that I was actually able to spend an uninterrupted hour talking to someone was unusual for the afternoon shift. This woman was divorced and had a daughter and a son the same age as mine. An inappropriate relationship quickly developed. I was then stopping by quite often to "check" on her, which progressed to stopping by one night after my shift. I had no business placing myself, or this person, a woman from my church, in a predicament such as this.

By the time I had left her house early in the morning, I had committed adultery. To some extent, I could not believe that I had done such a thing. But given the state of how I was living my life, the hardening of my heart, and my bankrupt spiritual condition, I wasn't surprised.

I was in a carnal state, a condition which resembled an unsaved person. However, this former state was about to be worse than my pre-Christian condition. Although there was guilt, for the most part, the guilt was overridden by the thrill and excitement of an inappropriate relationship. To compound the fact that I was now involved in an adulterous relationship, the relationship was with someone from the same church my wife and I were attending. The church we were attending was a small church and there was no way to avoid the awkwardness of being in the same church service as a person with whom I was committing adultery. Worse yet, this was the same church that I had made a covenant with my wife years before. The same church where, as a part of the service, we, as newlyweds had an invitation for those in attendance to receive Jesus as their Lord and Savior. So, there I sat with my wife, and only a few rows behind me was a woman with whom I was sleeping with.

> Throughout the Old Testament, the sin of adultery is used to symbolize spiritual bankruptcy. According to the prophets, in departing from their relationship to God, disobeying the Covenant and turning to pagan gods, Israel become a spiritual whore. While claiming the privileged relationship to God, Israel was apostate in their hearts and lives.[6] See Ezekiel 23:37

---

6 Ibid pgs. 32-33

My Own Way

By this point in my life, I was spiritually bankrupt. I was operating out of a dry well. I was apostate, a backslider, in a spiritual state that would resemble anyone who had never even professed to be a Christian. I know there are those who suggest that anyone who finds themselves living such a life of sin may never have actually experienced a spiritual rebirth and a genuine conversion. However, I can say that there was an authentic conversion. What I had done, and would remain doing was to put Jesus to open shame, which is equal to public disgrace (Hebrews 6:6).

Through my selfish choices and unbridled desire for sin, I was stepping into exactly what I had set up for myself. At this stage, although there were twinges of spiritual discomfort in what I was involved in, I was in a mode of managing these mixed up portions of my life, so there wasn't an explosion. I abandoned my commitment to my wife and the vows we took. I abandoned my commitment to the Lord.

I abandoned the role of a Godly father and Christian example for my children. The reality of it was I had long since abandoned each of these even before I committed the act of adultery. The physical adultery was now the evidence in the natural as to what had already occurred within me spiritually. The adulteress relationship had continued for several months before I confessed to my wife what was going on. The fallout was immediate and overwhelming. My wife was devastated. Our pastor and the church was also impacted. I would later learn, like anyone involved in such sin, that others around us were already suspicious and there was talk. I moved out of the house and moved in with my mom, and Jeff. The kids were young, but it was evident that they were being impacted by the wrecking ball going through their household.

My wife and I began counseling with our pastor as I was working to untangle the mess I had created. I could see the confusion on the faces of our kids when I would stop by, and I recalled the tremendous hurt I felt as a kid when my dad would stop by. To make matters worse, I didn't have much of a relationship with my dad, he was just "a" dad. As dysfunctional as I was, there was a bond between my children and me. Now, I had to face the fact, that I had fractured that bond. I knew I had betrayed them, my wife, and the Lord. I recognized that in a sense, I had now become exactly what I vowed I would never become - like my dad. There was also a vague understanding that I had damaged something that was far beyond my complete comprehension at the time. It was more than a cognitive or an emotional disappointment with myself, and the damage I had inflicted on everyone around me. Guilt would eventually set in, and it fueled a dislike for myself. Worse, the enemy (devil), would use my guilt and shame as a stronghold of believing God would never forgive me. Guilt is a powerful weapon, the devil enjoys using it against people, especially Christians. Unfortunately, this sentiment can be fueled by some well-meaning Christians, but mostly by those bound with a self-righteous attitude.

As you read this book, you will understand that I will make no excuses for my sin. Yet, there are times when Christians are a part of serious "messes" in this life. It is in these times that mature Christians should be willing to come alongside a brother or sister overtaken by sin and do whatever they can to usher in restoration.

"Brethren, if a man is overtaken in any trespass, you who are spiritual restore such a one in a spirit of gentleness, considering yourself lest you also be tempted." Galatians 6:1

In time, it was agreed that I should move back into the house as a part of the rebuilding of the marriage.

By March of 1994, mom had lost her battle with cancer. She slipped into a coma shortly after we had a gut-wrenching talk about her dying. A couple weeks before, believe it or not, I had led mom in a "sinners" prayer. I knew the plan, I just had my own struggles in living the authentic Christian life. While mom lay in the hospital in a coma, Jeff arrived at the hospital very drunk. He did not stay very long. Shortly after he left, I received a call from an officer, who had stopped Jeff driving through town. It was a tough call, I was not happy with Jeff but asked the officer to park the car and give him a ride home. I would pick up the car later. Mom passed away the following day.

> *By March of 1994, mom had lost her battle with cancer.*

During this time we lived on the near east side of Aurora. Unfortunately, the kids knew the sound of gunshots and routinely hid under the dining room table whenever they heard them. This was a response that they came up with on their own. We lived on a busy street near East High School, so there was always a lot of traffic. One night while I was assigned to the "patty wagon," that's what was used to pick up prisoners, I was driving toward my house when a car went through the stop sign right in front of me. The car was occupied by three subjects, and the person in the back seat kept looking back at the police van behind them.

The car sped up, and they were now fleeing from me. I hit the emergency lights and called out that I was behind a car that was taking off. We were not allowed to pursue in the transport vans, so I wanted another east side car to intercept them. What appeared to be three gang members were fleeing from the police as I drove right by my own house, my daughter out in the front yard waving at the police van as I whizzed by. Then, three blocks from the house, the driver hit the brakes, the rear passenger door popped opened and the backseat passenger took off on foot. I pulled the van ahead of the subject, who ran around the van, I jumped out and gave chase on foot. I was able to catch up to him and tackle him. I then discovered that he had a loaded pistol in his waistband. Turned out he was a juvenile gang member and they were most likely out looking for a rival gang member to shoot.

By then there had been two shootings in front of our house, we decided it was time to move. We relocated from the east side of Aurora to a far small town west of Aurora. The kids were attending a private Christian school and my wife was working a full-time job. As best as possible we were functioning as what may have appeared to be a typical American family. However, I was not providing my wife, or the kids with the love and nurturing they needed or deserved to remain healthy. I knew I was not loving my wife as husbands are called to:

"Husbands, love your wives, just as Christ also loved the church and gave Himself for her." Ephesians 5:25.

This is a selfless love that we as husbands are to give to our wives. This is not a love of convenience or in response to what we get. The Greek word used here is agapao, which, as one can assume from the text, is a love that is wiliness to deny self, and regard another above self. An agape love.

> *This is a selfless love that we as husbands are to give to our wives. This is not a love of convenience or in response to what we get.*

I was aware of the Godly responsibilities as a husband and father. But I was choosing to do everything my own way. Refusing to submit to a Godly order for a household. Although I was facing difficulties of a stressful, and unusual profession, it was no excuse for refusing to be the man God called me to be. Being a husband, and father is more than putting food on the table and a roof over the heads of those who depend on you.

As husbands and fathers, we are the spiritual gatekeepers for those who rely on us. This is a serious responsibility and is not to be discounted. As the husband, father, and leader of the house, we are also responsible for ensuring that the house is more than a structure for everyone to live in. It is to be a home, where your family has a sense of belonging. Where kids can grow up, make mistakes, and know that love and grace are always there. A home is where a wife also has a sense of belonging, and that agape love, not harshness radiates from her husband. I had provided little to none of the above.

When Joshua gathered the people (tribes) of Israel together (Joshua 24) he reminded them of all the Lord had delivered them out of, and as such, he took a stand, that he would not serve other gods. "…**But as for me (Joshua) and my house, we will serve the Lord.**" **Joshua 24:15** This is to be much more than a wall ornament that we hang on the kitchen wall. This is to be the heart of every man who has chosen to be a husband and a father. Also, Moses told the Israelites that they were to observe all that the Lord had commanded them.

"You shall teach them diligently to your children, and shall talk of them when you sit in your house, when you walk by the way, when you lie down, and when you rise up." Deuteronomy 6:7

Teaching our children the ways of the Lord should come from the heart of a man, who loves the Lord with all of his heart, all his soul, and with all his strength. The man of the house is to pursue the Lord and mentor his children in all that the Lord has "commanded," which is what we find in His word. The principle is to train up a child in the way he should go, and when he is old (adult), he will not depart from it. Proverbs 22:6. If we refuse to honor these Godly principles we should not be surprised by the harvest that is later reaped.

After being in patrol for just over two years, I was approached by the Lieutenant of investigations, who recommended I put in for an opening in the general assignment unit of the investigative bureau. In September of 1994, I was a detective with APD, and a month later I was the lead detective on a gang murder. One afternoon just after 3 PM, a call of shots fired had gone out on the east side. The neighborhood where the shooting occurred was known Latin King gang territory. There was a rival gang member who lived in that area. He had been standing on the inside of the front door waiting for a ride when three gang members walked by, one of which fired multiple rounds through the front door. The victim, armed with his own gun ran outside after being shot but collapsed on the sidewalk. He was later pronounced dead by the medics. When I and some other detectives arrived, the victim was still on the sidewalk, where he'd remain until the coroner reached the scene and did his job as we canvassed the neighborhood. There were some witnesses, but no one would offer any information. One woman remarked to me, "We can clearly see a person is not even safe in their own house, they'll (gang members) just walk up and shoot you." So, the cycle of gang violence would continue in the city of Aurora for years to come.

Over the course of the next 11 years, I would arrive at one crime scene after

My Own Way

another. I stayed in investigations until my promotion to sergeant. I did return to patrol for a year, after yet another affair, which I will cover later. During my tenure in investigations, I responded to virtually every type of death investigation imaginable. I would be involved in the investigations of murders, suicides, unexplained deaths, bodies found in fires, and in the Fox River. The manner and methods of death would vary but the routine of the investigations was similar. As detectives we would be called out to conduct a scene investigation, usually with the victim still at the scene. Valuable evidence can be discovered on or around the body. It was also useful in establishing the proper perspective for the detective to understand how the death occurred when the body was still at the scene. I would attend the autopsy and then continue the investigation. In 1996, Aurora would reach a record level of homicides, mostly attributed to gang violence. Each detective was assigned a night that they were on call after midnight. I was working the 4 PM to 12 AM shift, would get home about 1 AM. I usually got to bed after 2 AM. Then the phone would ring. It would be a dispatcher advising that there had been a shooting and someone was dead. I would get dressed, grab coffee and work on the new homicide for the next couple of days. Then head back home exhausted. This cycle would continue.

By this point in life, my role as a husband and father consisted of paying the bills, mowing the lawn, and setting the garbage at the curb. I attended some of the kid's events and programs, but with my work schedule, I missed some. There were no legitimate attempts on my part to maintain a healthy marriage. I had regressed into escape behaviors. Life had revolved around my depraved world of death and the investigation of death. During this time, I had been sent to several death investigation schools to learn more about the various causes and manners in which death can occur and how to testify of such. I had pretty much moved into the basement of the house and was sleeping on the sofa by this time. In the mornings I would drive the kids to the Christian school, they attended, as I either listened to *Disturbed,* "Down with the Sickness" (such sad irony) or Metallica. There were times that my daughter would even ask me to turn it off. Which I would but as soon as I dropped the kids off, I would listen to some sort of heavy metal music as I drove to the office. Out of the mouths of babes came a plea to turn off the evil that I allowed to contaminate their spirits. My daughter may not have understood at that time, but she recognized what she didn't want to hear. It was spiritual poison, and I was allowing it to infect her atmosphere. I had developed such a twisted view of life. By now, I had opened the front door of my spiritual house, and I might as well have put a sign out front that all demonic spirits are welcome. Understand once you've opened a spiritual door, you do not have to advertise. The demonic is aware, and more than ready to take advantage of such an invitation. The devil and his minions truly are roaming, or "walking" about seeking whom they may devour. 1 Peter 5:8-9. We are to resist them (demonic) not invite them in.

I had not been drinking for several years. I supposed that Jeff, being what I referred to as a non-functioning alcoholic, had some effect on me. Jeff was unable to function with even the rudimentary tasks of adult life. Knowing that alcoholism seemed to affect the males in my family line, and my previous experience with alcohol, I didn't want to fall into that trap. But by 2000, I was back on the afternoon shift and began going out after work for a couple of beers. I wasn't really in a hurry to get home anyway. Even if my home life had been "normal" everyone would have been in bed by the time I got there, and I would just be sitting in the basement channel surfing. But home is where I should have had my focus. Instead, I was going out to have a couple beers with a female "friend." We were friends. Regardless that both of us were married, and having a drinking buddy of the opposite sex is only an invitation for temptation. My rationale did not conform to the realms of "normal," let alone what would have been considered prudent Christian thinking. My aberrant mentality was driving me, and if something seemed contrary to anything wholesome, or Godly I was now pursuing it.

After a couple of months of bar hopping the suburbs and in the city of Chicago with my female "friend," we were sleeping together. Once again, I was in an adulterous relationship. However, I did notice a very distinct difference this time. There were no twinges of guilt, no sense of betrayal, and I eagerly pursued the morally depraved lie of an "open marriage" lifestyle. Although I did not admit to my wife that I was in an adulterous relationship, I knew that she eventually knew. I no longer cared. My heart had become so hardened, and my conscience seared that I gloried in what should have been my shame. I had not only turned my back on the Lord, but I had also denied that I, at one time, was in agreement with the covenant God had made with me, through His Son, and the blood He shed for me.

> *Once again, I was in an adulterous relationship.*

During all this, the Lord, in His unfailing love, sent a woman to my door with a prophetic warning. I knew this dear lady from the nearby church that I had attended years ago, and my wife attended at the time. She explained that the Lord had put it on her heart to tell me that the path that I had chosen was only going to lead to destruction. As she spoke, I thought that she was just too late. I'd already ventured down that destructive path. When she left that day, I knew that God had sent her to me, but I was puzzled by the timing. I rationalized that had she only been here a few weeks prior, perhaps I would have heeded the warning. So, I disregarded the warning. I thought it was too late anyway. God was stepping in, as He does. God is always speaking to us if only we would listen. At the time, in my ignorance, I was unaware that someone could be moved by Holy Spirit to give a word of warning. Meaning that they could receive a word of knowledge from the Spirit of God, and deliver a message of warning. Such a visit from a person filled with the Holy Spirit was out of the goodness of God. Whether I recognized it or not. After all, it is His goodness that leads us to repentance (Romans 2:4).

This was a dangerous and foolish position to place myself in. But by now the hardening of the spiritual arteries had blocked even the most fundamental truths of God's love for me, and His plan for my life. As a result of my open rebellion, I had surrendered myself to the enemy. The writer of the book of Hebrews writes:

> **If we deliberately keep on sinning after we have received the knowledge of the truth, no sacrifice for sin is left, but only fearful expectation of judgment and of raging fire that will consume the enemies of God.**
>
> **How much more severely do you think a man deserves to be punished who has trampled the Son of God underfoot, who has treated as an unholy thing the blood of the covenant that sanctified him, and who has insulted the Spirit of grace." Hebrews 10:26-27 & 29 (NIV)**

There is only one sacrifice acceptable unto God to cleanse us from our sins. That is the redemptive work of Jesus on the cross. I knew of the sacrifice made for me and had accepted, or entered into covenant with God to receive what had been done on my behalf (Romans 5:8). Yet, I had deliberately chosen to ignore my responsibility in honoring God. I had trampled underfoot, or despised the sufferings of Jesus, in pursuit of a sinful life. What an insult to the Spirit of Grace. I was a living example of the type of person Paul writes about in the first chapter of Romans.

"For this reason, God gave them up to vile passions…" Romans 1:26

The adulterous relationship eventually came to an end due to the difficulties of juggling such an affair. It certainly did not end because of repentance on my part.

I continued to live in darkness, and it was closing in on me.

I continued to live in darkness, and it was closing in on me. By this time, whenever I got a call to respond to a crime scene in the middle of the night, usually a shooting and someone was dead, that I would pop in one of my favorite CDs, *Drowning Pool,* and listen to the song, "Let the Bodies Hit the Floor." That was what I was considering normal. Everything seemed to be closing in on me and I did not fully understand what was happening. When I got home after work, I would sit in the basement and drink beer, every night. There were times I would just sit in the dark. Sometimes I felt as if I was going to come unglued. For the most part, I had isolated myself from everyone unless there a legitimate reason for me to interact with them. This included even my family to a large extent. I was a miserable person. Under a stack of books on an end table next to my recliner was my Bible. I could no longer bear to even pick it up.

One evening at work, we received a call of a shooting in front of an apartment complex. The call was that an adult woman pulled up in front of her parent's condo, got out of her car, and after getting their attention, shot herself in the head. There was a history of calls at this address, where the same daughter was either transported to the hospital for a psych evaluation or other domestic problems involving her. I responded and conducted a scene investigation, which did, in fact, appear to be a suicide. I then met the assistant coroner at the ER where she had been transported. We put on rubber gloves to examine the entry and exit wounds along with the gunpowder burns on the woman's right hand. I was putting the pieces of the woman's shattered skull back together in an effort to find the abrasion collar (the dark markings on the tissue of the entry wound where the muzzle of the gun had been at the time of impact). Although I had been involved in such forensic activities in similar investigations for years, this was the first time that when I had finished, I asked myself: "What am I doing?"

A few years earlier, the movie Sixth Sense came out. In the movie, young "Cole" asked his psychiatrist played by Bruce Willis: "Do you want to know my secret?" His secret was that he "sees dead people." I would often joke, even to my kids, that "I see dead people." It had become my tagline. When the phone would ring at home, immediately I would respond with, "I see dead people," assuming that it was a call out for a detective.

I didn't catch the sad irony then. Young Cole was haunted by seeing into the spirit realm of people who had died. In the movie, Cole tells Bruce Willis, his clueless psychiatrist, who himself did not know he was dead, that he sees dead people all of the time, "and they don't even know they're dead." Such was the state I was in.

I no longer had any understanding of the love of God. Even if someone had quoted Scripture about the love of God, it probably would have had little effect on me since I was so blinded. I had wandered so far from the truth of God's love I could no longer grasp it.

I did make efforts to get my life in order, but these efforts were self-seeking and distractions from my responsibilities as a "Christian," husband and father. I began working and riding horses. I told myself that I needed an outlet for the gruesome realities I was encountering all of the time with my job. Having such an outlet can be great therapy for anyone who needs to have some quiet time and a change of

My Own Way

focus. But I should have invested that time and energy into my marriage and my children. I discovered that while I was around the horses, I had to stay completely focused on the horse. Whenever I was around the horses, I thought of nothing else except the horse I was either riding or working within the round pen. In time, I was immersed in the culture, and life of a "cowboy." I began to barrel race at locals shows, joined the local sheriff's departments mounted search and rescue unit. I was also going to bars, and again drinking with female companions.

Then one day as I was driving my truck I broke out in a great sweat. My chest began to tighten and there was a crippling pain running down my left arm. I was having a heart attack! I managed to pull in the driveway. No one was at the house, so I called 911. By the time the medics arrived, it seemed like the heart attack symptoms had lifted. The medics took my vitals and although my blood pressure was somewhat high, they advised me that everything seemed normal. I was soaked with sweat and knew I had not been hallucinating. I was transported to the ER but released after the EKG and blood test did not reveal any indication of a heart attack. When I followed up with a cardiologist, I discovered that I had had a panic attack. The symptoms were identical to an actual heart attack. The cardiologist ran me through all of the tests and advised that my heart was fine (perhaps my biological heart). He suggested that I cut back on coffee but did not prescribe any other form of treatment.

I did not know what was going on with me. So, I reverted to stress management measures and relaxation techniques that I thought would help. I deliberately slowed down the pace of my life. I did the best I could to stop my anger outbursts and swearing. I spent time after work listening to instrumental music. But the panic attacks continued. They were getting to me. These panic attacks began to hit me at the onset of stress. Like testifying in court. I had always enjoyed testifying before. But now these attacks were crippling my ability to function.

Drinking didn't even seem to help. I was drinking even more after work to ensure I had a good enough buzz to sleep through the night. I would later learn that these panic attacks were the physical manifestation of a spiritual condition. "Panic attacks are a phobic, fear and anxiety disorder. A panic attack is an aggressive stage of a fear and anxiety disorder." "It is caused by a spirit of fear."[7] Fear comes to torment, and produces various disorders, such as panic attacks. My life of deliberate disobedience, and relishing in all that was contrary to God, was catching up with me. As with King Saul:

"For rebellion is as the sin of witchcraft, and stubbornness is as iniquity and idolatry. Because you have rejected the word of the Lord, He also has rejected you from being king." 1 Samuel 15:23

---

[7] A More Excellent Way by Dr. Henry W. Wright pg. 290

MOVE FORWARD

Although I was certainly not chosen to lead the nation of Israel as King Saul, I had given my life to serve the Lord, and turned my back on all that I knew was of the Lord. Saul had acted foolishly and refused to obey the commandments of the Lord (1 Samuel 13:13). Deliberate disobedience will bring consequences. So it appeared that I too would be under the influence of a troubling spirit.

"But the Spirit of the Lord departed from Saul, and a distressing spirit from the Lord troubled him." 1 Samuel 16:14

All of the self-medication, behavior modifications, and relaxing techniques were not going to rid me of this spirit of fear, or troubling spirit that was upon me. All of these efforts were nothing more thn me shadow boxing. I had rejected my first love and was in a dire predicament.

"There is no fear in love, but perfect love cast out fear, because fear involves torment. But he who fears has not been made perfect in love." 1 John 4:18

I had rejected the perfect love of my life and I was refusing the love of everyone around me. And, I certainly did not love myself. I had become a miserable person. I could not believe that after all the sin I had been involved in, after knowing the truth that there was any forgiveness for me.

There were times I would sit in my recliner, grab the NIV Bible off the end table, read Psalm 51, and desired the same forgiveness that David sought. I "wished" it was possible for me. But I lacked any hope that such forgiveness was possible for me. I would read through 2 Samuel where David, a man, who had a heart for God, committed adultery with Bathsheba. Then David, in a diabolical plan, had dinner with Bathsheba's husband and got him drunk. David, even after having a face to face dinner with the man (Uriah), whose wife he had been committing adultery with, sent orders for Uriah to the front lines of battle to be killed. Although the consequences of his sin would remain upon David, and David's household (2 Samuel 12:10-11), he was nevertheless forgiven. It was the desire of David's heart to be forgiven. David would eventually walk in that forgiveness and his restoration with God. Not so incidentally, it is often taught that this was a momentary lapse

> *All of the self-medication, behavior modifications, and relaxing techniques were not going to rid me of this spirit of fear ...*

for David, and a desperate plot to cover up his sin. I will tell you from my personal experience, and professional experience as a detective, that people don't just wake up one morning and find that sin like this just happens. Many will attempt to convince their audience, that "it just happened." It doesn't. I believe, as was the situation with David, this was not the first time he had spotted Bathsheba taking a bath. But it was the first time he was willing to send Joab out into battle while he remained home (2 Samuel 11:1). I will speculate, that David had already conceived the sin in his heart and when the opportunity presented itself he took advantage of it.

I presumed that I had gone too far. Surely God would not forgive me. There I was, operating out of place of hopelessness. A person without hope toils in a toxic environment. Their whole outlook on life, relationships, and even potentially inspiration of scriptures may have little effect. I am not suggesting that the Word of God is powerless (Hebrews 4:12). But people will reject the word of the Lord for a variety of reasons. And those who have come to place where they have lost "all" hope, will filter everything through that muck of despair so it won't breathe life on them. It may be great seed, but the soil of their heart is polluted.

> *I presumed that I had gone too far. Surely God would not forgive me.*

This attitude also carries a perverse sense of pride. Carrying this prideful attitude is to suggest that somehow the redemptive work of Jesus on the cross is insufficient to clean up our sinful mess. This is a lie from the devil, and to come into agreement with such a lie, is to empower the liar. Pride truly does come before the fall of one's own destruction (Proverbs 16:18).

I had reached a point in my life where I didn't feel I could take it any longer. The misery of life was too much, and I simply figured that with all the damage that I had caused everyone, my family would be better off without me. One morning, I went to workout out at the gym. While at the gym, I decided that this was the day. No one was home. So, I finished my work out and went back to the house. I was so resolute about what I was going to do, I was euphoric. I felt good for the first time in years. I had a sense of joy or gladness that soon it would all be over. What I did not know then, was that even the demonic can bring comfort to those who will fulfill its evil plans. False spirits of comfort will quickly seize the opportunity of a devastating event, such as the contemplation of suicide. The devil and his demon underlings really do roam about seeking anyone they may devour.

Once at the house, I walked down the hallway toward the master bedroom where I kept a 12 gauge shotgun in my closet. As I walked down the hall, I noticed my daughter's bedroom door was open. She never ever left her door open when she was at school. At this time my daughter was a senior in high school. I looked in her room, and on her floor, there were sorted piles of college brochures. She had been searching, and deciding what college she wanted to attend. Our daughter was about to graduate high school in only a few weeks. As I stood in the doorway, I clearly heard a voice: "You can't do this, you'll shatter her life." I closed her bedroom door. Went into the bedroom, and sat on the edge of the bed. Whatever that voice was. It was right. I couldn't do it.

The euphoria left me and I was frustrated. With that, I knew I needed to make some changes. I had been just a moment away from my own death. Perhaps to some, it was just one of those things (that my daughter's bedroom door was open). I knew then, as I do today, that once again, despite my own doings, God was intervening in my life. There was a real battle going on, and I didn't understand the spiritual significance of the battle. The enemy had not succeeded that day. It would certainly not be the devil's last attempt to take me before my appointed time.

Not long after my near brush with suicide, I had a serious horse riding accident. I had been practicing a barrel pattern with a barrel racing horse I owned at the time. On the very last run, the person watching me yelled: "Run like you have nothing to live for." I responded: "I have nothing to live for," as I cued the horse to run. At the end of the pattern, as the horse came to an abrupt stop, I was launched out of the saddle, hit the ground head and left shoulder first. My collar bone had been broken in four places, and I had a severe concussion. I had sustained a bruise to my cerebellum. This prevented me from laying down flat. Every time I tried to lay down everything would start spinning, and I would get nauseous.

It may have been just an accident, a riding mishap that occurs to anyone who rides horses. But I knew that for whatever reason, God must have had mercy on me. I knew I could have been killed or sustained a paralyzing injury. Since I was now off work for a while, I did spend some time reading my Bible. Although I enjoyed reading through Psalms, I was having a difficult time believing that God's love and forgiveness were for me. There was a desire for the words I read to be true for me and my life, but I had walked away. I had deliberately disobeyed what I knew to be true and went my own way. So, I remained in doubt.

Doubt will hinder faith, and one's ability to believe. When John wrote of the account where Thomas refused to believe unless he physically saw the wounds of Jesus after the crucifixion, John concludes that chapter (John 20) by letting us know Jesus went on to do so many more miracles that had not been written. But those that have been written were done so that we may believe, and in believing, we will have life in His name (John 20:30-31). Therefore, without believing, we will hinder, or even prohibit what the Lord desires to do in our lives. Thomas may not have come to fullness of understanding of what the Lord was able to do. But once he saw, he believed. The hopeless may simply refuse to believe, such as I did. I doubted it was possible to be forgiven. As obtuse as I may have been spiritually, I recognized that God, for whatever reason, must have prevented me from self-destruction again. I was a portrait of God's grace and didn't even know it.

Eventually, my collarbone healed, and my equilibrium returned to normal. Life resumed for me working and horsing around. I had become consumed with the lifestyle that revolved around the horse world. I was out at the barn where I boarded my horse three times a week. For the next couple years, it was horses, country music, and drinking beer. Going to bars on special occasions usually involved me drinking with some female companion, that I really had no business hanging around with, let alone drinking with. Eventually, I did the exact same thing that I hated my dad for. I packed up, and left the house, rented an apartment, and filed for divorce. The impact of a divorce will not only have immediate effects but will also have long lasting effects on everyone involved.

I had reached the pinnacle of failure. I had made an inner vow that I would never do what my dad did to me. I knew the hell I went through as a kid after my dad left. This period of time for me was more grievous than it may have appeared on the surface. I still worked the afternoon shift. I busied myself during the day with either lifting at the gym or being at the barn. After work, I would usually open a beer as soon as I got to the apartment. I was soon seeing a woman, Tonya, who I had briefly met a year earlier. Even though we hit it off when we first met, the relationship did not develop at that time. It wasn't as if I had a sudden case of morality then. We had met at a birthday party, at a bar, enjoyed a few beers together, and went our separate ways.

In time the relationship developed with Tonya. Also during this time, I was promoted to the rank of sergeant. I was assigned to the afternoon shift as a uniformed patrol sergeant. The transition from investigations back to patrol was a welcome change. It gave me a new focus at work, of which I was in desperate need.

Not long after the divorce was finalized, Tonya and I married. The first six months were a roller coaster ride for everyone. Tonya and I struggled, as two people sometimes do in a second marriage. She had been married before and had two children. Tonya's children were much younger than mine. All of the kids had been through enough in their given situations. It seemed unlikely that having a harmonious blended family would be possible. How would it?

Tonya and I had a tough time adjusting. Though we attended premarital counseling, we couldn't anticipate what it was going to be like unpacking all of our baggage together. Six months into the marriage, I left. I rented another apartment from the same landlord where I had previously lived. By this point, I had assumed I was a breeding ground for failure. How could I reasonably expect this marriage to be either blessed, or work, if I had not honored the covenant in my first marriage? I seemed to have a unique propensity to get mired in difficulties. I would often wonder why everything was ten times more difficult than reasonably necessary. Yet, I had no one to blame but myself.

Tonya and I were separated for six months. During this time we were going to counseling, but I was resisting making a commitment to the marriage. We eventually reconciled, and I committed to working on the marriage with Tonya. We were attending a Lutheran Church near home on a regular basis together. I had made a partial commitment to the Lord. I was reading my Bible every day, attending church every Sunday, and working on the marriage. At least, what I felt was necessary. What I lacked was a loving commitment to a relationship with the Lord and Tonya. Just going through the motions is not going to fool God, nor one's spouse. Fortunately, the Lord was not finished with me yet.

By this point, I had assumed I was a breeding ground for failure.

One Sunday morning the church choir was singing some old hymns. As was my usual mindset, I was making fun of the choir members in my head, when I clearly heard a voice: "And I love each, and every one of them!" The voice was so clear, I turned around to look at the people in the pew behind us. Clearly, they had not said anything to me. That was so freaky. It was much more than a random thought, and I knew it. The Lord was dealing with me, and I knew it. He was dealing with me about love. Which was not something I understood at the time. Over all the years in my backslidden condition, my heart had grown so hard, and calloused that I routinely said that I hated people. There were many times that I would read out of 1 John:

"He who does not love does not know God, for God is love." 1 John 4:8

I had concluded that since I didn't love anyone, and did not know love that I obviously was not a Christian. If my repeated sinfulness wasn't enough evidence that I was not a Christian, this was the most damning piece of evidence. But upon closer look, the verse correctly stated my condition. Since I did not love, I did not know God. I knew of Him for all these years. But I did not know Him, or His ways. However, in His grace, God was laying some simple foundation for me to get my spiritual footing, and lead me one step at a time. However, I was at times the one who had to learn everything the hard way. So, this process was still going to take a while.

Over the next few years, Tonya and I rode the roller coaster of good times and rough times in our marriage. Tonya had grown weary of the harshness of my demeanor, and in the way I treated her as a wife. Since I worked the afternoon shift, Tonya was left home during the evenings by herself. She would look forward to when I got home. But when I arrived home, still in uniform, I usually was in no mood for any face time. Unfortunately, all I wanted to do was to retreat into the basement, watch some old movie and drink beer. Tonya preferred, that her husband come home and simply loved her. I was setting myself up for the same failure. I saw that Tonya was fighting to have a relationship with me. I was willing to be engaged only far enough to be married in the legal sense but not in a healthy, loving relationship. I was in the same selfish pattern of doing whatever I wanted to do during my off-duty time. Go to work, and then insist on being left alone when I arrived back at the house after work. It's hard to believe that I was so dysfunctional in a relationship.

Tonya had grown weary of the harshness of my demeanor, and in the way I treated her as a wife.

The way I acted as a husband was out of a selfishness and a complete indifference to my wife, who I claimed to love. We were, reading our Bibles, going to church and I was in a routine of prayer every day. We showed up at church on Sundays and appeared to be a happy, well-adjusted couple. We were really struggling as a couple. I was missing any understanding of a loving relationship. If I was unable, or unwilling to love my wife, whom I lived with, how could I ever love God, who I didn't even know was present, and trying to get my attention.

"**Husbands, likewise dwell with them (wife) with understanding, giving honor to the wife, as the weaker vessel, and as being heirs together of the grace of life, that your prayers may not be hindered.**" 1 Peter 3:7

As a husband, we are called to love our wife, as Christ loved the Church and gave Himself for her. If we (husbands) refuse, we cannot expect much in the way of a meaningful relationship with the Lord. Holding resentment, and bitterness against our spouse will interfere with our relationship with the Lord. Peter points out that a husband is to dwell with their wife, give them honor, and to value them, though they may be a weaker vessel. Because together, they (as a couple) are heirs of grace in this life. Don't expect God to honor your prayers if you cannot honor

MOVE FORWARD

the covenant you (husband) have made with your wife. There are parallels with the natural and the spiritual, they are intertwined.

By the time Tonya and I had gone out for dinner that Wednesday night in 2014 we were both exhausted. Tonya was tired of the struggle to just be loved by her husband. I was too willing to give up on our marriage because it seemed so difficult to understand how to love; either myself or someone else. We had reached a crossroads. As Tonya and I drove home that night from the bar, there was nothing but silence. Neither of us had anything left to offer. Nothing else to say. Little did either of us know then, that in just a few days, a loving God was prepared to meet us, in a personal way at an altar during a tent meeting.

We, as humans, tend to use our accumulated life experiences, knowledge and even how we perceive who God is as the measure of what love is. We can read verses in the Bible which tell us that love is from God, that God is love. But how do we really understand God's love? God's love had been set into motion before the foundations of the world were ever spoken into existence.

"…just as He (God) chose us in Him before the foundations of the world, that we should be holy and without blame before Him in love." Ephesians 1:4

Because of God's eternal love, He chose each of us, before we ever stumbled into sin. Before we had a chance to fall short of His Glory (Romans 3:23), God made a provision to redeem each of us. God already knew some would refuse to accept His love, some of us would trample underfoot what He has done and bring shame to Him. God also knew some would thankfully receive what He has provided. Salvation has been provided for each of us out of His love.

Jesus illustrates what the love of the Father looks like in Luke chapter 15. This is part of the parable that is usually referred to as the prodigal son. We can see the love of the Father in this parable.

In summary (Luke 15:11-32), we read that a father had two sons. One was so ungrateful that he insisted on his portion of the inheritance before his father had even died. It was not customary to distribute the portions of the estate prior to the estate holder's death. The father granted the son's request to go his own way and gave him his portion of the estate. The son journeyed to a far country, squandered his money, and found himself in a desperate situation. Eventually, the son came to his senses, and told himself that although he was not worthy to be counted as a son, he would return to his father, and be satisfied if the father took him in as a servant. What stands out to me can be found in the following verse:

"…But when he (son) was still a great way off, his father (God) saw him and had compassion, and ran and fell on his neck and kissed him." Luke 15:20

My Own Way

The father (God) saw his son (us) while he was still a great way off. The father did not wait for his son to make his way home. The father ran to greet his son. The son was a "great way off." Just as we are so far off the standards of a Holy Father. Yet, the father met his son as he journeyed back to him. Despite the fact that the son put his father to open shame by disrespectfully demanding his inheritance before he was entitled to it, when the father greets his son, there is no reprimand. Rather the father greets him with a kiss, a sign, and a seal of the father's love.

The father ignores his son's rehearsed speech. He adorns his wayward son with all of the symbols of belonging to the father. The son is brought the "best" robe, a ring, and sandals. Then there is a celebration. The fatted calf, that most likely was to be reserved either this very occasion or for an offering, was killed. The father was filled with joy that his son who had been "dead" (in sin), was now alive, and no longer wandering lost.

Such a love is beyond comprehension to many of us. This is the love that met me at that altar. I stood there and wept in the Presence of a Holy God. In His Holiness and righteousness, He could have stood there with His arms folded, and rebuked me for ALL of the damage that I had done in His name. In spite of all that He had already done for me, out of His love, He met me at that altar. Who was I to stand before a Holy God?

Who was I? I was a lost son, who had wandered off and put my Father to open shame. But the day Tonya and I stood at the altar I positioned myself where He could touch me and bring me back to where I needed to be. The Lord saw me a great way off, and ran to meet me. Those moments at the altar demonstrated that He is truly a God of love! It is overwhelming to know, I encountered the love of God, I encountered God, for He is love.

4

Moving Forward

"And my speech and my preaching were not with persuasive words of human wisdom, but in demonstration of the Spirit and of power, that your faith should not be in the wisdom of men but in the power of God." 1 Corinthians 2:4-5

Having an undeniable encounter with the Presence of God will change a person forever. When I drove home that night from GGG 2014, it was then that I realized that I had just lived out a portion of scripture that were previously just words on a page to me. Although mired in sin and open rebellion there was still a small part of my heart that desired His forgiveness. However before, this encounter, I didn't have the faith to believe that forgiveness and being made clean was possible. As I drove home, I knew (had faith to believe), that the Lord had created in me a clean heart, and renewed a right spirit within me (Psalm 51:10). In the months to come, more revelation would come.

Revelation is not always mystical, or spooky, or for just a select few. Revelation is simply something that was previously unknown, now made known, in either a dramatic or undramatic fashion. This was a dramatic fashion for me. I knew I had been in the Presence of the Lord. My faith was catapulted to a place it had never been before. I was clean for the first time in my life, and in my spirit, all was right as I drove home.

Often when we refer to the "Presence" of God, we think of the term as singular, and not in the plural sense. I know I did. It's hard to understand the mystery of the nature of a Triune God, who is One, yet manifested in three distinct Persons; the Father, the Son, and the Holy Spirit. When I stood at that altar and experienced the Presence of God, it was the Spirit of God that moved upon me. When the Spirit of God comes upon, or fills a person, it is the power of the Most High God (Luke 1:35). This is what we read in 1 Corinthians 2:4-5. It was the demonstration of how the Spirit of God works, which is with power. Therefore, one's faith is not in men but in the power of God. I knew a mighty work of God had been done within me at the altar. It would take the next several months to even begin to understand the magnitude of that mighty work.

As 2015 started, I was still getting acclimated to the new job, and working as a virtual employee. The change was working well, and life outside of law enforcement was just what Tonya and I needed. We were attending a non-denominational mega-church. For the time being, we were content to stay at the church. However, in February we decided to try Living Stone Christian Church in Aurora after we heard they would be hosting a prophetic conference in March. We decided to check it out before signing up for the conference. During worship, the Holy Spirit came upon me, and I worshiped in the Spirit (tongues). I had never experienced the Spirit coming upon me during worship at a church service before. Pastor Gerry was given the message that morning. Before he started the message, he walked down from the podium over to Tonya and me and began to prophesy.

Pastor Gerry gave us a word that we were entering a new season. A season where the Lord was leading us and building a level of dependence and trust in Him. The word continued that we were to trust the Lord in this new season, and He would show us, piece by piece, what He was doing, and in the end, we would look back and say that it was the Lord who brought us through. God is so amazing. It was a prophetic word from the Lord that intervened in our lives, and He was still guiding us through a prophetic anointing. It appeared that the Lord had confirmed for us that this would be the church where we were to be equipped and fellowship.

Tonya and I were being led into a new spiritual dimension where the gifts and manifestations of the Spirit were to be a regular pattern and practice of a believer's life. This would be an area where the Lord was going to lead us, step by step, and show us, piece by piece. Our theological backgrounds and experience in this area were limited. We had been in what I would say, is more mainstream, or environments rather than charismatic. I will cover more on the gifts, and manifestations of the Spirit in another chapter of this book.

In this new season, Tonya

MOVE FORWARD

and I knew this training would challenge our spiritual understanding. It would force us to examine what we assumed Scripture taught, and challenge our long-held beliefs on how the Spirit operated. During this season of spiritual training, we would also have to realize that some of our "beliefs" of how the Holy Spirit works were not entirely accurate.

One morning, upon waking, I had a prompting from the Lord: "Build a website." Then: "For the glory of God, and inspiration of others." I laughed, as Sarah did (Genesis 18:12). I was not the most technically proficient person. I had barely muddled through all of the technical challenges of the new job. Now I was to build a website. My feet had just hit the floor, and I hadn't even had coffee to get my brain engaged. But I knew, even as a neophyte at the things of the Spirit, that what had just dropped was a prompting from the Lord. So, over the course of the next few days, I researched how to register a domain name, and build a basic website. Tonya had been away at a conference at the Hub (Chicago), at the time. By the time she got home, the beginning of psalm51ministries.com had been set into motion. Tonya would become the architect and administrator of the website. At the time, I didn't even understand the purpose of having a website. There are times when we are called to simply be obedient, and this was one of them. We are not always called to filter everything of the Lord through our own understanding.

Tonya, who had been away for a women's conference would arrive home with a fresh anointing of the Spirit. When Tonya came back, let's just say that she was "full" of new wine. Had it been another time in our life, I would have suspected that she had been riding a bar stool, and not the wave of the Spirit. For three days, Tonya just floated around the house. Nothing phased her. Nothing bothered her. She was simply basking in the Presence of the Lord. Tonya had a chance to see Carol Arnott, and Bonnie Chavda but unfortunately missed Heidi Baker. Nonetheless, Tonya was filled with the Spirit while at the conference, and for those three days had been under an anointing of the Holy Spirit. This anointing was a tangible measure of the Holy Spirit, which Tonya could sense was lifting after those three days. There was a work that the Holy Spirit had done in Tonya during that time. I recall that she only wanted to pursue the things of God, such as prayer, and staying in the Word, while she was under the anointing. The household chores mattered very little during this time for Tonya. This was a powerful encounter, which seemed to jump-start her spiritually.

As we began attending Living Stone Church, the Spirit of the Lord would frequently come upon me during the corporate worship time. Whenever this occurred I would start to weep. I didn't understand it at first but assumed that since GGG 2014 when I stood there and wept in the Presence of the Lord, this would become the benchmark for me to know when the Spirit had come upon me. Whenever this occurred there would also be a vision that came. One Sunday morning, during worship I had a vision of walking in what I assumed was heaven since I was walking on a pathway of gold. There was "someone" at my right side as if giving me a tour. I looked and saw, an endless supply of what looked like personal-sized pizza boxes. In the vision, I knew I was to give them out as I go along in life. In time, I would understand more fully what that would mean for me, and my walk as a Christian. I also knew that there was an endless supply of these personal sized boxes. I was just coming into a place of learning about the gifts of the Spirit. What may have appeared to look like personal sized pizza boxes were gifts, treasures of the Kingdom of Heaven. I would never exhaust this storehouse, so freely I have received, freely give. Please don't misunderstand. If you are not familiar with how God speaks in dreams and visions, He speaks parabolically (metaphorically). He will often use images that the person receiving the dream or vision will understand. I was not equating the gifts of the Spirit or the treasures of heaven to a personal size pizza box. That was the way the Spirit of God revealed it to me, and I how understood. It would take time for my understanding to grasp the revelation I was given. Eventually, when I stepped into personal one on one ministry with people (Chapter 8), it became apparent that I could never exhaust the storehouse of personal size gifts for anyone I encountered.

Not long after the visions began during worship, I was having vivid dreams. In time, I began to understand the difference between the dreams of my subconscience, and when the Lord was giving me something. Dreams are for the dreamer and usually will provide a warning, instructions or directions. Some of these instructions are given for the dreamer to deal with an area of their life.

We serve an incredible God, who is truly concerned with every detail of our growth. Each of us has, at times, blind spots. Areas that we don't see as a spiritual problem. But in the sight of the Lord, these may be the areas that need the most attention for us to properly grow in our walk with Him. So, while we are asleep, when our pride is set aside, and the distractions of the day are out of the way, God speaks (Job 33:14-18).

> Because dreams are produced through our subconscious minds, they will normally bypass our various self-defense mechanisms and preconceived notions about our strengths and weaknesses and go right to the truth of the matter.[1]

If you are a dreamer and recall them upon waking, I would encourage you to record them, then pray for the interpretation. For it is the Lord who provides the interpretation (Genesis 41:15-16). As you record your dreams, you will begin to see the pattern of parabolic language that the Lord will be using with you. This will give you a better understanding of the meaning of the images He uses in speaking warnings and instructions to you. I will cover dreams more in-depth in

1   Dreams and Visions by Jane Hammon pg. 68

Appendix B. Here is a quick word of advice in the area of dreams.

I believe dreams are often personal, so I would be careful in sharing your dreams with just anyone. People are sometimes quick to offer their own interpretation of the dream, and they may not have the spirit of wisdom to understand the personal revelation. Also, not all dreams and visions are necessarily from the Lord. Some may be more soulish in nature. Until you are confident in knowing the difference, I would maintain a record of them. Study them over a period of time to learn the patterns that either the Lord is using, or how your subconscious operates when you sleep.

As 2015 continued, Tonya and were asked to consider going to South Africa on a mission trip. Until then, I had no desire to ever set foot on foreign soil. We agreed to pray about it and see what the Lord would have us do. Then one Sunday morning during church worship service, the Spirit came upon me.

I stood there weeping, and in a vision, I saw myself standing in front of a gathering young black people. I was presenting to them the love of God. In my spirit, I knew this was an audience in South Africa. Visions can be more literal than the metaphoric language of dreams. I took this as a confirmation for us to go to South Africa. We then began making the arrangements to be a part of Go Missions Africa, who had a planned mission trip for August.

> *I believe dreams are often personal, so I would be careful in sharing your dreams with just anyone.*

Cape Town is a coastal city, and the second most populated in South Africa after Johannesburg. As we rode from the airport to our hotel, we passed, what seemed like, miles of shanty homes before we arrived in a more familiar urban area of Cape Town. Solomon, as founder, and director for Go Missions Africa had organized the mission trip and assembled a team from all over the United States. We would be preaching the gospel in the public schools, visit a men's prison, and do some street ministry.

In the months leading up the trip, we were well prepared as a team. We would meet, or conference call, with each other to pray. This would be the first mission trip for Tonya and I. It would also be the first time either of us would experience operating under a cooperate anointing outside of a church. An anointing is the tangible impartation of God's ability into our lives to do His work. Also stated: "…the anointing is a tangible measure of God's Holy Spirit imparted upon those He has chosen, and this anointing gives them the supernatural ability to fulfill

Moving Forward

God's call on their lives."[2] A corporate anointing carries significant power, as we minister in one accord.

Solomon had arranged with various schools, from preschool to high schools, an allotted time where an assembly was called, and one or two of us had an opportunity to give a brief testimony, preach, and have an altar call. The fact that we were given this opportunity in a public school was awesome. The response was always overwhelming. Virtually every hand would raise when we invited them to give their lives to Jesus. Throughout the trip, as we drove to each school, we were to pray in the Spirit to prepare for the ministry that day.

None of us knew on any particular day who would be called to give their testimony until the team leader would make the announcement.

One morning, we arrived at a high school, and were setting up in an outdoor courtyard. It was cold that morning. Yes, it was cold, in August, in Africa. The seasons in South Africa are the opposite of the US. I was told that I was to give my testimony to the high school students. After a time of music, I stood on a desk to give my testimony. At some point in the testimony, I realized that I was now seeing in the natural, as I looked out at the crowd of South Africa students, the vision I had in church a few months before. I continued with my testimony and the love of God. I learned a dynamic spiritual lesson that day. Each of us is "… **His workmanship created in Christ Jesus for good works which God prepared beforehand that we should walk in them.**" **Ephesians 2:10**. In other words, the reason I was able to see in the Spirit through a vision is that, in the Spirit, it had already occurred. I was now walking in that which God had prepared beforehand. That was an amazing spiritual understanding!

> *Virtually every hand would raise when we invited them to give their lives to Jesus.*

As I spoke, Tonya had her first "open vision." While I was giving my testimony, Tonya saw a golden glow around the whole body of one young man. At first, she thought it was the sun since we were outside. But the glow was only around one person. Tonya told Solomon what she saw, and he told her to speak "into," or share what she was seeing. So, after I finished my testimony, she stood on the desk, and pointed out the young man. Tonya told me later that she felt odd singling just one person out, but the glow was all around this one young man. As she began to speak out what she saw over this young man, who we will call "Sam," Tonya began to move prophetically relating that there was a call on Sam's life.

---

2 The Anointing of the Holy Spirit by Johann Melchizedek Peter pg. 9

MOVE FORWARD

That was why the Lord was highlighting him. It was incredible to see the hand of the Lord move upon this young man. We were blessed with an opportunity to pray with Sam individually after the altar call before he returned to class. Sam accepted the Lord, and we prayed a blessing over him before we left.

The next day, as we were traveling to the men's prison, I was flooded with the memories of the abuse I had endured as a child at the hands of an older brother at the sitter's house. I didn't have any idea what was going on. Why was I thinking about that now? But I wasn't just thinking about it. I knew the Holy Spirit was prompting me, and I knew, for the most part, why. I would be testifying to it at the prison.

I had not spoken of this abuse to anyone. Certainly, not in detail, and never publicly. These memories were locked deep inside of me. All the years since the abuse, the memories were buried so deep, it would require the Spirit of God to bring them forth, and He was. Situated in the day room at the prison, we were told that each of us would have an opportunity to testify to the group of prisoners. I did not want to do this at all. But when my turn came, I testified of God's love. It was in that love, He delivered me from the anger and shame of the abuse I had endured as a child. Most of the prisoners in that meeting were already Christians, so the prompting brought encouragement to any of the men who may have suffered similar abuse. By the time I walked out of that prison, I felt a massive release! God has a unique way of bringing restoration to what belongs to Him. These memories were so locked down that I didn't even know they needed to be released. I had been set free and there was a healing that day within me I didn't even know I needed. Once we were outside getting ready to board the bus, Solomon hugged me. It was all I could do not to fall apart completely. He knew that the Lord had just done a mighty work inside me ... again. Jesus did come to proclaim liberty to the captives (Luke 4:18). Praise the Lord! This part of my life had been buried for so long that I didn't see the need for it to surface in front of a ministry team. I wasn't prepared for this, but in His love and understanding, He knew what I needed. What an amazing prophetic picture, as I walked out of that men's prison in South Africa, the Lord had set me free from the past that had been on lockdown.

That was how the entire trip was. It seemed that everywhere we went, there was an opportunity for ministry. Tonya and two other team members had a chance to pray with a couple of women who had been selling bowls along the roadside. As Tonya was praying in the Spirit, one woman began crying. Tonya was able to minister further with the woman, and there was a sense that a deliverance had occurred for the woman. Then as we toured a cavern, our tour guide complained of knee pain. Tonya and I prayed for his knee, and afterward, he told us that the pain was gone. This had not only become a new season but a whole new lifestyle for Tonya and me. Little did we know then, that these would be the building blocks of an entirely new way of life. A life where ministry is not just something we do, it's the life we live.

One of the last schools we had visited was a primary school. After the structured ministry time, we had a chance to mingle with the kids. They all seemed to want hugs. They were so precious. The children ranged from toddler to fifth grade. Then it dawned on me: "Kenisha." As we walked around hugging the kids, I was asking what their names were. I did not find Kenisha. I was so sure I would have found Kenisha there as Tonya and I walked around ministering love to the kids. When we were on the bus leaving the school, I was lost in thought. "Kenisha" had to of been there. Where else would Tonya and I be to have a chance to hug and minister to a toddler, like I saw in the vision of "Kenisha." The vision was so vivid, and I knew the Holy Spirit had shown me that for a specific reason. But as we drove away, our final school of the mission trip, I was left to wonder. I would have to be patient; the vision was for an appointed time (Habakkuk 2:3).

By the end of the Go Mission Africa trip, there were 5000 souls added to the Kingdom of Heaven. It was wonderful to be a part of a terrific team to minister in South Africa. Upon our arrival back in the US, I will never forget, as we drove home from the airport, I literally could feel the anointing lift from me. The minor aches in my joints I usually carried with me, but had no evidence of throughout the trip, began to creep back in. I don't completely understand the lifting of an anointing, except that the mission finished. I would learn that there are levels of, and designated purposes for an anointing. I will cover this more in the chapter on the Holy Spirit. The ministerial anointing I had been operating under was lifting.

I had not heard from my brother Jeff in 18 years. Given his lifestyle, and since my previous attempts to locate him were unsuccessful, I assumed he was dead. In my searching for Jeff over the years I eventually searched unclaimed bodies through the various coroner's websites. Jeff had managed to live off the grid for a very long time. I finally managed to locate an address for him in Ogden Utah. In May of 2015, I sent him a birthday card with a short note. I did not receive a response. Then in November, I was surprised to get a letter from Jeff. Jeff explained that he had been having some health issues, and had been in the hospital. He had been staying at a homeless shelter in Ogden and was still alive. I recognized the handwriting on the letter and knew it was from Jeff. Shortly after I received the letter, Jeff was allowed to use the phone during an appointment with his social worker, and he called me. For the first time in 18 years, I spoke with Jeff. Wow! In December, Tonya and I arrived in Utah, and Jeff and I were reunited. It's difficult to explain my joy of hugging the brother I once hated, thought was dead, but now was reunited. God, in His goodness, made this all possible. Over the course of the next few days, we had Jeff stay with us at a hotel. We spent time together

MOVE FORWARD

catching up and Jeff showed us around Ogden. Once again, the Lord brought forth a healing that needed to occur, not only for me, but for Jeff. Looking back, for me to move forward in His purposes, this reconciliation between two brothers needed to take place. God's timing is amazing.

We invited Jeff to come back with us but he said he wanted to stay in Ogden. Even though he had been staying at a homeless shelter, he had his routine and would spend some time at a local motel since he had a disability income. One morning at breakfast, Tonya was prompted by the Spirit to speak to our waitress. After Tonya had given the waitress a word, we prayed for her. She was so touched by Jeff's story, and the word of encouragement, that she offered to be a contact person who would help look after Jeff.

> *... for me to move forward in His purposes, this reconciliation between two brothers needed to take place.*

I would learn on my return trip in 2017, that the waitress had honored her commitment. She had been giving Jeff breakfast vouchers, and he was able to come in the hotel restaurant and have breakfast. Before we left, Tonya and I lead Jeff in prayer, where he accepted the Jesus as his Savior and Lord.

On the return flight to Chicago, I noticed Tonya writing notes on a napkin. Once we landed, Tonya told me that she had a "word" for the passenger seated next to her in the window seat. Tonya began to share the word with the passenger. It turned out he was a young man was returning home after leaving home months ago. He wasn't sure how things would go once he arrived back home. Tonya's word was just the encouragement this young man needed. We also learned that he had come from a Christian home, but had been backslidden for some time. So, right there at a busy gate at Midway airport, we lead this young man in prayer. To our surprise, the Spirit of God got a hold of him, he began to cry, and took over the prayer himself and repented. Out loud, he confessed his sin and rededicated his life to the Lord as everyone else in that busy airport terminal went about their business. Praise God! Tonya was then prompted to give him some cash. He couldn't believe it. He told us afterward that he didn't have any money with him.

"But everyone who prophesies speaks to men for their strengthening, encouragement, and comfort." 1Corinthians 14:3

A prophetic word is powerful, and can change your life. My testimony is an example of that. For this young man, a couple, whom he had never met, gave him a brief but encouraging word from the Lord. It touched him so that he was willing to rededicate his life to the Lord. From what little he shared with us, this may have been exactly what he needed as he returned home to face his parents. God's timing is amazing. In the moments of leaving that plane, he was so unsure of the response he might receive when he arrived home, God intervened and gave him a word of strength, encouragement, and comfort. Stepping into moments like that make it so real that we serve a loving God, and the Kingdom of heaven is really at hand.

A few months later, Tonya and I attended an annual prophetic conference hosted by our home church in Aurora, Illinois. During one of the sessions, Eva Dooley was speaking, and Tonya leaned over and asked if I was "seeing that." I didn't have the faintest idea what she was talking about. After Eva Dooley finished speaking, it was the lunch break. Tonya had been assisting in serving the speakers in a conference room, so I met her there after lunch. Eva was gracious enough to meet with us while we were in the church office and Tonya shared with her what she had witnessed on the stage. Tonya told Eva, that as she was speaking, there was a "glow" around her as she moved on stage. Tonya explained that at first, she thought it was the backlighting from the stage. The glow originated from behind the large wooden cross at the back of the stage. Tonya saw that the "glow" lifted from the cross and followed Eva's every movement. If Eva bent over or turned to the side, the "glow" kept in perfect rhythm with her. Eva told us that others had said that they had seen angels on stage before with her, but never something like this. Eva believed that there was a reason that Tonya was allowed to see into the spiritual realm. Eva then gave us a prophetic word, which encouraged us as a couple for ministry. Afterward, Eva suggested that we would probably be a good fit for a group out of the St. Louis area that had a mission trip coming up for Jamaica. Eva recommended that we contact them, and consider being a part of that mission trip. We agreed to contact them and to pray about it.

A prophetic word is powerful, and can change your life.

During the next several months, I was busy with work, which took me throughout the Chicago and Milwaukee areas. I had bought a case of New Testaments and kept them in the car with me. Often, as I would exit one of the expressways, a homeless person would be working the intersection. I included a $10.00 gift card in each Bible, with a plan of salvation printout. As I drove to appointments, I would hand out the Bibles and gift cards to whomever I could. Sometimes I would simply hand the Bible out the window, tell the recipient that it was the bread of life and that there was a gift card enclosed for them. The person receiving the Bible was always delighted to see that someone took a moment to give them something.

One time, as I was leaving Milwaukee, I stopped under a bridge where an older man approached me.

I handed him a Bible. He looked at me and told me that he was a backslidden pastor. He started to explain the life choices that he had made but was too choked up to continue. We prayed together under the bridge, as the traffic went around us. In those moments, he needed to know that God still loved him, and needed to receive a word of encouragement. This man had a chance to see that the Kingdom of heaven could even be under a bridge in Milwaukee.

On one of my next appointments to Milwaukee, I was investigating a residential burglary. As I conducted my investigation at the insured's residence, I noticed that she had several Bibles set out and open. As I was about to leave, I asked the woman if she was a person of faith, and mentioned the Bibles she had laying open. The woman admitted that she had been raised in the church but had made a lot of poor life choices, and wasn't living the way she should. I sensed that she most likely involved in illegal drug activity. I knew the Lord was prompting me to ask her if I could pray for her. She eagerly exclaimed: "I wish you would." Without being prompted, she grabbed my hands and there we were, praying in her living room. The Holy Spirit gave me a word for her. The Spirit of the Lord touched her, and she began to weep. Then my mind kicked in. This was the first time I had prayed with an insured during an appointment. I thought, "What am I doing?"

What I was doing was what I had been called to do. I was now stepping out, taking the risk, and being the "church" outside of the walls of a church building. This was exciting, and it still is. To see people touched and positively impacted by a Spirit-filled believer in places where they may not otherwise experience a touch from the Lord. I believe each of us has a sphere of influence that we can reach for the Kingdom of heaven. As Paul put it in 2 Corinthians 10:13, this "sphere" is our very own mission field. When we operate in ministry or those works which the Lord has prepared for us before the foundations of the world (Ephesians 2:10), the flow seems effortless. To grasp our life "in Christ" is to understand that it is no longer just about us.

"I have been crucified with Christ; it is no longer I who live but Christ lives in me, and the life which I now live in the flesh I live by faith in the Son of God, who loved me and gave himself for me." Galatians 2:20

In those moments that I was stepping into "ministry," it was like stepping on those airport moving walkways. Once you step on, you just know you are headed in the right direction, and you go with it.

In May, Tonya and I went to Bethel Church in Redding California for a healing conference. The atmosphere was fantastic. Every day we were immersed in a Kingdom environment. There were a couple of huge takeaways for me. The Lord revealed to me: **"in this is love, not that we loved God, but that He loved us and sent His Son to be the propitiation for our sins."** 1 John 4:10 It wasn't as if this was the message preached, it was a healing conference. Nevertheless, in His goodness, the Lord revealed to me His mercy (Luke 6:36), and His grace (Ephesians 2:8) which all originated in His love for me (each of us). I don't serve Him because I love Him, I serve and love Him because He first loved me, even when I didn't deserve to be loved.

Perhaps that is fundamental truth for most Christians. When that resonated in my spirit, my heart's desire was to serve and love Him with all my heart, all my soul, all my strength, and all my mind, just because He loves me. I don't serve Him to show Him how much I love him. I operate out of a place of love because God is love (1 John 4:7-8). To honor and serve Jesus from a place of love is the Lordship that He desires. Jesus doesn't want us to serve Him out of obligation. Serving the Lord out of obligation is religious and lacks a commitment of the heart.

The second work that the Lord did with me at that conference was during the last evening of worship. As Tonya and I began to worship, I sensed that I was to let "it" go. In my spirit, I knew what "it" was. Over the years, I carried a tremendous amount of guilt over the life I once lived. There was a lot of guilt over the direct and collateral damage I had caused, particularly in the crippling effect of my rebellion on the faith on my first wife and my children. To carry that guilt is an oppression the devil will exploit. We may have to deal with the consequences of our sins but Jesus came to set the captives free, and we are free indeed. As this revelation resonated in my spirit, a guy grabbed me from behind and told me that the favor of God was upon me. He continued: "favor is not fair, it's just favor." I thought of the first prophetic word that had been given to me. "I had found favor with the most High God." It wasn't fair in the sense of justice but in the mercies of God; it was just favor. I would later read in a book written by Bill Johnson; "Face to Face with God: "Divine favor causes you to rise to the top in your sphere of influence, and the reality is that favor can be recognized more easily if you start at the bottom."[3]

I do believe that God is always positioning us into a place of victory. There is no one-and-done encounter with God. As His workmanship, He is ever shaping His masterpiece, and even making alterations along the way, so we will be better equipped for our assignments. By the time I left the conference, there was freedom, and a sense that in His love, God was still developing me for His purposes. Tonya and I were looking forward to what He would do next.

In one of the breakout sessions at the conference, I knew we were to go to Jamaica

[3] Face to Face with God by Bill Johnson pg. 51

on the upcoming mission trip that Eva had told us about. I had been back and forth on the decision, and the deadline had passed while we at the conference. The session we had been in at the time was about Kingdom living and learning to draw from the abundance of heaven rather from the limited resources of earth. Although nothing was directly spoken or taught causing me to commit, there was a "drop" in my spirit, and I knew we were to go to Jamaica, the mission field, and "as you go, preach that the Kingdom of heaven is at hand." When I leaned over to Tonya and told her we were to go to Jamaica, her face lit up. She said that she was sensing the same thing. The first prophetic word spoken over us was that one would get, and one will confirm. Simply amazing! That evening, Tonya contacted the trip organizer. We then learned that trip organizer had delayed finalizing the flight and we were added to the team. Tonya and I were now set to go on a mission trip to Jamaica.

Upon returning from the healing conference at Bethel, we had a renewed spiritual fervor for His Kingdom. I had been assigned a stolen auto claim in a small town in downstate Illinois. As I began the investigation I quickly learn that the vehicle had not been stolen as reported. Rather, a boyfriend who may have been dealing crystal meth had taken the vehicle, and after being awake for days, fell asleep at the wheel, and totaled the vehicle. The insured, who was married to someone else, allowed her boyfriend to use the vehicle to drop her off at work, and then the boyfriend crashed the vehicle as he attempted to drive home. Since the husband was on the policy, I arrived at his house to speak with him, and see what information I could gather. He explained that he had recently been in the county jail for burglary and possession of crystal meth. I sensed a prompting to speak to the husband on a personal level. In short, I learned that the husband "Joe" had been given a Bible while he had been in county jail but had not been reading it. I felt that the Lord gave me an analogy to use about his need to receive Jesus as his Savior. When I asked him if he would like to receive Jesus as his Savior and Lord, he accepted the invitation. So, right there on his front porch Joe, in small-town Illinois, who has struggled with drug addiction, and a wife who left him for a drug dealer, accepted Jesus as his Savior and Lord.

> *When I leaned over to Tonya and told her we were to go to Jamaica, her face lit up.*

Joe wept as he made his profession of saving faith in Jesus. I gave him some advice on where to start reading in his Bible. Just like that, I was off, following up on the information I had gathered for the investigation. I knew there was joy in heaven

Moving Forward

because Joe had just given his life to Jesus (Luke 15:7). There is another side to this spiritual battle that was not so thrilled about Joe's decision to accept Jesus. Shortly after I left Joe, his wife called my cell phone. She was upset. Apparently, Joe decided to call her and tell her about my visit. She blew up on the phone. She was upset about the investigation, and that I had spoken with her husband on a personal level. She was not pleasant to deal with originally and was now even more unpleasant. I was discovering that ministry can be messy. People who need the most in ministry often find themselves in a mess with life. Joe's wife wasn't happy about his spiritual breakthrough, or the fact that I was piecing together what really happened to her car. But I counted it all as joy.

Exactly one week before we were scheduled to leave for Jamaica, I was back in Milwaukee investigating a car-jacking claim. Our insured and her daughter had been in their car when two subjects approached. One stuck a gun to our insured's head, pulled her out of the car, and threw her to the pavement. The other subject pulled the daughter out of the car, and they fought before fleeing in the insured's car.

She was not pleasant to deal with originally and was now even more unpleasant.

The insured, "Letisha" had been so upset over the incident that she and her daughter had been staying with her sister, since she didn't want to be home alone. As I took the recorded statement from Letisha, she struggled with fear and anxiety over what had happened. Letisha felt that she had come close to getting killed, and was still terrified over it. There was a stirring in my spirit, and I knew I would need to pray for this woman. When we concluded the recorded statement, I asked if I could pray for her. Letisha welcomed the prayer. As I prayed over her, I knew the Presence of God had come upon her. I rebuked and cast out the spirit of fear, and I spoke the perfect love of the Father over her. Letisha was overwhelmed by the Presence of God. Once she was able to collect herself, she told me: "That's it, I'm going back to church." Letisha said that she had walked away from her faith. She made a fresh commitment to follow the Lord. Praise God!

As I drove back home, I was excited about what the Lord had done, and that I was a part of it. To see, and be a part of the Presence of God come upon someone was exhilarating, to say the least. I had been so caught up in thought that I missed my exit from the 94 to the 294 split going south of Chicago. So, I took the next exit, intending to turn around. When I reached the green light for the next

MOVE FORWARD

intersection, a truck went through the red light and struck me broadside. The impact spun me around, the air bags deployed, and my "bell" had been rung like I'd been punched in the head. Before the medics and the police arrived, I crawled out of the passenger side of the car since the driver's door had been crushed. Although I was disoriented, everything seemed okay except the soreness to the left side of my neck and shoulder.

I approached the driver of the truck, who apologized and asked if I was okay. We spoke briefly. I was pleasant with the other driver, thinking this would be a good time for ministry. The intersection was shut down by the police, fire department, and two totaled vehicles. When the other driver said it was "nice to meet you," I responded jokingly: "I wish I had never met you."

My comment was in jest. But at that moment I missed the opportunity to step into His Kingdom purpose. Apparently, the Lord was trying to make an emphatic point that we meet, or the enemy was beginning to tire of my pestering into his territory. In either case, I sensed that I had dropped the ball with that obvious opportunity. We need to be ready in-season and out of season, meaning that our representing Jesus, who lives in each believer, is to be "re-presented" whether it's convenient or not. I then became busy with calling my boss and the fleet services to authorize a rental. We both went our separate ways that day. By the time I was driving home in the rental, I was praying that the Lord would grant me an opportunity to pick up that fumble and represent the Kingdom of heaven to the other driver at another time.

Tonya and I drove down to St. Louis to meet the team flying to Jamaica. Everette and Faye were the leaders of that team who were from Victory Church, of Pevely Missouri. They had made this mission trip over 30 times. We were excited to be a part of such an impressive group.

On the morning of the first full day of ministry, I tried to put my contacts in after I showered. When I walked away from the mirror I realized that everything was blurry. I had worn contacts for 16 years and just assumed that I had switched the contacts around and had them in the wrong eye. So, I took them out and switched each contact. Still blurry. I stood there in front of the mirror switching the contacts back and forth from eye to eye. I finally got so frustrated that I put the contacts back in the case. I figured I wasn't driving anywhere, all I had to do was ride on the bus and go to our ministry stops. My eyesight is not that bad, but I am nearsighted. I wear contacts to see far away, and they are helpful to read upcoming road signs when I drive.

After breakfast, we loaded onto the bus and were off to Ocho Rio for our first ministry of the day. As we drove, I realized that I could read all of the road signs as if I had my contacts in. I looked at my Bible, and realized that I could read without my "cheaters." Apparently, for this mission trip, the Lord had restored my eyesight. That was the reason everything was blurry with the contacts in. This was a blessing of the corporate anointing. Throughout the entire trip, I never needed to put my contacts in. I was able to see as if I had 20/20 vision during the whole trip. I didn't need to understand; I simply enjoyed the supernatural blessing!

For our first scheduled ministry on the island, we went to Teen Challenge in Ocho Rio. Similar to our previous mission trip, we would be asked at various places to give our testimonies, but we did not know until we arrived who would be called upon. On this morning, I was called to give my testimony. I gave my testimony, and then a local pastor gave a brief sermon, and the altar was opened for anyone who desired prayer. Tonya and I had an opportunity to pray with three men who had asked for prayer. These men were eager for God to intervene in their lives supernaturally. It was a powerful time of ministry.

During the trip, we had been working in partnership with a local church out of Port Maria. The next day, we arrived at a school to host a VBS for the village children. When the church bus arrived, I was introduced to a young woman named Kenisha! I didn't know what to say. We spoke briefly and then went about our business of teaching the kids. Initially, I wasn't sure if this was the Kenisha that I had a vision about two years prior. In the vision, Kenisha was a toddler and dressed in a white dress. A few days later, the pastor, myself and another team member went to a store to pick up rice and beans to distribute to the neighborhood the next day. As we were out, the Pastor mentioned Kenisha and explained that she had come to the church recently, and was now in charge of the house they operate. I knew in just a moment, that Kenisha, now an adult, was the one whom I had seen in the vision two years before. It was like a download from the Holy Spirit. The words that came to me were: "God was calling her to have a childlike faith. The Lord also sees Kenisha dressed in white, for her sins are washed away, and this is how he sees her. Where her sins were as scarlet, they have been washed away. She is now dressed in white." (Revelation 19:8).

On Sunday, after the church service, the team was invited to pray for anyone that desired to come forward for prayer. I could see Kenisha was busy with the kids near the back of the church. I requested that Kenisha come forward, and asked Pastor Winston to accompany her. I had never done something like this before. I was excited to share with Kenisha the vision God had given me two years ago. It seemed important to share with her the circumstances surrounding who I was at the time He gave me the vision. I was nervous, but confident that the Lord wanted me to step into this. I was aware that Pastor Winston moved prophetically, and wanted him to hear everything, so that the prophecy may be judged. With Tonya at my side, I explained to Kenisha the vision God had given me, and how at the time, I had no idea what it meant or why He would give it to me. But now

MOVE FORWARD

I knew that the Lord wanted me to give Kenisha this word. Kenisha said that the word resonated with her, and Pastor Winston confirmed that the word given was accurate. He later told me that the word the Lord provided did indeed resonate with Kenisha.

To this day, I am not sure why exactly God chose me to deliver this word to Kenisha in the way He did. But the magnitude of what God did is more than amazing. At the time I had the vision, Kenisha had not even given her life to the Lord. She had been in a challenging situation living with a relative and had been subjected to a difficult life. Kenisha was learning to trust God for the ordinary things of life and needed the reassurance of how God views her. I was learning how the Lord operates for those who are in the Spirit. At the time I had the vision, I had just encountered the Lord at an altar and been filled with the Spirit. There was a flood of the Spirit within me, and I was being shown how this new life in the Spirit would flow.

"Hear now My words: If there is a prophet among you, I the Lord make Myself known to him in a vision, I speak to him in a dream." Numbers 12:6

Although I do not consider myself as one who holds the office of a prophet, the Lord was training me in His ways. The vision of Kenisha was the first of many visions, and the Lord has since spoken to me in many dreams.

One afternoon, the team had off from ministry, so we were free to swim, or otherwise do what we wanted. Tonya and I decided to take some time, and enjoy the ocean at the resort. Tonya swam out to a huge raft anchored about 50 yards off the beach. It wasn't long before it was evident that something was wrong. Tonya returned to shore quickly and showed me her forearms. Her forearms were red, swollen, and she was shaking. Tonya explained that she felt as if she had been "whipped" or stung. She had what looked like bright red "whip" marks across both arms. Tonya had been stung by a jellyfish. I grabbed her by the wrist and commanded the swelling, and any poison to leave her body in Jesus name. We then decided to go to the nurse's station at the resort but found that it was closed. I knew nothing of the effects of being stung by a jelly fish. I knew

> *I was learning how the Lord operates for those who are in the Spirit.*

how sensitive Tonya was to poison ivy, and assumed this could potentially be even worse. However, within a half hour, the bright red welts had almost entirely disappeared. She did not have any ill effects and had no pain from the stings. God healed her! I was as surprised as anyone, but very thankful. Since I have not seen many healings and certainly did not sense this was a gifting the Lord had endowed me with, I believed that this healing fell under the corporate anointing we were functioning under at the time. The enemy took a swipe at Tonya to hinder her, but what he meant for harm turned into a testimony throughout the trip. Praise the Lord!

One of the ministry stops was in Trelawny. This was a home for girls of all ages. Some were there because they had been incarcerated. Others were there because they had no family to take them in. After three of the girls from the team gave their testimonies, and an altar call, there was a time for us to minister to any of the girls who chose to remain in the day room. I encountered a girl who didn't go forward during the altar call but did want to speak with a team member. As I finished ministering to this girl, Tonya was waving at me to come over where she and Abby (another team member) had been witnessing to two girls.

One of the girls had burns over a large portion of her body, and as Tonya was praying, the girl made sounds as if she was just learning to speak. Since I wasn't aware of what was going on, I didn't realize what was happening. The other girl was excited and crying as Abby was teaching her to pray for the little girl with the burns. Then the team was called to leave for the bus, and all of the girls were exiting the day room. Tonya and Abby were in tears as they told me that the girl with the burns did not know how to speak. The other girl was so thrilled that Jesus was healing her friend, she received Jesus. Abby taught the girl how to continue in prayer for her friend that she may receive full recovery of her vocal cords. Neither Tonya nor Abby wanted to leave but we had to go to the bus, and the girls to their dorm. God

> *Tonya and Abby were in tears as they told me that the girl with the burns did not know how to speak.*

was working a miracle in that little girl's life, and her friend was so moved by the hand of God that she eagerly gave her life to the Lord. This new believer received a quick discipleship lesson from Abby.

It was an amazing trip. However, once we were at the airport, going through customs, I found that my patience had worn thin. Traveling is less than enjoyable to me most times. I've learned that it is a process of getting to one place to another, and I "function" through the "process." As we stood in line I was looking at the flight board on the wall; everything was blurry! I wasn't wearing my contacts.

MOVE FORWARD

Apparently, the corporate anointing was lifting. I just shook my head and told Tonya that the board was blurry. I laughed and made my way through customs with a smile.

A few weeks after we returned from Jamaica, the court date arrived for the driver of the truck that went through the red light and crashed into me the week before the Jamaica trip. The driver was ticketed for disobeying a red light. I knew I was to go to that court date. I intended to just sit in the courtroom, and afterward, apologize to the driver, Chris, for making a comment about wishing I had never met him. When I arrived, Chris was sitting there waiting. When I entered the courtroom, the bailiff insisted that I check in.

We were called up right away. This is not what I wanted. I did not come to the court appearance to testify against this guy, but testify to him. As we approached the bench, we each had to identify ourselves. The judge turned to me and asked if I wanted to proceed with trial, or just let the insurance handle the matter. In all my years of appearing in court, I had never heard a judge open a bench trial like this. Usually, the judge would simply ask if each party was ready to proceed. I responded that I would just allow the insurance to handle the matter. The judge then said to Chris, "I suggest you thank this man as you leave." The two of us walked out of court together.

I explained to Chris that I did not appear in court to testify against him but to testify to him. I went on to explain that I was a Christian and believed that the Lord must have been emphatic for the two us to meet. I apologized for saying that I wished the two of us had never met. Chris was gracious and told me he knew right away that I was a Christian. He then said that he too was a Christian. Chris said that he didn't think anything of the comment, and felt that I had a good sense of humor under the circumstances. Before we parted, I asked Chris if I could pray a blessing over him. There we were, standing on the sidewalk in front of the Cook Court District court building in Skokie, Illinois, two Christians praying for each other.

There are times when what has been laid before us just doesn't make any sense. Although I wasn't sure if the accident was backlash from the intercessory prayer that I had been involved in Milwaukee just a few of hours before, or if it was just an "accident." Perhaps the Lord was testing my faithfulness under difficult circumstances. Either way, I do not believe that my response is to falter. I am called to remain steadfast in the Lord.

"Therefore, my beloved brethren, be steadfast, immovable, always abounding in the work of the Lord, knowing that your labor is not in vain in the Lord." 1 Corinthians 15:58

Moving Forward

As I resumed work, my heart was torn at times. I desired to be in full time "ministry," rather than working in the insurance industry. However, I knew in my heart that the Lord had provided this job. With this job, there are tremendous opportunities to interact with people all over the country. But there are days when I am stuck in my office hammering out the details of insurance claims. On days such as these, it is tough to see past the insurance portion of the job. Although I enjoyed the investigative part of the job, I don't find the actual nuts and bolts of the insurance industry very exciting. On one of those, "less than exciting" days I believe the Lord prompted me with: "Look past the insurance and look for the opportunity." That, of course, may have been obvious, but on this particular day, the Lord's timing was perfect. I needed to see the big picture. To set up investigations that would take me to the needs of people, I had to handle other claims duties in the meantime. After all, I would never know which investigation the Lord may desire me to be involved in until they were assigned. Eventually, I developed a habit of praying over the various file assignments I would receive.

Moving forward would mean that I would be stepping into areas where the Lord would stretch my faith. I had been assigned to investigate a claim of minor front end damage to a car in Rockford, Illinois. When I arrived, I met with the insured, and her boyfriend. During the recorded statement, the female, "Rachel" was unable to sit still for more than a few minutes at a time. When we were done with the statement, she explained that the day after we scheduled this appointment, she "threw" her back out at work. Rachel explained that she works on an assembly line at a nearby factory. She said that she had been in such pain she went to the ER and had been in the hospital. She was diagnosed with a herniated disk in her upper back, and there was no relief from the pain.

While we were outside for the vehicle inspection, I noticed Rachel was unable to find any comfort from the pain. I knew that I would be praying for her and her healing. However, I could sense a reluctance on my part. There are many times, that the insured is just not happy with me as an investigator and the questions I have to ask. This was one of those times. The damage on the vehicle suggested that the vehicle had been in motion at the time. But Rachel was insisting that it occurred while it was parked. I knew my investigation would conclude differently than what the insured was claiming. In such cases, there are times when the insured complains because their policy will reflect fault and possibly impact the coverage. Also, neither Rachel nor her boyfriend had been very friendly. I'll say politely, that they were definitely not "church" people. So, when I asked to pray for Rachel, I had no idea how that was going to go over. I had hoped for a word of knowledge at this point to give me some insight on how to move forward with the request to pray. But no word of knowledge came.

However, I told Rachel and her boyfriend that I had been at a "church" conference

MOVE FORWARD

earlier in the year, and I saw people healed during prayer. (As I was talking, I recalled at the Bethel healing conference we were told to pair up with someone we did not know. The person I was paired with said she had neck pain for 15 years. The moment I touched her neck, she started jumping around and praised God that the pain was gone! There was a healing anointing throughout the service, and a lot of people were getting healed). I asked them if they would be willing to try prayer. The boyfriend to my surprise seemed very eager, and said: "Yeah sure." Rachel also agreed. So, I had the boyfriend place his hand on Rachel's back where the pain was, and I placed my hand over his. I commanded the pain to leave in Jesus name. I prayed some more and then asked Rachel if there was any improvement.

She shrugged her shoulders around and said, "not much." I responded by saying that if Jesus prayed for a blind man twice, then we can pray twice. The boyfriend also agreed, and we prayed again. Once again, I commanded the pain to leave in Jesus name. When I asked "Rachel" how she felt, she said the pain was much less. Rachel walked around in the driveway shrugging her shoulders and said it was much better. She then walked into the house.

I explained to the boyfriend that Jesus was healing Rachel and encouraged him to keep praying for her if the pain returned. He agreed and walked into the house after Rachel. I don't know if she had ever received complete healing. Neither ever complained about the results of the investigation. But I knew, I was doing what the Lord had spoken to me about: "Look past the insurance and see the opportunity."

I knew this was risky. But I also knew that I could not just walk away without stepping into praying for Rachel's healing. I had to move forward in order to advance the Kingdom of heaven. In those situations when we "know" in our spirit we are to act, we simply need to act. I believe our obedience is critical. Before I stepped into praying for Rachel, I was hoping for a "sneak preview"

> *The moment I touched her neck, she started jumping around and praised God that the pain was gone!*

through a word of knowledge. Not getting a word of knowledge didn't mean that the Lord left me hanging, rather, moments like these are building blocks of faith. In these moments, it's a complete dependence upon the Lord. I recognized the need and placed a demand on heaven. Neither Rachel nor her boyfriend apparently had considered prayer for the herniated disk. So, the Lord sent me, to access the Kingdom of heaven on their behalf.

Moving Forward

Through someone at our church, Tonya and I were invited to be a part of a prophetic conference at the HUB Ministries. We were asked to be a part of the prophetic team where we would be assigned to provide prophetic words to anyone who signed up to receive a word at the conference. I'll admit, I was very reluctant at first. Sure, I had given a word here and there, but this would be on the spot, giving someone word from the Lord. As I prayed about it, I knew this was again, something that Tonya and I both needed to step into. This was the Hub's Face to Face conference, where they had lined up some well-known conference speakers: Mahesh and Bonnie Chavda, Rodney Howard Brown, and Will Hart were on the itinerary, among others.

We were scheduled for the Friday session prophetic team. When Tonya and I checked in as part of the prophetic ministry team, I thought: "Well Lord, I'm relying on You." As team members, we were paired up by gender. I was paired with a guy from Crusaders Church in Chicago (Pastor John Eckhardt's church). "Melvin" told me that he had been a part of these conferences for years. Thank you, Lord! I was apprehensive at first. Then the doors opened, and for the next two hours, Melvin and I provided prophetic words to whoever we prayed with. Melvin was a veteran at the prophetic. There was a prophetic anointing upon him as he flowed effortlessly given prophetic word after prophetic word. As I mentioned previously, when I am around the prophetic, it seems easier for me to flow prophetically. When the Spirit of God is moving prophetically, any Spirit-filled believer can also flow prophetically. Even those not inclined to move prophetically can be stirred by the Spirit of God, such as the messengers Saul sent when they encountered a prophetic anointing (1 Samuel 19:20-21).

A few weeks later, Tonya and I attended a Global Awakening conference in Urbana, Illinois. The main speakers were Randy Clark and Bill Johnson. During the first session, I went up to the altar for a fresh anointing of the Spirit. I received an outpouring of the Holy Spirit. As a member of the altar team was praying for me, he recognized the Presence of the Lord upon me. At first, it was a wave of peace, then euphoria. I thought I was fine until I tried to walk back to my seat. People were laying all around on the floor, and stepping over them was difficult, but I managed to get back to my seat. There, I just soaked in what the Spirit of the Lord had for me. The next night, after the evening session, when Tonya and I stopped by the hotel front desk to check on a billing question, the clerk complained about her knees as she hobbled behind the counter. Tonya and I prayed for healing in her knees. I prayed that the meniscus be restored and the pain to leave. The clerk was shocked and wanted to know how I knew to pray for the meniscus. I told her that was what the Lord gave me as we prayed. To the clerk's delight, and to our joy, she said that the pain was gone. Praise God!

One of the first appointments I had set up after being back to work from the

MOVE FORWARD

conference was a stolen auto claim in Fort Wayne Indiana. I met with the insured, "Alisha," in the cafeteria where she worked. Once we finished with the recorded statement, I asked her if I could pray for her. I had a sense that she was dealing with anxiety. Alisha eagerly accepted the offer for prayer. So, there in the middle of the cafeteria, I prayed for her. The Lord had given me some words of knowledge to pray into, and the Presence of the Lord came upon Alisha. It took her a few minutes to compose herself. She told me that she hadn't heard prayer like that before. I explained that the Lord was doing a work in her. I also gave her some insights that I believed the Lord was doing with her. I could tell, Alisha, who had been through some tough times over the years, was now being blessed by the Presence of the Lord. A week later, she called me to follow up on her claim. Although I suspected that was not the main reason she called. Alisha told me that she had gone to church Sunday, and had been prayed over. She was very excited and knew that the Lord was seeing her through everything. Alisha thanked me for praying for her.

Moving forward is simply to advance the kingdom of heaven here on earth. Jesus said: "And as you go, preach, saying the kingdom of heaven is at hand." (Matthew 10:7) Moving forward, for me, means that where ever I go, the Kingdom of Heaven is within anyone's reach. I am there to help facilitate that encounter for someone. That person may be broken, wounded or even blind, so I will stand in the gap and access the Kingdom of heaven on their behalf. Faith is the currency of heaven. I believe that when we step in and pray with someone, a spiritual transaction occurs. Whether the person realizes it or not, we have brought someone to the throne of grace and Jesus is there to receive, and intervene. Even if we step into what seems like a valley of dry bones, as we pray, a prophetic word may come, and those who have been "slain" and seem dead can come alive (Ezekiel 37).

In January of 2017, I was notified that my brother, Jeff, was in the hospital. Tonya and I met with Gary and Gail York the night before I was scheduled to drive to Utah to see on Jeff. Gary and Gail led us in prayer and asked for an anointing to be poured out upon me for the ministry and responsibilities I may encounter at the hospital. Gary and Tonya had an impression that while I was at the hospital, people would "see" Jesus in me. Shortly afterward I had a strong impression that I was to "stay in the moment" for the duration of the trip.

In chapter 8, "As you go," we will pick up my journey to Utah. As we go about our business of life, we represent Jesus, wherever we go. As we go we also know that the Kingdom of heaven is truly at hand.

Section II

5

Our Walk in Him, The Newness of Life

"And Jesus said to her, Neither do I condemn you, go, and sin no more." John 8:11

As you read the testimony of my life, you may wonder how was it possible for someone who said that they had been born-again and made a genuine commitment to the Lord to fall into such a depraved level of sin. That's a fair question. I believe, as we read through Scripture, my life choices, although shocking to many, did not catch the Lord off guard. After all, there is nothing new under the sun (Ecclesiastes 1:9). The above Bible reference from the book of John was from the Lord speaking new life over the woman who had been caught in the act of adultery. Moments before her encounter with Jesus, she was in jeopardy of being stoned to death. The Pharisees used a woman, possibly even set her up, with the evil intent of trapping the Lord, and then planned to dispose of her when they finished. However, Jesus was not surprised by the scenario. Once the woman's accusers fled, Jesus declared powerfully. "Go, and sin no more." The woman's accusers were gone. She had been relieved on the legal judgment required for her sin. The woman, in the presence of Jesus, had been forgiven, and her life changed forever. Although in the natural, she could rise to her feet and walk away, forgiven of her sin, and, of her own will, return to a life of sin. In her moment of dire need and shame, she was in the Presence of the Lord. Whenever someone is in the Presence of the Lord, their very character changes. They have a burning desire to walk in the newness of life He gives.

Jesus declared, as she went her way, "Sin no more." If you were to study the original text, it means just what it says. Basically, "hereafter, and no longer miss the mark, or wander from the path of uprightness." In those moments at the feet of Jesus, everything changed for this woman. Yes, she had a responsibility to live a life fitting to what had just happened. She was not to take this personal encounter with Jesus for granted. I believe that personal encounters with the Lord are life changing and can be the same for anyone who seeks Him.

Our Walk in Him, The Newness of Life

The point here is simple, as profound as a personal encounter is with the Lord, Jesus knew exactly what needed to be said to this woman before they parted company. Jesus made a declaration of who this woman would be from this point forward. He spoke life over her, not an admonishment. The love of God was displayed to her, as Jesus told her that He did not condemn her. Jesus' parting words were life-giving, not rule-binding. This was to be a change of heart, not an obligation to keep. As Jesus declared over the fig tree that it would no longer bear fruit, at the word of the Lord, it was so. So, this woman was completely changed in those moments and the declaration of her new life had been made. For her, she had to rise and walk in the newness of life.

For many who come to know Jesus as their personal Savior and Lord of their lives, it may have initially seemed like a rather non-dynamic event. Not everyone has the same experience that I did at the altar in 2014 when they receive Jesus as Savior and Lord. When I accepted the Lord back in 1983, it was in the quietness of my bedroom and appeared to be a "non-dynamic" event. However, accepting Jesus as Savior and Lord is a spiritual rebirth, a miraculous, supernatural work of God. A person's spirit has been born-again, this time able to commune with God who is Spirit (John 4:24). Let's look at what some other authors write about the born-again experience.

... accepting Jesus as Savior and Lord is a spiritual rebirth, a miraculous, supernatural work of God

> When people give their lives to Jesus and become Christians, a miracle takes place. Jesus Christ Himself comes to live inside them. A transfer of power and ownership is made. Those who once belonged to the "ruler of this world" (John 14:30) now belong to Jesus and it is He who rules their lives. All has become new (2 Corinthians 5:17) in the deepest part of their being – their spirit. The central and most important part of each person, the part that died when Adam sinned (Genesis 2:17), is now made alive and becomes the home of Jesus.

> Jesus, the new ruler, rescues them from the kingdom of the enemy and places them in the Kingdom of God. Our Lord won the right to do this by defeating Satan at the cross and the tomb. From the moment people decide to give their lives to Jesus, the Holy Spirit who lives within them is greater than the former ruler, the one who is in the world (1 John

MOVE FORWARD

4:4). New believers still have a lot of work to do to achieve the goal of becoming "conformed to the image of Jesus. They must still contend with their old sin nature.

> For reasons we do not understand, our sin nature is not eradicated when we accept Christ." We must fight for every inch of sanctification. But with the Holy Spirit within us to help us, we can make great progress.[1]

I also liked the way Henry Blackaby put it:

> Salvation is more than going to heaven when you die. Eternal life is an intimate, personal, progressive relationship with Almighty God and his Son (and Holy Spirit). When salvation comes to your life, God radically and immediately reorients you for the rest of your life to Christ's right to be Lord.[2]

Once salvation has come to us, we are to cherish the eternal significance of what God has done for us. We are to "walk" in honor of what Jesus went through to bring eternal salvation to us. Paul wrote to the church at Philippi in the second chapter of the magnitude of what Jesus did for us. Jesus set aside His divinity, took on the form of a bond-servant, being in our likeness to restore that which had been lost. He humbled Himself to an open shame, being put to death on a cross. Jesus fulfilled what we could have never done even in all of our best religious efforts. The Lamb slain before the foundations of the world came to be The Lamb that takes away the sins of the world. Therefore, so great a plan of salvation that we should "work out your own salvation with fear and trembling." (Philippians 2:12) As we read the entire second chapter of Philippians, Paul uses Jesus as our example of how to live. Doing all things without complaining or disputing that we may be as blameless children of God (v14-15). Even in the midst of a crooked and perverse generation. Jesus is our example and model of the Christian life. In the likeness of Christ we live, so in humility we serve.

Paul's encounter with the Lord Jesus is probably the most dynamic and radical life-changing encounters recorded. In Acts chapter 9 we read that Paul, then called Saul, was still breathing threats and murder against the disciples. Saul was so obsessed with destroying Christianity that even after consenting to the death of Stephen, he sought letters of approval to imprison more Christians. Indeed, any of these Christians that Saul would have bound would have also been imprisoned if not murdered. However, Jesus stepped in.

As Saul, a Pharisee of Pharisee's, rode near Damascus: "suddenly a light shone around him from heaven." When Saul fell to the ground, Jesus spoke to him…

---

1   Defeating Dark Angels by Charles H. Kraft pg. 73-74
2   The Man God Uses by Blackaby & Blackaby pg. 35

Our Walk in Him, The Newness of Life

"Saul, Saul, why are you prosecuting me?" In response to Saul's confusion, Jesus responds: "I am Jesus, whom you are persecuting. But rise and enter the city and it will be told you what you must do." Acts 9:3-6

Personal encounters with the Lord, literally meet the person where they are. They are life changing. Having a personal encounter with the Lord will redirect anyone's life. The woman who had been brought to Jesus in John chapter 8 received just what she needed in those critical moments. She received forgiveness, not condemnation. She received relief from those who accused her and were using her. She also received life-giving direction in Jesus' parting words. Saul received an intervention in his misguided zeal and a new direction. He was made blind in the natural so that his eyes would be open in the spiritual. Saul, a fanatical zealot of the Pharisees, would now learn dependence among God's people as he was lead by the hand as he walked into his new life. Saul would experience a healing at the hands of a servant of the Lord, and understand how the Lord moves among His people in visions and words of knowledge. Saul would learn his new calling despite his murderous past, he was a chosen instrument of the Lord to bear His name before the Gentile world, and Saul's name would be changed to reflect a new identity in Christ Jesus.

Paul would then go on to write what we would refer to as the pastoral epistles. Wherein, Paul uses action metaphors to describe our responsibilities as Christians. What I have learned, even as a result of my past failings, and my encounter with the Lord in 2014, is to follow Godly instructions. Following Godly instructions not only fulfills His purposes in and through us but also edifies us in the process.

Paul would go on to write to the Galatians what he was teaching them had been given to him by revelation of Jesus Christ Himself (Galatians 1:12). Therefore, his instructions in the epistles to the various churches had originated from Jesus Himself. Jesus was making good on His declaration that Paul was His chosen instrument to the Gentile world.

Let's cover some of the instructions Paul wrote that will have a significant impact on how we live our Christian lives. We certainly cannot cover all of Paul's instructions to the Church, but the following are some of which I have found to be very beneficial in my walk. Albeit, many of which I had to learn the hard way as I reflected back on my wandering in the wilderness.

In this chapter, we will examine Paul's metaphor, "walk."

Our first text will be: **"For we walk by faith, not by sight." 2 Corinthians 5:7.** The Greek word used here is "peripateo," which means "to walk." Clever right? It also means "to make one's way, progress," and figuratively "to live one's life." As we move forward, you will see why I take the time to dissect the original Greek word used. In any event, I believe from the text that Paul wants the reader to understand that in our Christian walk (life), we are not to be dependent on what we see in the natural. There is a spiritual reality that exists whether we can see it in the natural or not. Remember, when Paul had his encounter with the Lord he had lost the use of his natural eyesight for three days. Then when Ananias laid hands on Paul (Acts 9:17), Paul was filled with the Holy Spirit, and that which had covered his eyes, something like scales fell, and he received his natural sight back. I do not believe the Bible contains trivial details. Rather, this was a time for Paul to begin understanding his new life, a life of faith, a life depending upon the Lord, and not so self-reliant. Paul would explain to the Galatians (1:16-17), that he had spent three years in Arabia where he did not confer with flesh and blood (man) before returning to Jerusalem (society). I'm sure the point was that he spent a lot of alone time with the Lord.

Although I don't want to debate who wrote the book of Hebrews, for the sake of this writing, I'll assume that Paul was the author. So, in Hebrews 11:1, Paul writes:

"Now, faith is the substance of things hoped for, the evidence of things not seen." Here again, the faith we are to walk in every day is not to be dependent on what we see in the natural or comprehend with our natural senses. I firmly believe that the principle of living a life of faith is to rely on the promises of God regardless of what may seem either more real or even contrary to the promises of God. The Bible is full of examples of faith, but let's quickly look at an excellent example of standing firm on a promise of God. In the book of Numbers, chapters 13 through 14, God told Moses to send men

... the faith we are to walk in every day is not to be dependent on what we see in the natural ...

to spy out the land of Canaan. What is very interesting is in Numbers 13:2, God told Moses to send out spies into Canaan, the land "which I am giving to the children of Israel." The promise of God seems very clear, yet God was testing the faithfulness of His people. Moses then selected men from each tribe to: "... **see what the land is like, whether the people who dwell in it are strong or weak, few or many..." Numbers 13:18.** Moses added for the selected spies to be, "of good courage." However, when the 12 spies returned, only two of them, Joshua and Caleb, were completely trusting in the Lord to protect them as they entered the land. God already said that He was giving them the land. That was the promise. Ten of the spies were more focused on the obstacles rather than the promise of

Our Walk in Him, The Newness of Life

the Lord. As we read the story, the bad report given by the ten spies contaminated the atmosphere to such an extent that the people cried out and they wept that night (Numbers 14:1). Fear and doubt will always destroy faith. But Joshua and Caleb saw this lack of faith in the people as rebellion (Numbers 14:9). Joshua and Caleb were walking by faith and not by sight. Later, because of Caleb's faith, God would honor him and his descendants and bring them into the land that He had promised.

> "But because my servant Caleb has a different spirit in him and has follows Me wholeheartedly, I will bring him into the land where he went to, and his descendants will inherit it." Numbers 14:24 (NIV)

Faith is the currency of heaven. It is recognized and accepted as what is needed to complete a spiritual transaction. Without faith, we cannot please God, Hebrews 11:6. Faith is an absolute trust in God. It transcends logic, intelligence, and reasoning. It transcends our natural understanding. Therefore, we do not lean on our own understanding but trust in the Lord with all of our heart, Proverbs 3:5. That may seem offensive to those who think of themselves as intellectual. But be assured, as a people of faith, it's not that we set aside our God-given ability to act wisely. Nor does it suggest that we neglect to use the mind God gave us. However, it does mean our thinking, and our minds must be transformed or renewed to grasp the ways of the Kingdom of heaven. It means that despite what we may see, we remain faithful in what God has promised.

Faith is the currency of heaven.

Faith believes His promises, allowing us to move forward, even when the present realities suggest in the natural something other than God's promises. Paul would use Abraham as an example. Despite the fact that it seemed impossible for him and Sarah to have children, let alone father many nations (Genesis 17:4), God was able to give life to the dead (womb), "and call those things which do not exist as though they did." Romans 4:17. We can declare the promises of God, out loud, from His word, calling something forth, though it may not exist in the present, as if it does. Such as when we seem to have been battered by life to the extent we wonder if God is still listening, or even cares.

> For I am persuaded that neither death nor life, nor angels nor principalities nor powers, nor things present nor things to come, nor height nor depth, nor any other created thing, shall be able to separate us from the love of God which is in Christ Jesus our Lord. Romans 8:38-39

Incidentally, it is significant to note that with all Paul mentions in these two verses that could cause us to doubt, there is no mention of the past! That should not even be a consideration for a Christian. Our past (sins) have been forgiven. Life may at times be difficult, but we can be certain that our past has been dealt with at the cross!

There are numerous other verses you may choose to declare out loud in the midst of your circumstances, even though the answer may not seem to exist at the time. For we walk by faith, and not by sight.

Next, let's look at: **"If we live in the Spirit, let us also walk in the Spirit." Galatians 5:25. NKJ.** The NIV translates it in a very applicable manner, "Since we live in the Spirit, let us keep in step with the Spirit."

The NIV translation is actually more accurate to the original Greek word "stoicheo," which means to proceed in a row, as the march of a soldier, to go in order, to direct one's life. This is a significant word difference. Our lives then, since we live in the Spirit, we are to remain in alignment with the Holy Spirit. We operate, function, and act in harmony with the Holy Spirit. We should always be in proper formation with the Holy Spirit. Our lives then, should never grieve the Holy Spirit. They should never be out of step with how the Holy Spirit moves, flows, or otherwise be contrary to Him. The picture here is how a group of soldiers, when they march, remain in perfect step with each other as if they are one unit. Picture the soldiers in harmony as they move, and function as a powerful unit, even though they are individuals, they remain in step with each other. Together they move impressively. There is even a cadence with the Spirit even as words are spoken.

For the New Testament believers, Paul was addressing in the text, living in the Spirit was a given. As you read the first two chapters of the book of Galatians, Paul is bringing a correction to the Galatians since they were apparently returning to their ways of Judaism, or works, rather than the gospel of grace that Paul brought to them. Paul also had to remind the Galatians that the Spirit they had received, was received by faith, and not works. As Christ lives in each of us, Galatians 2:20, so does the Holy Spirit (1 Corinthians 6:19). Being Spirit-filled is evidenced by the fruit described in Galatians 5:22-23. This is not just external evidence of an inward working. These are the very attributes of God Himself. The fruit, singular, here is the by-product so to speak that we have been filled with the Spirit. In the same manner, a person can walk up to an apple tree, and without any understanding of the type of leaves, or texture of the bark, when they see the apples hanging there they know they are standing in front of an apple tree. No one has to convince the onlooker, they can see it for themselves. Suffice it to say that if we "live" in the Spirit of God, we are to be sensitive to the Spirit, and do not walk in a manner that could possibly bruise the fruit we see listed in Galatians 5:22-23.

Our Walk in Him, The Newness of Life

Continuing in our walking metaphors of the Christian life, we will next turn to **Colossians 1:10: "…that you may walk worthy of the Lord …"**

Paul lets the believers at Colossi know that he does not cease to pray for them, and among the petitions he brings before the throne of grace is that they may be able to "**... walk worthy of the Lord, fully pleasing Him, being fruitful in every good work, and increasing in the knowledge of God …**" Walking worthy, or living a life worthy of the Lord as a Christian would include being fully pleasing to Him, being fruitful, in every good work, and increasing in our knowledge of God, and His ways.

Although some usually associate being worthy with service or good works, which are birthed out of a "religious" obligation, such efforts miss the point. I believe from the text, Colossians 1:9, as we receive "all wisdom and spiritual understanding of His will," we will be better able to move or walk in those "works" He has established for each of us to complete (Ephesians 2:10). Walking worthy is to walk every day is such a manner that we would hear the Father say: "In him, I am well pleased."

We are to be fruitful. Walking worthy of the Lord is a life of bearing fruit. Jesus said: "**I am the vine, you are the branches. He who abides in Me, and I in him, bears much fruit; for without Me you can do nothing." "By this My Father is glorified that you bear much fruit, so will be my disciples." John 15:5 & 8.**

This is a picture of intimacy with the Lord. It is out of that place of intimacy, and communion we abide and bear fruit. Real fruit from the Kingdom of heaven is not born of our own efforts, independent of Jesus. Fruit bearing is the product of our walk. Our life should leave a trail of fruit that whoever we have come in contact with may be nourished. We will explore this much further in the last chapter "As we go." The original commission to man (Genesis 1:28) remains in effect, "be fruitful." God did not engineer us to be spectators in life. We were designed and equipped for a Kingdom purpose.

Increasing in the knowledge of God was not an admonishment to the Colossians, or us to merely gain more knowledge of God. Rather the spiritual understanding, as Paul prayed, was to know God more. Paul would make a very similar prayer known to the Ephesians that he did not cease to make mention of them in prayer that God would give them the spirit of wisdom, and revelation in/of the knowledge of God (Ephesians 1:16-18). This spiritual wisdom and understanding to know Him better are so that our eyes of understanding Him will be enlightened that we may have a better grasp of the hope we have, and His calling on our lives. Such an increase in the knowledge of God brings a deeper level of intimacy with God. We should be as it was said of Moses.

MOVE FORWARD

"He made known His ways to Moses, His acts to the children of Israel." Psalm 103:7.

God regarded Moses so highly, that He spoke to him face to face (Numbers 12:8). Not so with the children of Israel, they were only privileged to witness the acts of God. Although God spoke to the prophets in dreams and visions (Numbers 12:7), which are in a parabolic language, not so with Moses. God spoke to him plainly. There was a greater level of intimacy between God and Moses. Remember, Moses operated under the rule of God's law, where sin(s) separated one from such an encounter with a Holy God.

"But your iniquities have separated you from your God, and your sins have hidden His face from you." Isaiah 59:2. Prophets were subject to death for disobedience, even if they were deceived to believe otherwise (see 1 Kings 13:18 & 24-26). Moses' character was of one whom God was well pleased, which allowed for such a deep relationship. Albeit, even Moses went through a season of training as he faced Pharaoh, and led the people to the Promised Land.

We are so blessed to be operating under the rule of grace where the veil has been torn, and we have full access to God through the redemptive work of Jesus on the cross. "... **having made peace through the blood of His cross.**" Colossians 1:20. Therefore, let us walk in a manner that is worthy of what Jesus paid for.

The last of the walk metaphors we will cover is to walk in love. Our text is **Ephesians 5:2 "And walk in love, as Christ also has loved us and given Himself for us..."** Because of Paul's personal encounter with Jesus on the Damascus Road, he was a new creation. Prior to this meeting, Paul had been breathing threats and murder against the disciples, looking to bring anyone, whether men or woman, bound to Jerusalem if they were a follower of Jesus (Acts 9:1-2). Years later, Paul writes to the Ephesians teaching them to "**Let all bitterness, wrath, anger, clamor and evil speaking be put away from you, with all malice. And be kind to one another, tenderhearted, forgiving one another, even as God in Christ forgave you.**" Ephesians 4:31-32 Therefore, be imitators of God (Ephesians 5:1). God is love, so walk in love. It was love in the encounter that Paul had, and now Paul is exhibiting the very attribute of God: love. Paul would also write to the church at Rome that it is the Holy Spirit that pours out the love of God into our hearts (Romans 5:5). Paul had clearly been filled with the Spirit and the love of God.

> *... let us walk in a manner that is worthy of what Jesus paid for.*

We also read that Paul moved, and functioned in all of the gifts of the Spirit. He spoke in tongues more than any of the Corinthians. He had even raised the dead (Acts 20:10-12). But he knew that without love we are nothing more than noise (1 Corinthians 13:1).

The one thing that will truly set us apart from anyone else is love. Jesus knew this because His Father is love. Therefore: "By this all will know that you are My disciples, if you have love for one another." John 13:35 A person can have a life-changing experience when they follow the precepts of one religion or another. But they will not be able to truly display the love of God without knowing God, who is love. They will just be religious, following the disciplines of their belief system. That is why Jesus makes the distinction as people will recognize you as His disciples. At the time of Jesus, there were numerous religions and philosophies. None of which would demonstrate the love of God as Jesus did. John would later write:

"He who says he abides in Him ought himself also to walk just as He (Jesus) walked." 1 John 2:6

Jesus walked in and demonstrated the greatest of love known. **"Greater love has no one than this, than to lay down one's life for his friends." John 15:13**

Although it may be difficult to wrap our understanding around it from the very beginning, it was in the love of the Father that set in motion Jesus, who would eventually walk as the lamb slain before the foundations of the world.

"For God so loved the world that He gave His only begotten Son that whoever believes in Him should not perish but have everlasting life." John 3:16

So, our walk, as Christians revolves around love. Because God is love (1 John 4:8). This is what I had such a difficult time with in the past. But without love, we don't know God. And it does not revolve around our "love performance" so to speak. God simply loved us first, and we love Him as children love their parents because they know they are loved. It's this sort of Godly love that we, in turn, love others as Jesus did. Paul, went from a Pharisee bent on destroying anyone who followed Jesus, to a bond-servant who no longer operated out of a religious obligation. Paul knew love. Because it was love that knocked him off his donkey. Paul would eventually understand that it was out of love that Jesus appeared to Him on the Damascus Road. That is what amazing grace is, it is love and not justice. Ultimately, "Christianity is a love relationship with a living Person."[3] Therefore, "walk in love as Christ has loved us…"

Our walk with the Lord should never become one of obligation. The Christian life is not a religious endeavor. We live and walk out our faith from a place of intimacy with the Lord. I will go into greater depth on intimacy with the Lord in chapter 6. Our life in Christ is an interactive relationship much the same as our lives with our spouse ought to be. I realize there are periods in our marriages where we seem to be just going through the motions.

I have been through periods in my walk with the Lord, even since GGG 2014, that seemed stagnant. But that is a place we can never stay for any length of time. We need to learn to recognize whatever may be hindering our walk. Once we recognize a hindrance, it must be eradicated. I believe God always wants us to be positioned in a place of growth. The entire Bible reflects that God's heart is to grow His people into all that He originally intended us to become. Our walk as a Christian is to always be moving forward.

Even after my dynamic encounter with the Lord at the altar in 2014, it took time to recondition my way of thinking. There have been times since then that I lost my spiritual focus. I tend to default on the problem and not on what God may ultimately be doing in a given situation. For many of us, before we made a commitment to the Lord, our lives, our way of thinking, our minds were opposed to God and His ways. The thoughts and ways of an unrighteous, or natural man, are not those of God (Isaiah 55:8). Nor can they be. I know that most my life, my way of thinking has been to default into the problematic side of any given situation. The phrase I would often use was: "Why does everything have to be ten times more difficult than reasonably necessary." However, our walk, in the newness of life should reflect a new way of thinking.

"And do not be conformed to this world, but be transformed by the renewing of your mind, that you may prove what is that good and acceptable and perfect will of God." Romans 12:2

The word transformed in this verse is "metamorphoo" which in the Greek means "to change into another form." This is where we get the word metamorphosis. Of course, it means the same thing. As Christians, we are to no longer have the same way of thinking as the world does. Our minds and our way of thinking are to take on a whole new nature, to be transformed into something other than what it is accustom to. We are to have the "mind of Christ." 1 Corinthians 2:16. Having the mind of Christ is not for just a select few, it's for all believers. This new, heavenly mindset, is an established attitude to be held by each believer. Having this Christlike mindset allows us to fulfill the commission that Jesus gave.

---

3   The Man God Uses by Blackaby & Blackaby pg. 43

Our Walk in Him, The Newness of Life

> And these signs shall follow those who believe: In my name they will cast out demons, they will speak in new tongues, they will take up serpents (handle demons), and if they drink anything deadly (ingest, come into contact the demonic as they handle/cast out), it will by no means hurt them, they will lay hands on the sick, and they will recover. Mark 16:17-18

This is not just in concept for the believer. Rather we are to believe in the supernatural, and spiritual authority we carry. Always understanding that as these signs follow those who believe, they should stem from our right relationship with Jesus. Not merely believing in His name to do the works as those cited in Matthew 7:21-23, who did not have a relationship with the Lord. For every believer, we are to have a renewed mind. That renewed mind allows us to grasps that the remainder of our natural life shall be a "supernatural" life because it is the Spirit, who raised Jesus from the dead that dwells in us (Romans 8:11). Get over yourself, it's not you or me it is the power of God (1 Corinthians 2:4-5) to him who believes. Our minds need to be changed, or renewed, to know that all things are possible with God. For He is the God of the impossible (Luke 18:27).

Pastor Bill Johnson of Bethel Church in Redding California has written a book and produced a video series on "The Supernatural Power of the Transformed Mind," which I would recommend for further study. In the book, Pastor Johnson tells of a ministry team that had been in South Africa (pg 69 -70), and when they were on their own time walking to a restaurant, they encountered a homeless man. I won't recount the whole story, but during the meeting they learned that the homeless man had been paralyzed for 11 years, and was unable to walk. The details of the story are dramatic and worth reading. As the team prayed for the man, he was healed, and the person that had been with the man gave his life to the Lord after witnessing the miraculous healing. This all occurred in a parking lot, and not in the comfortable setting of a church. More ministry broke out because of a group of team members, "on their own time," recognized what the Father wanted to do in the life of a paralyzed man. This does not occur unless there is a fundamental shift in thinking. We can see things differently. Not the problem of a paralyzed man, but the potential for a mighty move of God.

> That's called putting revelation into practice. You see, renewing the mind is not merely reading words on a page and having the moment of revelation about a particular verse. That passes for renewal of the mind in many churches, but at the best that's only half of the equation. Renewal comes as a revelation leads you into a new experience with God, as those people had that day in South Africa." "To renew the mind we must not just think differently but live differently, in a new experience of the

Having a renewed mind enables us to have a godly, or heaven's perspective in situations. Where "let thy will be done on earth as it is in heaven" is more than a repetitive prayer; it is our heart's desire. The renewed mind enables a person to take/give from God's world and bring it into this world. Most of us as believers are the closest some people may ever get to heaven's realm, so we need to be prepared to share it. Jesus said that the Kingdom of God is within us (Luke 17:21). Having a renewed, or transformed mind is one that takes this from a concept, and understands that the Presence of God does not dwell in the temples made with hands (Acts 7:48). The Presence of God dwells/abides in His people.

> *Having a renewed mind enables us to have a godly, or heaven's perspective in situations.*

"Do you not know that you are the temple of God, and that the Spirit of God dwells in you." 1 Corinthians 3:16

Having a renewed or transformed mind is not a new twist to the secular understanding of the power of positive thinking. Although it is a conscious choice in many incidences, it is also a supernatural work we need to allow and not hinder. It is by the Holy Spirit (Titus 3:5) that brings such a renewing. The regeneration is our new birth into the spiritual, and the renewing (Greek -anakainosis) is a renovation, a complete change for the better. Not just a new and improved version of the old. We become a brand new creation in Christ.

That being so, then the Most-High God, in His sovereignty has chosen to partner with His people to achieve the purposes of His Kingdom. This may not be something that we can really wrap our brains around. By faith, we can seize what cannot be seen, it's what has been demonstrated by the power of the Holy Spirit (1 Corinthians 2:4).

Closely associated with the renewing of our minds, are the words we speak. Jesus said: "…**For out of the abundance of the heart the mouth speaks.**" Matthew 12:34. The words we choose to speak will reveal the inner workings of who we are at our spiritual core. Our words either reveal treasures that produce life or a lack of understanding of the spiritual realities our words carry.

"**Let the words of my mouth and the meditations of my heart be acceptable**

---

4   The Supernatural Power of a Transformed Mind by Bill Johnson pg. 69-70

in Your sight O Lord, my strength, and my Redeemer." Psalm 19:14. As Jesus taught, our mouths and hearts are closely connected. I once heard it taught that our mouths are our spiritual barometers. This is an accurate picture since a barometer measures the atmospheric pressure. The words we speak will certainly affect the atmosphere around us.

As life goes on, there are times we each need a spiritual course correction. This is usually evident in the words we use. Trust me, I know from experience that this is an area that has revealed the level of toxic waste residing within me in the past. There was a time when I joked about verse 36 of Matthew chapter 12. That it was a good thing I had all of eternity to give an account for all of the "idle" words spoken on the day of judgment. I no longer find the topic something to joke about. The Lord has since shown me how powerful words are.

> *... there are times we each need a spiritual course correction.*

"But shun profane and idle babblings, for they will increase to more ungodliness." 2 Timothy 2:16

God created everything in the natural, and the spiritual with a spoken word. You can't get more powerful than that. Understandably, one would expect something powerful to occur at the command of God Almighty. Yet, we have a tendency to diminish the tremendous significance that our words carry. We say, "sticks and stones may break my bones but words will never hurt me." Perhaps many us may be largely unaffected emotionally by the words of others. However, even the strongest of people do get tired of hearing complaints, criticism, and sarcastic comments.

As born-again Christians, we each undergo a spiritual transformation. The Holy "Spirit" has taken up residence within each of us. We then believe, even at a basic level, that upon our physical death, our spirit will go to heaven. But when we discuss the spirit realm around us, some Christians bristle, assuming that such talk is a little "too much."

> Scripture is clear that there is a close connection between the spirit world and the human world. In spite of our habit of regarding spiritual things and human things as separate, in Scripture these realms are not compartmentalized. They are tightly interrelated, with events in the spirit realm having repercussions in the human world and vice versa.[5]

---

5   I Give You Authority by Charles H. Kraft pg. 132

MOVE FORWARD

Jesus brought this to the attention of the disciples after teaching that He is the bread of life. The Jews and the disciples were having a difficult time with this teaching (John 6:48-67). Jesus explained: **"It is the Spirit who gives life, the flesh profits nothing. The words that I speak to you are spirit, and they are life."** John 6:63. When Jesus said that the words He spoke are spirit, does not refer to His teaching on the subject. Literally, Jesus is saying that His words are "spirit," and they are life. So receive them. Many did not receive and abandoned Jesus (v 66). But Jesus was bringing to life the following proverb:

"Death and life are in the power of the tongue. And those who love it will eat its fruit." Proverbs 19:21

Our very words we speak will either bring justification, or condemnation upon ourselves (Matthew 12:37).

It is by the spoken words that we offer prayers, give, and pass on blessings, pass curses, make vows, take an oath, or vocalize personal judgments. These are not just words that tumble harmlessly into the atmosphere. They carry a spiritual significance. Our words bring either benefits or penalties in the natural when they manifest or are not fulfilled as spoken. It is through our words that we enter into an agreement, both in the natural and spiritual realm. Do you remember the words spoken just before my horse riding accident? I came into agreement with the person watching who suggested that I ride like I had nothing to live for. I said: "I have nothing to live for." Had it not been for the grace of God, I could have been killed that day.

During our everyday lives, our words will reveal to those around us the treasures of our hearts. Our words will reveal if we really are serious about walking a life worthy of the Lord, or in the Spirit, or a life of faith. Certainly, our words will reveal whether we are walking in love for anyone other than ourselves. On the other side, our words will also reflect our attitude about ourselves. This was a very real stronghold for me in the past. I was full of negative self-talk, and usually had nothing good to say about myself. Allowing this poison spill out infected the spiritual atmosphere around me. It is counterproductive to someone who seeks to grow spiritually. Such negative self-talk will not benefit anyone around us either. We can be free from much spiritual bondage if we would simply stop speaking our agreement with them aloud. Self-image is a favorite target for the devil. So we do not need to give the devil permission to lock down a stronghold upon us.

"Do not let ANY unwholesome talk come out of your mouths, but only what is helpful for building others up according to their needs, that it may benefit those who listen." Ephesians 4:29 We are not exempt from this verse. Whether we realize it or not, our minds will capture (listen) to all of the negative self-talk, or worse, any self-condemnation we speak. Even in jest, such words should not be uttered about ourselves, it only serves to cripple our spiritual growth. In addition, it will grieve the Holy Spirit (Ephesians 4:30), who is at work within each of us to complete the spiritual renewal mentioned in Titus 3:5. Such a conflict is self-destructive and wars against our spiritual growth.

Before GGG 2014, where I encountered the Lord at the altar, I can honestly say that I didn't know what I believed about a Christian needing deliverance from demon spirits. I know that my theology leaned more towards the idea that it would be impossible for a Christian, who has the Holy Spirit, to also have any demon spirits in them. It didn't seem to make any sense that the two could exist in the same person. How would the Holy Spirit and a demon(s) spirits reside in the same person? Besides, if I, as a believer was the temple of God (1 Corinthians 3:16), demon spirit(s) could not dwell where God dwells. This may make for neat theology. But my genuine experience, in the Presence of the Lord would later give me serious insight into a subject I had not considered much before.

As I drove home that night from the Give God Glory tent meeting, I noticed that I felt "lighter." It's difficult to explain, except to say that a weight had been lifted off of me. Whatever had been so oppressing on me was gone. Before this "weight" being lifted off of me, I always seemed agitated. Like I always had too much coffee in my system. I was ready for a confrontation and didn't know why. But since then, that which had me so agitated is gone.

There was a bitter, hateful, angry side of me that was always there. In private, my mouth would reveal the evil in my heart. I would actually turn from an encounter with someone and say out loud how much I hated people. Where did that come from? Now that it is gone, I can clearly recognize the source of all that hostility that had been bottled up in me for all those years. I was no longer blinded, or dismissive of what had such a grip on me. I had been demonized.

This is still an area where I am learning so this portion will not be an all-inclusive lesson on deliverance. Hopefully, this will be a launching pad for you to begin further research on the subject if it is new to you. Please don't fall into the misconception that a believer cannot have a demon. This is a dangerous misunderstanding in the Church. Of course, such a falsehood is enjoyed only by the devil since he is the father of lies. However, I have also come to understand that not every Christian who struggles with sin, or behavior that is less than godly can blame it on demons. That would be convenient but not always accurate. However, unrepented sin or continually being involved in sin by a Christian will open the doors for demonization. Generally, most Christians who are in need of deliverance have encountered the demon spirit(s) prior to their conversion.

> The vast majority of the demonized Christians to whom I have ministered brought their demons with them into Christianity. Though it is certainly

MOVE FORWARD

possible for Christians to become demonized, I have dealt with few whose infestation was not connected to pre-Christian attitudes and behaviors.[6]

Such was the case with me. Demons are evil and have nothing but hatred for God's most precious creation, people. So, the devil and his minions will seize upon any opportunity to destroy or inhabit a person. Often, suffering trauma, abuse, abandonment, or any number of devastating events can be open doors for the demonic to enter. As you read in chapter 2, I possessed a strong impulse toward anger, violence, and self-destruction from an early age. As I matured I learned to better manage the anger, but that was only because I knew there were consequences for that type of behavior. But my enjoyment of violence did not lift until after GGG 2014.

This book contains a sanitized version of my testimony; it was only by God's grace that I did not self-destruct. Sharing all of my destructive behaviors and details would have been just too much for the purposes of this book. Looking back, it seems easy to recognize what was driving me as a child, in my teen years, and then when I willingly walked in defiance to anything godly after I had become a Christian.

Often, people do learn to manage or control those "impulses" without even realizing what may be going on. I, like many people, had no understanding of the spiritual effect that my childhood had on me as I entered young adulthood, and into my born-again experience. Although your childhood experiences may have differed, if you either overtly, or privately have a sin issue that you cannot seem to conquer, you may need to consider

> *Demons are evil, and have nothing but hatred for God's most precious creation, people.*

deliverance. Again, I am not suggesting that anyone who struggles with a repeated pattern of sin has a demon. But if you have genuinely committed yourself to living a life worthy, fully pleasing to the Lord, and still find yourself in a place of sin, repentance, sin, and repentance, you may need to have deliverance.

As I entered known sinful behaviors after becoming a Christian, I cannot blame it all on the devil and his demon cohorts. I had entered into the sin willfully, and knowingly. It wasn't as if I was so out of control I could not say no.

"For the good that I will to do, I do not do, but the evil I will not to do, that I

---
6   Defeating Dark Angels by Charles H. Kraft pg 83

Our Walk in Him, The Newness of Life

practice. Now if I do what I will not to do, it is no longer I who do it but sin that dwells in me." Romans 7:19-20

But there were times I possessed a drive, even a real relish for sin. I believe this was beyond the usual struggle with sin we as humans have at times, as Paul refers to in Romans. Even back then, I knew that I had ventured beyond struggling with the frailty of being a human being who has a flesh that desires what is contrary to the Spirit. So, how does it work for a Christian who has the Holy Spirit to also have a demon(s)?

> Often people ask me how a demon could possibly be in a Christian if the Holy Spirit is there. My response is with a question. How can sin and evil thinking be where the Holy Spirit is? Sin is the flesh, the mind, will and emotions. Turmoil is the result. Demons cannot enter the spirit of man, just as sin could not enter the holy of holies. But demons can and do gain access to the flesh and soul of believers! This is a battle, and it is not disclosed by most preachers. Hence, many Christians live defeated because they are not even aware of what the battle is.[7]

I had been one of those defeated Christians. I had been caught in what seemed like an endless cycle of sin, repentance, sin, repentance. Then I would just give up, and give in. Nothing was more frustrating than to hear a three-point sermon that proclaimed that true repentance was to turn away from sin, just don't do that again. That may have been great, and even obvious advice if you were not the one tumbling down the sin side of a cliff. As you tumble down that cliff you may cry out, "Oh I hate this!" Okay, just stop. But the momentum and circumstances have already been set in motion. By that time, something, or someone may have to step in and break the fall. I will reiterate here, just because you or someone you know seems to be caught in this cycle, does not always mean they require deliverance. For it is out the heart that proceeds every form of evil (Matthew 15:19). There are times when people just make poor choices. Christians may not be safeguarding their walk and allowing too much of the world to influence them. When that happens, it's hard to see them as separate from the world. This may be a case where as mature Christians, we can come alongside the one overtaken in their sin (Galatians 6:1). However, any Christian who openly continues to sin has opened the doors for the demonic and given it a legal right to not only gain entry, but remain until cast out.

But there were times I possessed a drive, even a real relish for sin.

---

7   When Pigs Move In by Don Dickerman pg. 134

MOVE FORWARD

> Demon oppression or demonization is common among believers. Obviously, it is not demon possession. Possession is ownership, and we are owned by the Lord Jesus. We have been bought and purchased with a price. Possession is not the question. Demons gain access to the body or soul by many different doorways. My experience is that they stay until they are commanded to leave. They enter by deception and become squatters. They take and take, until in the name of Jesus Christ someone put an end to it.[8]

So how does someone know if deliverance is needed? Let me start by saying that the visible indicators may be a cycle of sin, that a person is simply not able to curtail on their own. Whether this is your, or someone else, there will have to be an acknowledgment that a problem does exist. This may be the most difficult step in the deliverance process. Most people know that they have a problem with a particular sin or ungodly habit. In the past, I was good at hiding behind a veneer of polished "Christianese." For the most part, I looked the part, carried my Bible, spoke the Christianese very well. I knew the Bible addresses if asked, but there was a definite problem inside. Once one acknowledges that a potential problem exists, there must be a willingness to be free of any demonic oppression, demonization or strongholds. Without the willingness to be free, the demon(s) have a legal right to be there. The demonic kingdom is very litigious and has to be dealt with in that fashion.

One does not need to be gifted to move in deliverance ministry. All believers are called to cast out demons (Matthew 10:8 & Mark 16:17). One does not need to be gifted, just an obedient believer. What I have learned, is that it is best to have someone who is either experienced in deliverance ministry or has a solid understanding of their identity, power, and authority in Christ. Also, I would seek someone who is not likely to get frustrated when challenged. This usually requires someone who is confident in who they are in Christ, and their personality even if they are not that experienced in deliverance ministry. I have seen people yelling and screaming while conducting a deliverance. When I have witnessed this, it is simply the person overcompensating for their lack of experience. Demons are not hard of hearing. They are demons, and will at times resist, protest or bluff to determine if you have any idea what you are doing. The bottom line is that they will submit to the authority a Christian carries in the name of Jesus.

I have since looked back at that first arrest I made for DUI as a new police officer. At that time, I had never arrested anyone before and was unsure of everything I was doing. But the subject that I had arrested recognized that I carried the power (gun/handcuffs), and the authority (badge/law) to make the arrest, book him and have him charged. As I mentioned, the demonic kingdom is a litigious realm

---

8   Ibid pg. 134

and understands the power and authority a Christian carries even if the believer doesn't. A word of caution needs to be emphasized here. If the person you are praying with or ministering to begins to manifest, you must take authority. It can be a battle. Remember that the person must be willing to be set free of the demonic. "If consciously or unconsciously, the person does not want to be free, it is very unlikely that it will happen."[9]

Whether it is you or another believer, don't allow shame or the stigma of the need to be set free potentially hinder your spiritual growth. Although I am not condoning behavior that is contrary to walking worthy of the Lord, I am aware that each of us can, and will make mistakes, and possibly open doors we would wish we never had.

> All of us have need of deliverance from time to time. There are no exceptions. As we grow in the Lord and in our discernment, we can begin to understand when we need spiritual victory in certain areas of our lives. Many times as believers we can sense hindrances in our lives that keep us from living fully in the Spirit. Deliverance is an ongoing process in the life of a believer. It is a gift to us from God to keep us from being tormented by the enemy and living in our own cycles of bondage.[10]

I began this chapter with two compelling examples of an encounter with the Lord. This book is a result of a powerful encounter that I had at an altar with the Lord. This encounter, like so many, was just the beginning of a new life. I have not been the same since that day at GGG 2014. Probably the most exciting part of this new life in Christ, is how we can continually experience Him. By experience, I am referring to more than a one time encounter, or an experience during worship, or when the Spirit lays us out. To experience the Lord, is to partner with Him during our "ordinary" or routine duties of the day. As you read in the chapter, "As you go", these experiences, as we move out in faith, we can take what we have learned, apply it, and continue to grow. This is where we as believers really grow, where we experience faith. Paul wrote to the **Ephesians in 4:15, "…may grow up in all things into Him (Christ)…"** this portion of the verse follows Paul explaining the apostolic offices that have been given for the equipping of the saints for the work of ministry. We are all called to do the work of ministry. I believe our lives, which we no longer live just for ourselves (Galatians 2:20), are to be used in ministry.

To experience God, and know Him, is to take that risk, and ask the person you may be talking with if you can pray for them. Reach across the table, grab their hand, and pray. When the Holy Spirit begins to lead you, the power of God will touch that person. Whenever we access heaven on behalf of another, we boldly appear before the throne of grace for that person. When the Holy Spirit brings

9   Defeating Dark Angels by Charles H. Kraft pg. 220
10   Deliverance and Spiritual Warfare Manual by John Eckhardt pg. 19

MOVE FORWARD

conviction, or restoration, healing, or deliverance, you and the person you are with, have just experienced God. These are the moments that mean the very most to me. It is my hope that you will take whatever you may learn and step out. Live your faith, and move forward.

6

Intimacy & Identity

"My sheep hear My voice, and I know them, and they know Me." John 10:27

Jesus had been confronted by the Jews, who demanded that He tell them plainly if He was the Christ. Jesus' response was not an exposition of the scriptures. He didn't point out the prophecies that were being fulfilled before their eyes. Rather, Jesus explained the very thing they were missing. When one has a personal relationship with the Christ, the Anointed One, that person knows who Jesus is. Jesus used the analogy of sheep, who have been in the presence of the shepherd and had become familiar with their shepherd. These sheep are so familiar with the shepherd, they even know his voice and follow. As Jesus points out to the Jews, they are not His sheep. These Jews who were confronting Jesus at the temple during the Feast of Dedication knew the scriptures. Although they should have recognized the fulfillment of the scriptures standing before them; they didn't know who Jesus was.

As Christians, it is in a relationship with Jesus where our walk as Christians begins. If this were not an autobiography, I would prefer this to be the first chapter. Because without an intimate relationship with Jesus, we can find ourselves following the "principles" of Christianity rather than following Jesus. For example, when Jesus called Peter and Andrew, He called them first to follow, and then He would make them fishers of men. I had lost sight of a relationship with the Lord and became more of a follower of the principles of Christianity. In time, I treated Christianity more as a sin management program rather than the pursuit of a relationship with the Lord. Although I had knowledge of the scriptures, I had little understanding of a relationship with a personal Savior and Lord. Such was the case with the religious Jews of Jesus' day, and such is the case with religious people today.

Sadly enough, we can know the scriptures but miss the very fulfillment of the scriptures. The Christian life is not a walk of knowledge of a "book," but a relationship with the author and finisher of our faith (Hebrews 12:2). There was a time, that although I knew the Word intellectually, I was still mired in a life of sin, and disobedience. The knowledge did little good to effect life change within me.

It wasn't until I had an encounter with God that I was brought into a "relationship" with Him. I was aware of my sinfulness and labored under the dark cloud that the face of God was hidden from me. It was my sins that separated me from God (Isaiah 59:2). It was true, my sin, and deliberate disobedience did adversely affect my ability to have a relationship with a Holy God. I did not comprehend the love and grace of God. I only saw the barrier. I carried a dark cloud around with me everywhere I went. This barrier was also a wall that I had erected, brick by brick In a perverse sense of pride, I assumed that the barrier I had erected was too great for God to penetrate, that my sins and disobedience were too much for God to forgive, and bring me back into a right relationship with Him. I have met, and spoken with people who have the same false notion. It is a real barrier, but it can be destroyed. Jesus came to destroy the works of the devil (1 John 3:8).

"Is not My word like a fire? Says the Lord. And like a hammer that breaks the rock in pieces." Jeremiah 23:29

For me, it was a "Rhema" (prophetic) word that broke through that brick wall that I had erected around my heart. Similarly, tragic are those who, like the Jews and Pharisees of Jesus' day, believe they too are doing the work of God, and yet have never given themselves to have a relationship with Him, or have lost sight of the relationship. In my opinion, one of the most frightening verses in the Bible is:

> Not everyone who says to Me, Lord, Lord, shall enter the kingdom of heaven, but he who does the will of My Father in heaven. Many will say to Me in that day, Lord, Lord, have we not prophesied in your name, cast out demons in Your name, and done many wonders in Your name? Matthew 7:21-22

But here is Jesus' response, after naming off the deeds that they did in His name: "And then I will declare to them, I never knew you; depart from Me, you who practice lawlessness!" Matthew 7:23

We as 21st century Christians have the luxury of the written Word to use and guide our understanding of theology, and the ways of the Lord. However, with Bible in hand, we can still miss that which I believe is the most important aspect of a personal God, Savior, and Lord. A personal relationship. What I find significant about the events that unfolded as the Lord walked through the Garden in the cool of the day "looking" for Adam is in verse 9 of Genesis 3.

"Then (after walking through the Garden) the Lord God called to Adam, and said to him: "'Where are you?'"

I take from this, that the Lord was calling for Adam, because this was not normal. For the first time, Adam had hidden himself from the Lord. Adam had not done this before. Meaning, as the Lord God customarily walked through the garden, Adam would join Him, and the two would walk together. This is the picture of a genuine relationship. The creator of all things, God Almighty, would walk through the garden with Adam. This was the way it was intended to be. To have close, personal communion with God. We know that sin broke the fellowship we were intended to have with the Lord. This was not a social arrangement between God and man. It was a covenant (Genesis 2:15-17) between the Lord and Adam.

As we continue to read in Genesis 2, God was discipling Adam, as He gave him the freedom to exercise his authority to name all of the creatures of the earth (verses 18-20). Adam spoke into existence the names of every creature His Father had made out of the ground.

Adam was to then recognize that although he was no longer alone in the garden, none of the marvelous creatures His Father created would be a fit helpmate for him. Every animal which God had created was wonderful, but not suitable or designed to have a personal relationship with Adam. God's next creation would not be made from the dust of the earth but from Adam himself. It would be a "personal" creation. Each of us has been created in the image and likeness of the Triune God to have a personal relationship with Him. I believe God created us in His image out of adoration for man (mankind), not as an impersonal creation such as an animal.

God in His goodness was aware that the covenant had been broken and still sought out Adam. God pursued Adam out of His love, not His anger. God, in His mercy then provided an atonement for Adam. I believe that as we read through the Bible, we can see the Lord has pursued man, ever since. If we would only listen for that still small voice. It took me a long time before I began to listen.

Jesus commended Mary as she sat at His feet, that she had chosen "that good part," which will not be taken away from her. Jesus counseled Martha on being troubled with so many things (Luke 10:38-42). Martha welcomed or invited Jesus into her house. I sympathize with Martha. After all, Jesus was the honored guest in her home. So, she was distracted with much serving. Certainly, it would be understandable that Martha wanted everything set out, and the food served. But Mary had chosen to hear the words of Jesus as she sat at his feet. It would be fair to assume that Jesus was teaching. Since Martha was distracted with "much serving" it would seem that listening to Jesus was less of a priority than making sure everything was set out or served. How often do we get focused on all of the things that need to get done instead of waiting and listening to what the Lord may have to say? I still struggle with this at times. I have been learning to stop, and take time to be still with the Lord. Spending time worshiping the Lord for who He is has been amazing for me. The Lord truly does inhabit or dwell in the praises of His people (Psalm 22:3).

When Miriam and Aaron criticized Moses for marrying an Ethiopian woman God personally descended in a cloud at the door of the tabernacle. He then called Aaron and Miriam forward for a rebuke.

> **Hear now My words: if there is a prophet among you; I the Lord, make myself known to him in a vision; I speak to him in a dream. Not so with my servant Moses; He is faithful in all My house.**
>
> **I speak with him face to face. Even plainly, and not in dark sayings; and he sees the form of the Lord. Why then are you not afraid to speak against My servant Moses? Numbers 12:6-8**

God is making a clear distinction that Moses is more than a prophet to Him. To God, Moses was the faithful servant, who had the privilege of speaking with God face to face. This means that there was a genuine relationship there. God was being protective of Moses, as He called out those who were criticizing His faithful servant. From the text, Moses found such favor with God, that God conversed with Moses plainly. Prophets carried the word of God to the people. They were important for the purposes of the Kingdom. But there was a certain order that was to be followed. God spoke to His prophets in an established order, in visions, dreams, and the parabolic language of heaven. But with Moses, there was a kinship, a relationship that allowed God to speak with him plainly. Moses had a similar relationship with God as did Adam. Moses, in fact, spent so much time in the Presence of the Lord that he had to have a veil cover his face for the Glory of the Lord was upon him; just from being in the Presence of God (Exodus 34:35).

When Samuel brought a rebuke to King Saul for disobeying the Lord, he also prophesied that the Lord had sought for Himself a man after His own heart(1 Samuel 13:13-14). That man turned out to be David. The Lord instructed Samuel not to look at the outward appearance. For He does not see man the way that man sees. Rather, God told Samuel that He looks at the heart of man (1 Samuel 16:7). Since those instructions came from God Himself to direct Samuel on who to anoint as king over Israel, I believe, that in order to better help us have a personal relationship with the Lord, we should have an understanding of the heart of David. This is an essential example for us.

As we read through the Psalms, we are given insight into the heart of David. I believe what set David apart was similar to what set Moses apart. It was all about being in the Presence of God. David understood the significance of the Presence of God early in his life.

He knew even as a youth, before he was king, that he represented the Lord, and that the Lord was with him. David credited the Lord with delivering him from the bear, and the lion. David knew as he stood there, and declared the defeat of Goliath (1 Samuel 17:34-37), he was in the Presence of God. We read, as David repented of his sin, he feared being cast away from the Presence of God and having His Spirit take 30071 n from him (Psalm 51:11).

David learned to covet the Presence of God. For it was His Presence that brought David comfort (Psalm 61:1-4), through his trials. I believe, for the most part, David lived and walked in a manner that reflected his awareness of the Presence of God. David behaved wisely in all his ways, and the Lord was with him 1 Samuel 18:14. Although David did fall into sin. That should serve as a reminder that we can choose to turn away from the His Presence. For David, I believe, remaining in the Presence of God was what captured his heart.

> *You can't be in the Presence of God, and not worship.*

"One thing I have desired of the Lord, that will I seek; that I may dwell in the house of the Lord all the days of my life, to behold the beauty of the Lord." Psalm 27:4

As Pastor Bill Johnson writes: "It's important that we all find the 'one thing' that can become the reference point for the rest of the issues of life. And that one thing is the Presence of the Almighty God, resting upon us."[1]

Since David had such a tremendous understanding of the Presence of God, it is no wonder why he had such a heart of worship. You can't be in the Presence of God, and not worship. When I encountered the Presence of God at the altar in 2014, it was my spirit that recognized the holiness that I had encountered. My intellect was not processing what had happened until afterward as I sat nearby. When my spirit encountered the Presence of God, I wept. I repented and was confident that by just His word I could be made clean. In the Presence of God, I surrendered, I worshiped Him who was Holy. Jesus told us:

---

1   Hosting the Presence by Bill Johnson pg. 21

"God is Spirit, and those who worship Him must worship in spirit and in truth." John 4:24

For the first time in my life, I entered into such worship of God. The Greek word used for worship in this verse is "proskyneo," which means that in such a reverence, it is to kiss the hand as in homage to him who is superior. That's why people tend to "buckle" under the weight of God's Presence. We will revisit this in chapter 7. But the essence of worship comes from our spirit. David revealed throughout the book of Psalms that he had a heart of worship. This came from his spirit.

... the essence of worship comes from our spirit.

"Oh come, let us sing to the Lord! Let us shout joyfully to the Rock of our salvation. Let us come before His Presence with thanksgiving, let us shout joyfully to Him with psalms." Psalm 95:1-2

"Make a joyful shout to the Lord, all you lands! Serve the Lord with gladness, come before His Presence with singing." Psalm 100:1-2

When we read Psalms such as these, we can also understand how David, a king danced before the Lord with all of his might (2 Samuel 6:14). David recognized that this was not a religious exercise. When David sang, shouted, and danced before the Lord, he did it with the understanding that he was in the Presence of the Lord. This would not be an impersonal religious exercise but an expression of David's spirit. It was the "one thing" he desired, and it was with all of his heart.

Although David had been aware of the Presence of the Lord upon his life since his youth, he still had to learn how to "carry" the Presence of God. We see this in the account where he danced before the Lord. In 2 Samuel chapter 5, and then into chapter 6, we read that David had just defeated the Philistines. After the victory, David gathered 30,000 choice men of Israel to bring the ark of God, where the Lord of Host dwelt between the cherubim (2 Samuel 6:1). Before David had decided to have the ark of God brought from Baale Judah, he had inquired of the Lord on how to proceed in the battle with the Philistines (2 Samuel 5:19 & 23). David then heard directly from the Lord as to how to handle the battle. David was an experienced warrior by this time. Nonetheless, David, in his faithfulness, wisdom, and awareness of the Lord's Presence followed His directions. David often inquired of the Lord as to how he should handle such matters.

When David decided to reclaim the ark of God from the house of Abinadab he allowed the ark of God to be placed onto a cart (a man-made transport). This was to be time of celebration as the musicians played (2 Samuel 6:4-5). However, the oxen that had been pulling the cart stumbled, and Uzzah took hold of the ark of God. As a result, God was angered, and Uzzah died right there next to the ark (2 Samuel 6:7). There has been confusion as to why God would, in His anger strike Uzzah dead for apparently not wanting to see the ark fall off the cart. However, the ark of God was not to be carried upon a cart; a man-made transport. In Deuteronomy 10:8, we see that the ark was to be carried on the shoulders of the priests. The Presence of God is to be carried by the priest, not a manufactured work. I believe this is a prophetic picture for us as New Testament believers. Further, the Presence of God is not to be manhandled. The Presence of God is to be carried! Just because Uzzah died for his error does not mean that he had been condemned. What do you suppose would have happened to Moses if he had not removed his sandals as he approached the burning bush (Exodus 3:5)? Though Uzzah died, I would guess the error did not rob him of being in God's Presence for all eternity. God sees the heart (1 Samuel 16:7).

We then read that the ark of God had been at the house of Odeb-Edom before David brought it into the City of David. It appears that David had either consulted with the Lord, checked the Torah, or decided to make a second, more careful procession of the ark. As they entered the city, David danced with all of his might, along with the whole house of Israel 2 Samuel 6:14-16). Except for Michal, David's wife. She was indignant and despised David in her heart. David was without remorse as he danced, played music, and humbled himself before the Lord. Michal was bound and refused to let go of her indignation. As a result of her self-righteousness, (religious attitude), she remained barren (no fruit).

Though David made mistakes, we see that he had an intimate relationship with the Lord. David was not ashamed to express himself in the worship of the Lord he loved. David lived the life of a shepherd, a warrior, a fugitive, a king, a prophet and a worshiper of the Lord. David had found favor because of his heart, not because he was perfect. David was not religious, rather, he intuitively followed the Presence of the Lord. David pursued an intimate daily walk with the Lord.

> I will praise the Lord who counsels me, even at night my heart instructs me. Because He is at my right hand (walks with) I will not be shaken. Therefore, my heart is glad and my tongue rejoices, my body also will rest secure because You will not abandon me to the grave, nor will You let your holy one (faithful) see decay. You have made known to me the path of life, You will fill me with joy in Your Presence, with eternal pleasures at Your right hand. Psalm 16:7-11 (NIV)

David is a prophetic picture of what the New Testament church is to look like.

As we read the Old Testament, we see the people gathered around the Presence of God. David sought to worship, and bless the Lord, knowing that he was in the Presence of God. Worshiping the Lord can bring us into the Presence of the

Intimacy & Identity

Lord. Being in the His Presence brings us into true worship. For He is there, He dwells in the genuine praises of His people. David knew this first hand. David expressed his heart; a heart that was after God's heart. David worshiped the Lord with reckless abandon. This type of worship is much more than an amazing song service. The worship that God Himself will inhabit emanates from the core of our very being. It emanates from our spirit, and we should seek to live a life of worship of the Lord.

To have true intimacy with the Lord, it must be our heart's desire. It cannot be a casual pursuit. We must hunger for relationship, and seek His Presence.

Somewhere, over the years, we have learned to assemble together, and our gathering has become centered around a sermon. Don't misunderstand; good teaching is necessary for the equipping of the saints. But how much more could we enter into when we are in corporate worship. How many encounters would there be as an entire assembly worships in one accord? Let me encourage you to spend time during your day, just worshiping the Lord. Set aside time to spend in His Presence. These moments that I take out of a day to worship Him, bring a refreshing.

Before Jesus worked a miracle, fed a multitude, or announced in the synagogue that the Messiah had arrived, God declared that He was well pleased with His Son (Matthew 3:17 & Luke 3:22). I find it interesting that in David's case, and then with Jesus, God the Father revealed that he knew a man's heart. The Spirit of God came upon David just before his anointing. David was a shepherd boy, served as an armor bearer, and then an aide to King Saul (1 Samuel 16:16-23). Once David had been anointed, and Spirit of God came upon him, he stepped further into his training for Kingship. At the baptism of Jesus, the Holy Spirit descended upon Jesus, and a voice came from an open heaven, **"This is my beloved Son, in whom I am well pleased."** God knew the heart of Jesus. As a youth He diligently attended to His Father's business (Luke 2:45-49). Jesus had been trained to follow in His father's business, as were many youths of His day (Matthew 13:55 & Mark 6:3). However, at an early age, He recognized that His heart's desire was to follow His heavenly Father's business (Luke 2:49).

Having a pure heart, to love and serve the Lord, for no other reason except that He is God, will certainly bring us into, and keep us in a right relationship with Him. David desired a pure heart as he repented of his sin (Psalm 51:10). Jesus proclaimed that it would be the pure in heart who will see God (Matthew 5:8). There can be no ulterior motive. Simply a love for the Lord, because He is Lord!

As you have read my testimony, and the incredible "supernatural" experiences in my life; such "experiences" should never be the focus. I will touch more on this in the chapter on the Holy Spirit. God, Elohim, Jehovah, is an all-powerful, and self-existing God who created all things, including each of us. So, it is to be our heart's desire to pursue Him and not just the experience of Him.

God, in His love, has made a way for us to be redeemed from our sin and provided a way to live an abundant life, here on earth, and in heaven to come. Therefore, He is worthy of our worship, our devotion, and even our lives. We are to present ourselves as a living sacrifice (Romans 12:1).

As much as I have enjoyed what the Lord has shown both Tonya and me through His Spirit, this can never take over our devotion to the Lord. My experience has been that there are seasons of a mighty "move" of the Spirit, and then there are seasons of quiet. Much like in the natural, there is a season of rain, which produces growth. Then there is a dry season of summer, which seems to be a time to endure. I don't personally like the heat. My point is that we should never measure our "closeness" to the Lord based upon the move of the Spirit or the anointing upon our lives. This is not an accurate barometer. In Charismatic circles, there is a tendency to either look at one's own life, or the life of another and surmise "closeness" to the Lord based on the moving of the Spirit, or the spiritual gifts one possesses. I would caution against such an indicator. I have seen some very anointed people, who had areas in their life that needed correction.

There can be no ulterior motive. Simply a love for the Lord, because He is Lord!

I have also seen some people who I am convinced have a very close, personal relationship with the Lord, who did not exhibit much in the way of gifts of the Spirit. I know those gifts are there, even if they are not exercised, for they are irrevocable (Romans 11:29). Lest we forget, spiritual gifts are just that. They are gifts of the Spirit, given, and intended to be used for the purposes of heaven. The same with a particular anointing on one's life. An anointing is also intended to be used for the purposes of heaven. The absence of either does not necessarily suggest fault on the believer, although it may. Perhaps this sounds like the logic from a conservative charismatic. Regardless, we need to remain anchored in that which is an absolute: **"Great is the Lord, and worthy of praise!"** (Psalm 96:4 & 145:3).

Worship, and praise of the Lord, from a pure heart, will bring us into an intimate relationship with Him.

In Luke 5:15-16 we read that after a report about Jesus had circulated, a great multitude came together, to hear Him, and be healed by Him. So, Jesus left!

Intimacy & Identity

Actually, verse 16 reads that Jesus, as He often did, withdrew into the wilderness to pray. From the text, I believe that Jesus perceived in His spirit that there would be a significant need for the multitude. There would also be a supernatural demand. So, Jesus withdrew to ensure that He was properly prepared for the ministry and the demand of the multitude. Jesus would later explain that this type of preparation (Mark 9:29), was needed when a great demand was placed on the Kingdom.

When the disciples asked Jesus in Mark 9:28, why could they not cast out the demon from the boy, it was not because of their lack of training or even experience; these were the disciples, the students of the Master. At the time this stubborn demon manifested and refused to submit to the authority the disciples possessed. The disciples were probably the most experienced in this area other than Jesus. So, in the private setting of a home, the disciples asked Jesus "why couldn't we cast it out?" Jesus' explanation was not one of technique, but of preparation. He responded that the disciples needed to be better prepared spiritually. Perhaps the disciples did not recognize the supernatural demand that would be placed on them by this stubborn demon.

Prayer can be more than bringing our request, and petitions to the Lord.

We also see from the gospels, that Jesus would often withdraw from the chaos that most likely surrounded Him so He could have quiet time with the Father. This is essential for us as well. We need to withdraw from the chaos of life, work, and even family demands to spend quiet time in prayer, and His Presence. As you will read later, my heart's desire has become for the Lord to prepare me to meet whomever He has prepared to meet Him. God will bless ministries and projects, but it is His servants that He anoints. Each of us needs to be a prepared vessel, able to handle whatever may come our way.

Prayer can be more than bringing our request, and petitions to the Lord. Although that certainly is a part of our time in prayer. Prayer is also spending time communing with the Lord, just communicating with the Lord in a very personal way. Sharing our hurts, burdens, thoughts, and desires of our hearts with the Lord. Life will undoubtedly lead us into areas of uncertainty, so we will always need to rely on the Lord for direction.

"In all your ways acknowledge Him, and He shall direct your paths (steps)." Proverbs 3:6.

Having a pure heart and motives are very important to God. We read in Luke

16, that the Pharisees, who were lovers of money, overheard Jesus teaching His disciples that no servant can serve God and money (Luke 16:13-14). The Pharisees criticized Jesus for such a teaching. Jesus responded that God knows their hearts and what they (men) esteemed highly was an abomination to God (verse 15). Jesus then moves into "the" better pursuit, which is the Kingdom of God.

"...since (John) that time the kingdom of God has been preached, and everyone is pressing into it." Luke 16:16

The Pharisees were misguided in their priorities. They had the appearance of righteousness as Pharisees, but their love was not for God, but for money, and status. Jesus previously addressed this same issue of the heart and the proper Kingdom perspective.

"But seek first the kingdom of God and His righteousness, and all these things shall be added to you." Matthew 6:33

The principle is that our priority should be in the pursuit of the Kingdom of God, and His righteousness instead of needlessly worrying about the natural provisions that our Father already knows we need. Here in Luke 16:16, Jesus is more emphatic that the Kingdom of God is something to be pressed into.

In both Matthew 6:33 and Luke 16:16, there is an emphasis on an active pursuit of the Kingdom of God. If we, as Christians, truly desire to have an abundant life, which is why Jesus came (John 10:10), it must be pursued. The world around us has far too many distractions and burdens that can entangle us. So, what is this life in the Kingdom of heaven (God) here on earth? Jesus said:

"...For indeed, the kingdom of God (heaven) is within you." Luke 17:21

Paul would later write to the church at Rome: **"for the Kingdom of God is not of eating or drinking, but righteousness and peace and joy in the Holy Spirit." Romans 14:17** The Kingdom of God is not the satisfaction of our carnal desires. There is a higher calling than to go through life with the desire to satisfy the appetites of our carnal, or human, nature. As Christians (Christ followers), we follow Jesus' example. That is, to work for that "food" that does not perish, understanding that we are to have a heavenly, not just an earthly, perspective. The life of the believer, who knows the Kingdom of heaven is within them, should approach all of life as Jesus did. Knowing that there is an eternal significance to almost everything we are involved in.

Although I've already touched on this in a previous chapter, we need to take the verse that "the Kingdom of heaven is within you" beyond being just conceptual. We need to move that into a practical arena; a place of understanding that affects our entire life. I realize that there are times where this can be difficult, such as in those seasons where we feel we are either walking alone or in a dry season. In the days, and weeks, following GGG 2014, it was easy to know that the Kingdom of heaven was within me. I just had a personal encounter with God.

I was in tune with the Holy Spirit. I was a new creation, and my spirit was alive. I was "charged." I was on spiritual overload. But we can't wait for the next "experience" to practically walk in the spiritual reality that the Kingdom of heaven is within us. Jesus gives us the best illustration of the simplicity of Kingdom life here on earth.

"Assuredly I say to you, whoever does not receive the Kingdom of God (heaven) as a little child will by no means enter it." Luke 18:17.

This verse is most often referred to as the means in which we enter heaven at the end of our life. It is by having a childlike faith to believe in the gospel message. Although this is true, I believe to enter into a life of Kingdom living, as Jesus demonstrated for us, it requires the simple faith that a child would have. As adults, we allow too much of our reasoning, logic, and even cynicism to interfere with God's purposes. Jesus said that these signs will follow those who believe, in my name they will cast out demons, they will speak with new tongues … they will lay hands on the sick, and they will recover (Mark 16:17-18). Just because I lay hands on someone, pray my best prayer, or command a demon spirit to flee, and nothing happens, does not invalidate what Jesus said.

As adults, myself included, we tend to go back to the drawing board, and re-work our theology so it fits into our practical experience. It's more comfortable that way. It's easier to explain when the lack of miracles have a reasonable, and even "biblical" foundation to fall onto.

Although I have seen God do mighty works, there have been times I was expecting something "dynamic" as I concluded the prayer "in the name of Jesus," and nothing! Well, that doesn't invalidate the words of Jesus. I don't know and can't explain why someone didn't receive their healing, their deliverance, or become overwhelmed by the Spirit of God. But I will not blame God. I simply do what the disciples did. I go to the Lord privately and seek His counsel on the matter (Mark 9:28). Life in the Kingdom of God is righteousness, peace, and joy in the Holy Spirit; not in having all of the answers. So, I will not be moved from the realities of heaven.

"Therefore, my beloved brethren, be steadfast, immovable, always abounding in the work of the Lord, knowing that your labor is not in vain in the Lord." 1 Corinthians 15:58.

It is also much easier to step out and press into the Kingdom of heaven when we simply get over ourselves. In other words, recognize it is not us, or our abilities, or

MOVE FORWARD

even talents that effectively access the Kingdom of heaven. It is Jesus, the hope of Glory that resides in each of us.

"But we have this treasure in earthen vessels, that the excellence of the power may be of God, and not of us." 2 Corinthians 4:7.

"Do you not know that you are the temple of God and that the Spirit of God dwells in you? If anyone defiles the temple of God, God will destroy him. For the temple of God is holy, which temple you are." 1 Corinthians 3:16-17

God dwells in each of us. This is not theoretical, this is a spiritual reality. It is no longer I who live, but Christ who lives in me (Galatians 2:20). The same Spirit, that raised Jesus from the dead dwells in each of us (Romans 8:11). What more could we ever ask for? There is an entire Kingdom of Heaven within each of us that needs to be released into the world around us. For most of us, for that to occur we need to think completely differently.

Not to think from a human perspective, but from heaven's perspective. No wonder Jesus didn't panic when the multitudes approached him to be fed, healed, and delivered. In Luke 5, when Jesus withdrew, He needed time to pray, to be refreshed, and renewed in order to face the multitude. As is for us, it's not about our humanity or our natural abilities. It's about what dwells within each of us spiritually. Because of what Jesus did at the cross, the veil has been torn, and access has been granted into the holy of holies (heaven).

> *God dwells in each of us. This is not theoretical, this is a spiritual reality.*

As quoted in chapter 5, "Salvation is more than going to heaven when you die. Eternal life is an intimate, personal, progressive relationship with Almighty God, His Son (and Holy Spirit). When salvation comes to your life, God radically and immediately reorients you for the rest of your life to Christ's right to be Lord."[2]

However, in the midst of life, there are times we need to ensure we are properly oriented in the direction God has pointed us. Being in right relationship with the Lord will help us fully understand our identity; who we are in Christ. Having a true understanding of who we are in Christ will keep us in a right relationship with the Lord.

Often, I've heard Christians refer to themselves as sinners saved by grace. I feel that this is worth covering again because it's more than an image of who we are; it's our identity. Our identity is who we actually are whether we realize it or not.

2 The Man God Uses by Blackaby & Blackaby pg. 35

In Proverbs 23:7 we read:

"For as he thinks in his heart so is he…"

After all that Jesus has done for us at the cross, would I still consider myself as a sinner? We were sinners, saved by grace (Ephesians 2:8). But after our confession of sins, God is faithful in His forgiveness of our sins, and to cleanse us from all unrighteousness (1 John 1:9).

> … and by Him (Jesus) to reconcile all things to Himself, by Him, whether things on earth or things in heaven, having made peace through the blood of His cross. And you, who were once alienated and enemies in your mind by wicked works, yet now He has reconciled in the body of His flesh through death, to present you, holy, and blameless, and above reproach in His (God's) sight. Colossians 1:20-22

This is not just a promise of someday as we stand before the throne of God, it is a promise to each of us, as a believer can walk in today. Because of the work of Jesus at the cross, in God's sight, we are holy, blameless, and above reproach. When the Father looks at each of us, He sees the finished work of His beloved Son. It's an offense to view ourselves otherwise. Perhaps there may be areas that we know we need to work on. But that does not change God's view of us. Remember, God does not see man as man sees (1 Samuel 16:7).

Because of the work of Jesus at the cross, in God's sight, we are holy, blameless, and above reproach.

When Paul greeted the churches at Rome, Corinth, Ephesus, and Philippi he addressed the believers as "saints." Paul uses the Greek word, "hagios," which means, most holy thing. For example, when Paul greets the church at Philippi, he writes: "To all the saints in Christ Jesus who are in Philippi…." Paul does not distinguish those who may be more devout, or more mature in their faith. Paul called all of the believers at Philippi, as he did in all the other churches he would write letters to, "saints." Paul even greeted the church at Corinth as "saints."

"To the church of God which is at Corinth, to those who are sanctified in Christ Jesus, called to be saints…." 1 Corinthians 1:2

This is the same church that Paul goes on to rebuke for their carnal, and immoral behavior. Paul also rebuked them for their disrespectful behavior when partaking of the Lord's table. Corinth was, at the time when Paul founded the church, in an immoral and idolatrous culture in Greece. Though they had been sanctified in Christ, they still needed come to the full understanding of their calling as saints in middle of a pagan society. Although their behavior may not have accurately reflected who they were. They were saints (a most holy thing) nonetheless. They simply didn't recognize their own identity. I believe had they truly recognized their new identity as saints their behavior would have reflected it.

Having a full understanding of who we are in Christ will positively affect every aspect of our lives. The benefits of having an accurate understanding of our identity in Christ will release us from our past, sustain us in the present, and bring us assurance for the future.

I wrote in chapter 4, that on the last day of the conference at Bethel there was a sense to release the past. This was manifested out of God's love. It is not that I have become self-absorbed and no longer care about my past. But to go back, and wallow in past sins as if they are still an entanglement is to not understand what being forgiven means. In the sight of God, because of the work Jesus did, our sin debt has been paid. We are redeemed, bought back, no longer a slave to our painful past. We are free indeed. Therefore, we are to live a life that is free from the commendation and guilt of the past.

Being a new creation in Christ means just that. We have been transformed from the old into a brand new creation. The old has passed away, it is dead. All things have been made new (2 Corinthians 5:17). Do not pick up your old identity. Only the enemy wants us to retreat and pick up our old identity. If the enemy can get us to re-identify with what, and who we used to be, then he can steer us back into the old habits, and even the old lifestyle. We resist the devil as we move forward, not in going backward. Understanding our true identity in Christ will keep us focused on who we are in Him, how He has defeated the power of sin and guilt.

"He (God) has delivered us from the power of darkness and conveyed (transported) us into the Kingdom of the Son of His love, in whom we have the redemption through His blood the forgiveness of sins." Colossians 1:13-14

This is not a someday promise. We no longer need to be subject to the power, the allure, or grip of darkness (sin). Properly identifying who we are in Christ means we belong to a new family. We belong to His Kingdom and have been positioned spiritually in His Kingdom. The redemption by the shed blood of Jesus means we have been taken out of that which we once were enslaved in. We now have full access to His Kingdom.

I heard a story of a man who bought a ticket in the 1900's on an ocean liner to take him across the Atlantic from Europe to America. He was a man of meager means, so he packed enough crackers and cheese to sustain him for the two-week journey. About a week into the trip, he spoke with someone on the deck and discovered that his ticket allowed him full access to the meals provided every day in the dining area. Although he had a ticket which allowed him full access to wonderful meals, three times a day, he was unaware. So, he lived in a manner in which he was accustom. Although he would reach his destination, during the journey, he just barely got by. There was so much more available to him.

We have full access to the Kingdom of heaven, and all that Kingdom can provide. Understanding our identity in Christ frees us from our former ways of living. Over the years, I struggled with a habit of self-condemnation. If something would not go right, or not as I had planned, I was quick to berate myself. In the past, the self-condemnation was vile and came from a self-hatred. Although the self-hatred is no longer there, the habit of criticizing myself is a default when I lose my focus. This is not the mindset of the Kingdom of heaven. Whether we realize it or not, we will attract spiritually exactly what we release.

"Now thanks be to God who always leads us in triumph in Christ, and through us diffuses the fragrance of His knowledge in every place." 2 Corinthians 2:14

When we walk in the knowledge that God always leads us in the triumph in Christ, the Spirit of God is able to release the "fragrance" of Christ in every place we walk. The fruit of the Spirit is evident to all. There is, in the spiritual, the diffused fragrance of life, peace, and joy, and all that is associated with Jesus. However, when we use condemnation, either to ourselves or others, we release a foul odor that will attract that which enjoys decay. During the years I spent working as a detective, there is one odor that I will never forget. It's the odor of decomp. Decomp means death, and it always attracts flies, which enjoy feasting on decay and death. It's the same in the spiritual realm. Inadvertently we can open ourselves up to the demonic realm when we spew, anger, frustration, and condemnation into the atmosphere.

This is not how the Kingdom of heaven operates. So, we need to be ever mindful, not to come back into agreement with those habits that were once associated with our old self.

Having a full understanding of our identity in Christ will help sustain us in the present. If we do not fully comprehend who we are in Christ, our true identity in Him, we will most likely seek our identity in something else. However, when our identity is in Christ, and His Kingdom purposes, we will not be crushed by our failures, weaknesses, fall into pride from our successes, or despair over the disappointments or even tragedy. Although the past three years have been an incredible period of spiritual growth, it comes with growing pains. I have experienced setbacks, and even what seems like defeats in life. It's so natural for me to battle feelings of despair and defaulting into a mindset that is not of Christ. But my identity in Christ is not just when everything seems to go my way. It is in Jesus. In those challenging times, I need to remain faithful in what I know to be true, and not give into thoughts of failure, pride, or despair.

> For I am persuaded that neither death nor life, nor angels nor principalities nor powers, nor things present nor things to come, nor heights nor depth, nor any other created thing shall be able to separate us from the love of God, which is in Christ Jesus. Romans 8:38-39.

Knowing who we are in Christ, assures us that we have nothing to fear about the future. We may not know the future but we can trust in Him who holds our future. As Paul said in the above verse, he was persuaded, that nothing can separate us from the love of God, which includes those things to come. Although the future can hold uncertainty, we do not need to give into fear or anxiety. As I wrote of my travels to Utah when Jeff was in the hospital, God prepared me to remain in the moment. If I had not remained in the moment, I would have been more likely to fall into the anxiety of how to work out all the "logistics" that I thought needed to be worked out. Knowing who we are in Christ, and that we always operate *from* a place of victory, we don't have to work *toward* a place of victory.

Knowing who we are in Christ, assures us that we have nothing to fear about the future.

All of us have many decisions that we must make every day that affect or pertain to the future. But we need not give into fear or dread about the future. Whether it is in our personal lives, or even the state of affairs of the country, or the world. We can remain confident in Him.

"For God has not given us a spirit of fear, but of power and of love and of a sound mind." 2 Timothy 1:7

It will take time to fully understand, and live out of our identity in Christ. When I lose my focus, I tend to default back into self-critique which is never healthy.

When I read Nehemiah chapter 4, I see a prophetic picture of what a Christian can look like. Under the direction of Nehemiah, the citizens of Jerusalem were determined to protect themselves from a life of attacks by the enemy (devil). We read in Nehemiah that when the enemy (Sanballat) heard they were rebuilding the wall around Jerusalem he was furious, very indignant, and he mocked the Jews. Sound familiar? Once the enemy realizes that we are no longer going to identify with our past, he loses that stronghold.

The same with the Jews who were determined to rebuild the wall around the city. The wall was one of their layers of defense. Once it was rebuilt, and the gaps in the broken wall repaired, the enemy would be unable to access the city. The enemy mocked the Jews for their effort. But they realized that they were fortifying themselves from attacks (verse 2). The Jews were undeterred and continued in their efforts. They prayed and set up a watch during the building process (verse 9). Meaning, their first priority was prayer, their relationship with the Lord. They were also vigilant in watching for any attacks, which were sure to come. They needed to be prepared to defend themselves. So, with a trowel in one hand, and a weapon in the other, they built the wall around Jerusalem (verse 17).

"Every one of the builders had his sword girded at his side as he built..." Nehemiah 4:18

As we come into the full understanding of who we are in Christ, as a new creation, our identity is a new foundation for us to build on. We are not remodeling the old self into a new person. That is what the world does with all of the self-help gimmicks. As Christians, our foundation is the stone (Jesus) which the builders rejected. He is our cornerstone.

We are not remodeling the old self into a new person. That is what the world does ...

I will praise You, for You have answered me, and have become my salvation. The stone which the builders rejected has become the chief cornerstone. This is what the Lord is doing, it is marvelous in our eyes. This is the day that the Lord has made, we will rejoice and be glad in it. Psalm 118:21-24

As we continue in understanding our identity in Christ; how it relinquishes us from our past, allows us to persevere in the present, and allows us to rejoice over the future, the spiritual wall is built. Our cornerstone is just that. Jesus is our foundation that joins the walls together. The enemy may mock us, but our defenses have been fortified, the gaps repaired, and access for the enemy is denied. But we do need to be vigilant. This is not a one and done.

So, with our spiritual trowel in the one hand, we build. In the other hand, we use the weapons provided when an attack approaches. Knowing that God always leads us in triumph through Christ, our Rock, and Redeemer (Psalm 19:14). As the Jews built the wall around their city, so we build our identity in Christ our rock. Nehemiah was aware that the enemy would not be happy with them building the wall. He instructed the people to prepare themselves for the potential battle that may come their way as they built the wall. The battle strategy was the best way to remain in a state of readiness for the people of Jerusalem.

When we understand our individual identity in Christ, regardless of our "status" in life, we are secure in who we are. We each have an eternal Kingdom purpose to fulfill in this walk of life. Many of us tend to look at others or their ministries, and at times, feel that we are lacking. Giving into comparing is not only destructive, it can be evidence that we have lost sight of God's purposes for our lives.

"For we dare not class ourselves or compare ourselves with those who commend themselves. But they, measuring themselves by themselves and comparing themselves among themselves, are not wise." 2 Corinthians 10:12

Each of us has a Kingdom role to play. Thus, we each need to steward that which we have been given. Whether in talents, opportunity, or an anointing for a particular ministry. I have been blessed to have tremendous opportunities to press into the Kingdom of heaven for people as I go about working as an insurance investigator throughout the country. I will cover more of this in detail in chapter 8.

However, there are many days where I am just going through the nuts and bolts of the insurance business, and trust me, that is not very exciting. During those days I am stuck in the office typing, on the phone, or otherwise sorting out a coverage issue for a customer, I too wonder, "Is this really what You want me to do for the rest of my life?" Well, perhaps it is.

In those times when I am not praying for someone, I greet them with a blessing, and leave them with a blessing. I don't know how many times I have departed from someone after "talking insurance," and told them to have a blessed day. They seem so surprised, but they receive it. My point is, just because I have not been called into a mega-ministry, the Lord has a designated purpose for me, and I will gladly honor whatever He has for me. It is the call for every one of us just to step into what He has for each of us.

My identity is no longer in what I do to earn a living, as it was when I worked as a police detective. Often, men especially, identify with what they do for a living as who they are. At times it is difficult to separate, but our identity is in Christ, not a profession. Recognize that whatever we do, and wherever we go, we are ambassadors for Christ (2 Corinthians 5:20). We represent Jesus, and His

Intimacy & Identity

Kingdom wherever we go, and in whatever we do.

So, whether we are employed at the local box store, manage a business, or investigate suspicious insurance claims. We do all things as a representative of the very Kingdom we belong to, not just the company who employs us.

"And whatever you do in word or deed, do all in the name of the Lord Jesus, giving thanks to God the Father through Him (Christ)." Colossians 3:17

Not only are we to represent the Kingdom of heaven as an ambassador, but we are also citizens of heaven (Philippians 3:20). Our citizenship should be apparent to anyone who sees us going about our daily business, living our lives and working at our jobs. Just as we can recognize someone we encounter, and know immediately that they are from another country, so should those around us recognize that we are citizens of heaven. Everything we set our hands to do, is unto the Lord.

"And whatever you do, do it heartily, as to the Lord, and not unto men." Colossians 3:23.

When we recognize that each of us has been chosen by God, before the foundations of world (Ephesians 1:4), to be in Christ, or identified with Christ because of the love of God. How can we not walk in the utmost appreciation for Him, and desire to fulfill His purposes through us?

Our life, ministry, or livelihood was never intended to resemble anyone else's. Before the foundations of the world, God knew each of us, and formed us (Jeremiah 1:5). This did not just pertain to the prophet Jeremiah. God knew each of us. He formed (created), each of us. Which includes our own unique personalities, talents, and strengths.

"For we are His workmanship, created in Christ Jesus for good works, which God prepared beforehand that we should walk in them." Ephesians 2:10

We can be sure that whatever God has called each of us to do, He has equipped us to perform. God in His sovereignty and wisdom has chosen each of us to co-labor with Him (1 Corinthians 3:9), in His victory over the devil. God could have smitten the devil at the very moment of his rebellion. But He chose us, and given us the privilege to work in Him, and through us to bring about His purposes. What a blessing.

As Christians, we are blessed. We can have a personal relationship with God Almighty. We have been forgiven of our sins, we can live an abundant life, and will spend eternity with Jesus in heaven. Our intimacy with the Lord comes from spending time in His Presence. Our identity comes from recognizing what Jesus did for us at the cross, and how God sees us because of His redemptive work.

MOVE FORWARD

When the reality of what God has done for us in His love, how could we do anything but rejoice?

"Rejoice in the Lord always. Again, I say rejoice." Philippians 4:4

We are called to rejoice, always. "Rejoice in the Lord, o you righteous!" Psalm 33:1 Let us rejoice in the Lord, in who we are, and the life He has given us.

Our calling, our life's purpose goes beyond rejoicing in the Lord. I know for myself, it is easy to rejoice in those times when everything seems to be going along according to plan, usually my own. When the Lord is granting the desires of our hearts, we rejoice. We can be thankful to the Lord for all that he has done, and will do, and we should be. I believe our ultimate expression of who we are in Christ (since He redeemed us), and as a new creation in Him, means we are made to worship Him.

Our calling, our life's purpose goes beyond rejoicing in the Lord.

"This is written for the generation to come, that a people yet to be created may praise the Lord." Psalm 102:18

We, who have been created as a new creation in Christ are the generation to come that David speaks of. As I mentioned before, when God rested from all His creation (Genesis 2:3), He rested because all had been created. Yet, David speaks prophetically of a generation yet to be created.

"Therefore, if anyone is in Christ, he is a new creation, old things have passed away, behold all things have become new." 2 Corinthians 5:17

We are that people. Ultimately, we have been created to bring Him glory and honor (Isaiah 43:7). So, as we grow closer to Him, and in our identity in Christ, we will certainly better represent Jesus to the world around us everywhere we go.

7

Life in the Spirit

"The angel answered, "The Holy Spirit will come upon you, and the power of the Most High will overshadow you." Luke 1:35 (NIV)

When I accepted the Lord in the summer of 1983, I did so kneeling in the privacy of my bedroom. By all outward appearances, it seemed to be a non-dynamic event. However, in those few moments, my spirit had been born-again. There was a new birth, a spiritual birth. I was made into a new creation. This new creation was made possible by the Holy Spirit.

"…not by works of righteousness which we have done, but according to His mercy He saved us, through the washing or regeneration and the renewing of the Holy Spirit." Titus 3:5

Holy Spirit is the power of the most High God (Luke 1:35). When the Holy Spirit came upon Mary, new life was created within her, which brought the birth of Jesus. At our conversion, there is a new birth. A spiritual birth which then grants us a birthright into His Kingdom. We were once of the kingdom of darkness (Ephesians 5:8), but now we belong to the Kingdom of Heaven. The Holy Spirit sets His seal upon us (Ephesians 4:13), as a king uses his signet ring to seal something official. The seal represents that "this" belongs to the King. Once we have been made alive in our new birth, we are then able to see and enter into the Kingdom of heaven (John 3:3-5). Upon being born-again, the Holy Spirit then dwells in us (1 Corinthians 6:19). He then becomes an abiding presence within us. This is different than a manifest Presence of the Holy Spirit, which will be covered later in this chapter.

But this is just the beginning. As Jesus said, a day will come for new believers when rivers of living water will flow from their hearts.

"He who believes in Me, as the Scripture has said, out of his heart will flow rivers of living water." John 7:38.

Life in the Spirit

"But this He spoke concerning the Spirit, whom those believing in Him would receive, for the Holy Spirit was not yet given, because Jesus was not yet glorified." John 7:39.

Although we receive the Holy Spirit at the time of our conversion, there is a still a separate, and distinct baptism in the Holy Spirit. Once a believer is baptized in the Holy Spirit, they will understand fully what it means to have rivers of living water flow from their heart. This is a supernatural work of the Holy Spirit that nourishes everyone the living water touches. This baptism in the Holy Spirit should not be an area of any confusion. For it was one of the reasons that Jesus came, and accomplished through His finished work. John declared:

"I indeed baptize you with WATER unto repentance, but He who is coming after me is mightier than I, whose sandals I am not worthy to carry. He will baptize you with the Holy Spirit and fire." Matthew 3:11

Although I had received the Lord over 30 years before GGG 2014, I had not been baptized in the Spirit before that day. I had been sealed by the Holy Spirit at my conversion and belonged to the King. But of my own will and rebellion, I chose to live in the ways of the flesh rather than in the Spirit. Then in His mercy, and grace, the Father saw me while I was yet a far way off (Luke 15:20). He met me at that altar. I was baptized in the Holy Spirit as I stood there at the altar.

"His winnowing fork is in His hand, and He will thoroughly clean out His threshing floor, and gather His wheat into the barn, but He will burn up the chaff with unquenchable fire." Matthew 3:12

Jesus cleaned His threshing floor of my soul, gathered what was His, and burned up (fire) that which did not belong in His Kingdom when I was baptized in the Spirit. I was clean for the first time in years. I was lighter; that which did not belong to the Kingdom of heaven had been removed (delivered). Although I already touched on the topic of deliverance and Christians having demons in chapter 5, I will quickly review.

When a person becomes a born-again believer, it is their spirit that has been made alive; born-again spiritually. Therefore, their spirit has been sealed, and the Holy Spirit dwells in the believer's spirit. However, the new believer may have brought some of his demons with him, which inhabit the soul (mind, emotions, and flesh). Other believers, may open the doors to the demonic along the way, and need deliverance at some point. But for me, that day, standing at the altar, in His mercy, Jesus filled me (baptized) with the Holy Spirit and, by fire. By His hand, He cleared the threshing floor (the place where wheat (good grain) is separated from the tares). Jesus drove out all that was defiling the temple (Matthew 21:12-14). The barn (soul), and the temple (prayer center) had been completely cleansed and made ready for His purposes. Then, the supernatural life began for me. Once baptized in the Spirit, the Holy Spirit will introduce every believer to a supernatural life.

In my early years as a Christian, I attended a small four square Pentecostal church. Although it was a Pentecostal church, there was little emphasis on how the Holy Spirit moved or operated in the life of a believer. There was an occasional tongue, and then the interpretation given. However, as I recall, the messages were usually a rebuke of sorts for the assembly as a whole. As a new Christian, I studied my Bible and knew the scriptural addresses of who the Holy Spirit was, and the Spirit's functions. But I did not have a relationship with the Holy Spirit. Over the years as a Christian my understanding of the Holy Spirit like the remainder of my biblical understanding became academic. If our understanding of the Christian life is academic it is anemic. It simply is without life, or real understanding, and not likely to be lived out. The same with the Holy Spirit. He is a person. The third person (not in order) of the Trinity. There is God the Father, God the Son, God the Spirit. We are to have a relationship with the Holy Spirit just as we do with the Father, and the Son.

Benny Hinn explains that after he was saved, then filled with the Spirit that he discovered there was so much more.

> So many Christians have received that same experience (baptism in the Spirit, and speak in tongues), and stop right there. They fail to realize that what happened at Pentecost was only one of the gifts of the Spirit. But what I want you to know is this; beyond salvation, beyond being baptized in water, beyond the infilling of the Spirit, the third person of the Trinity is waiting for you to meet Him personally. He yearns for a lifelong relationship.[1]

Our natural man will not comprehend the things of the Spirit. This is not a journey into the logical, or an intellectual understanding. It's an intimate relationship with the Spirit of God. Having a relationship with the Holy Spirit will lead us into a

---

1   Good Morning Holy Spirit by Benny Hinn pg. 46

deeper understanding into the ways of God. Our natural mind can not fully grasp the ways of the Spirit, but our spirit can.

"But the natural man does not receive the things of the Spirit of God, for they are foolishness to him, nor can he know them, because they are spiritually discerned (understood)." 1 Corinthians 2:14

In the previous verses of 1 Corinthians 2:10-13, Paul tells the Corinthians that the ways of God are revealed through His Spirit. It is the Spirit who searches the deep things of God. It is the Spirit of God who reveals the deep inner workings of God. As it is with man, it is our "spirit" that reveals our inner workings. Jesus rebuked His disciples about what spirit were they when they suggested that they should call fire down from heaven on the Samaritans who did not receive them (Luke 9:54-55). It is through our thoughts, words, and actions that will reveal our spirit. So, it is with God. "**...Even so no one knows the things of God except the Spirit of God." 1 Corinthians 2:11**. In order to know the "things" of God, we need to cultivate a relationship with the Spirit of God. Not merely read about Him, and cite the applicable Bible references.

> **Now we have received not the spirit of the world, but the Spirit who is from God, that we might know the things that have been freely given to us by God. These things we also speak not in words which man's wisdom teaches but which the Holy Spirit teaches, comparing spiritual things to spiritual. 1 Corinthians 2:12-13**

The Spirit we have received is from God, and not of the world. It is through His Spirit so that we would know (discern) what we have been given is from God. By God's very nature, His thoughts are not our thoughts, nor are His ways our ways (Isaiah 55:8-9). Therefore, we need a Spiritual Helper (John 14:16), who will help us navigate into the ways of His Kingdom. Being born-again is just the beginning of this wonderful journey of life in the Spirit.

As we continue in this chapter, we will cover what has been given to us through the Holy Spirit (1 Corinthians 12:7).

I believe very strongly that we need to fully understand what we have access to in the Holy Spirit. If we don't, we run the risk of falling short of our full potential for the Kingdom of God. This understanding comes from having a relationship with the Holy Spirit. As Paul continues, what we have in the Holy Spirit is not man's wisdom. It certainly is not an academic knowledge that the Spirit of God teaches us. If it were, Paul would have exhorted us here study to show ourselves approved in the ways of the Spirit. He did not. We have been made spiritually alive, and it is the Spirit of God that will lead us to compare, or know spiritual things. An in depth understanding of the deep things of God is spiritual, not intellectual.

MOVE FORWARD

Before being baptized in the Spirit I only had an academic understanding, and even that was at an elementary level; it lacked spiritual depth.

Therefore, we need to be baptized (immersed) in the Holy Spirit. The same as those in the early Church as they began to witness for Jesus. It was the first order of business for those gathered as the Lord commanded. Wait for the Promise of the Father in Jerusalem, which they heard from Jesus (Acts 1:4). They were waiting for the baptism (filling) of the Holy Spirit. There was a time that I thought that the infilling of the Holy Spirit was a euphemism for when we receive the Spirit at conversion. Being filled with the Spirit (Ephesians 5:18), is to be filled with clean water which will flow as a river from our innermost being. Once the apostles and those gathered on the day of Pentecost were baptized in the Spirit, rivers of living water began to flow through them.

> *We have been made spiritually alive, and it is the Spirit of God that will lead us to compare, or know spiritual things.*

Just before Jesus ascended into heaven, He explained to the apostles the reason they needed to wait in Jerusalem for the baptism in the Holy Spirit.

"But you shall receive power when the Holy Spirit has come upon you, and you shall be witnesses to Me in Jerusalem, and in all Judea and Samaria, and to the end of the earth." Acts 1:8

But were these not the same apostles that Jesus had already breathed on that they may receive the Holy Spirit? Yes, they were. After Jesus rose from the dead, He appeared to them, and after greeting them:

"...He breathed on them (apostles), and said to them, receive the Holy Spirit." John 20:22

Jesus breathed on the disciples the same Holy Spirit, who raised Him from the dead (Romans 8:11). The disciples had been with Jesus in ministry for three years. They were familiar with the Holy Spirit because the Spirit had dwelt among them since Jesus had been anointed by the Spirit without measure (Acts 10:38). But now the disciples were given the Holy Spirit to dwell within (Titus 3:5) them as well. Although the disciples received the Holy Spirit as Jesus breathed on them, this did not exclude them from the baptism in the Spirit that would be poured out on the day of Pentecost and birth the church.

Life in the Spirit

"The Spirit of truth, whom the world cannot receive, because it neither sees Him nor knows Him, for He dwells with you, and will be in you." John 14:17

The same disciples (apostles) who had dwelt with the Holy Spirit, through Jesus' ministry had received the Holy Spirit in them as Jesus breathed on them. Just as God had breathed life into Adam from the dust, Jesus breathed Spiritual life into His disciples. I suppose this would be similar to us receiving the Holy Spirit upon our conversion. However, the baptism in the Holy Spirit was still to come for the disciples and those who had gathered with them in the upper room. Of course it was fitting for such an event to be poured out on the day of Pentecost. Pentecost was one of the great Jewish feast celebrated yearly, the seventh week after Passover in gratitude for the first fruits of the latter season harvest. So, when the disciples and those gathered received the gift of the Holy Spirit (immersed), they became witnesses for Jesus. The events that followed that day, in front of those gathered from all over, witnessed the hand of God.

Then the preaching of Peter and 3000 souls were added to the Kingdom of heaven. What a tremendous harvest as the Holy Spirit was poured out on those gathered. When those in the upper room were filled with the Spirit on Pentecost it was like a fulfillment of a prophetic picture were read about in 2 Chronicles 5:11-14. There were 120 priests, worshiping the Lord (ministering to Him). They made one sound and were in one accord. Then the house of the Lord was filled with a cloud (His Presence), and the Glory of the Lord filled the house of God. We continue to read that fire came down, and the Glory of God was upon the temple (the New Testament believer is now the temple of God, 2 Corinthians 6:16). Those gathered, bowed at the Glory of God, and worshiped, and praised Him (2 Chronicles 7:3). They were "magnifying" and praising God.

In the upper room, on the day of Pentecost, all 120 gathered, were in one accord, when the whole house was filled with a sound, which was like a mighty rushing wind, and tongues of fire rest upon those gathered (Acts 2:1-3). They began to speak in other tongues as the Spirit gave them utterances. The languages they were speaking were not learned languages but languages that the Spirit gave them. Those gathered for the feast of Pentecost were from elsewhere and recognized their native tongue magnifying and praising God (Acts 2:11).

It was the devout men who were amazed, but there were those who began to mock and make the excuse that those speaking in tongues were drunk. Unfortunately, still today, there are those who ridicule or criticize the move of the Spirit because it seems to be foolishness (1 Corinthians 2:14). If you have been one of those, you were not alone, I too was one of those critical thinkers who took offense at the Holy Spirit. Until I was baptized in the Spirit.

When Peter stood up and addressed the crowd, he explained that those filled with the Spirit, speaking in tongues were not drunk, as some had supposed. Peter then pulled from Joel's prophecy that in the last days God will pour out His Spirit upon all flesh (Joel 2:28-32). I have found it interesting that in Peter's use of the prophecy from Joel, that tongues were not mentioned. Nonetheless, it was obvious that the Spirit of God had been poured out that day.

Peter brought his sermon to a close with the need for repentance, to be baptized in water, and the same gift of the Holy Spirit would be received. There was an anointing that day, and the Spirit of God would fill anyone willing to receive. There were 3000 people that gladly received salvation. Although it is not written, you can be sure, those saved that day were also filled with the Spirit. This was to be the standard practice for the early Church (Acts 8:14-17 & 19:1-6).

Although I had been baptized in the Spirit at the altar, I did not speak in tongues until five months later. It seems to be my custom that I don't follow ordinary or traditional protocol. However, in my previous academic pursuit of Christianity, I believed the Lord, in His wisdom, had to take me down an unconventional route. Otherwise, I would have possibly been hung up on a formula theology in how to receive the baptism of the Spirit. I like everything to fit neatly into an orderly structure that I can make sense of. The Lord, through His Spirit, would in time, dismantle every preconceived notion I had once held about how the Spirit would or should operate. So, for me, there were other immediate manifestations of the Spirit. I had a prophetic word for a woman (a complete stranger), as we passed by each other at a grocery store. Then there was the vision of Kenisha. It wasn't until the appointed time (Habakkuk 2:3) that the understanding of that vision was given.

Then dreams began. Not just the nonsense from my subconscious. But dreams that would unfold in segments, usually in three segments. I knew the Lord was providing instructions and warnings for me. Ever since then God has given me vivid dreams. I will cover in dreams in Appendix B. Once I had been filled with the Spirit, my experiences resembled what Peter quoted from Joel. I was given visions, dreams, and prophecy (Joel 2:28). I found it humorous that I was given visions and dreams. I guess the Spirit gave both for balance since I was neither a

Life in the Spirit

young man nor an old man.

When Jesus concludes His explanation of the born-again experience, He describes what life in the Spirit will resemble in John 3:8

"Just as you can hear the wind but can't tell where it comes from or where it will go next, so it is with the Spirit. We do not know on whom He will next bestow this life from heaven." (The Living Bible).

Since Jesus uses the analogy of the wind for the Holy Spirit, I believe He is referring to the life in the Spirit, and the manifestations, not the abiding Presence of the Spirit in the life of the believer. The word in the Greek for wind here is "pneuma". This is the same word used for Spirit. The Spirit of God will move, or manifest, in the same manner as the wind. No wonder that when the Holy Spirit arrived as promised on the day of Pentecost, there was a sound of a mighty rushing wind. Then there was a manifestation of His Presence (fire & tongues). As I have discovered that the Spirit of God will move and operate like the wind. You will see, and hear the evidence of His Presence, but you don't know who may be touched, or who may not. You can be assured that there is a Kingdom purpose for whatever the Holy Spirit is doing. It may not make logical sense. The Holy Spirit, like the wind, can be unpredictable when it comes to manifestations. Yet there is always a divine purpose, whether we understand it or not.

"But the manifestation of the Spirit is given to each one for the profit (benefit/common good) of all." 1 Corinthians 12:7

When the Spirit of God is manifest, or is given to each of us, although we may not understand the work He is doing, you can be sure the Holy Spirit's work is for the individual person's benefit, and will benefit all those of the Church. In 1 Corinthians chapter 12, Paul outlines for the Corinthians, and us the gifts of the Spirit so we would not be unaware of what they are.

Also, Paul lets the Corinthians know, that by the same Holy Spirit, the gifts are diverse, there are different ministries of the Spirit, and different activities of the Spirit. Yet, they all originate from the same Holy Spirit.

"There are diversities of the gifts (nine) but the same Spirit. There are differences of ministries, but the same Lord. And there are diversities of activities but the same God who works all in all." 1 Corinthians 12:4-6

There is usually little debate that there are nine different, or distinct gifts of the Spirit, which we will cover. However, with the different ministries, or methods of operation of the Holy Spirit there is at times questions as to the authenticity of their manifestation. Regarding the different and distinct activities of the Holy

Spirit, there can be misunderstanding and even real skepticism. Although there should be little wonder that the same God who created the enormous, and diverse heavens, earth, and creatures would also be diverse in how He ministers to His people. I would not expect the Spirit of God to use a "cookie cutter" approach to touch people, who have been created in His image, yet are so diverse. The fact that there are various activities of His Spirit as He moves, and operates should only reveal His nature. It is only us, who want to contain how the Spirit should operate so He fits neatly into our preconceived theology or our own comfort zone. I have found what seems to really throw us out of our theological comfort zone, is the various ways in which people react to the Presence, or moving of the Holy Spirit. So, let us cover some of these manifestations of the Holy Spirit as I have experienced and witnessed.

In my testimony, you read that when the Presence of God came upon me at the altar in 2014, I stood there and wept. This was a significant reaction for me. At the time, I refused to cry. Let alone show such emotion in front of a crowd of people. Tonya recalls, in the few times she saw me display even tearing up, I would be so agitated that I had allowed myself to express this kind of emotion. However, since then, when the Spirit of the Lord comes upon me, I often begin to cry. Many times, the weeping intensifies as the Spirit of God gives me a vision, or otherwise begins to stir within me. As I read through the book of Acts, and 1 Corinthians I can't find a single verse that explains that tears will begin to fall as the Spirit of God moves upon a person.

> *... what seems to really throw us out of our theological comfort zone, is the various ways in which people react to the Presence, or moving of the Holy Spirit.*

Depending on the concordance and translation of the Bible you use, there are 34 to 64 verses where weeping or tears are mentioned. However, they are virtually always associated with suffering, repentance, or sorrow. None of the references that I could find would explain, from a Bible-based citing, as to why I weep when the Spirit of God comes upon me. In those occasions, I am not repenting, or experiencing tears of joy. I have simply learned, that when this occurs, the Spirit of God has come upon me for a purpose. On those occasions, there is a deep work of the Spirit is occurring. In charismatic circles, tears have been a long-standing manifestation of the Presence of the Lord. Such a manifestation of the Spirit, or perhaps my reaction to the Presence of the Lord, may be offensive to the theology of others. Nevertheless, it does not diminish the reality of the work of the Spirit, because these tears for me are like living waters to my spirit. The best example for me was in South Africa when we as a team were heading for a prison ministry. The Spirit of God came upon me. I was weeping, and flooded with the memories of abuse from my childhood. I didn't understand what was going on. By the end of the ministry that day, I had been set free from something that I didn't even know still existed. It had been buried so deep, it took the Spirit of God to search it out, and at the right time provide a cleansing flood. That was a deep work of God that man does not know, but the Spirit of God does (1 Corinthians 2:10-11). Those tears in the natural were a release of living waters for healing in the spiritual for me.

> *I was weeping, and flooded with the memories of abuse from my childhood.*

The term "being slain in the Spirit" is sure to conjure up images that could be debatable as to the origin of such a manifestation of the Holy Spirit. But to fall either face down, or backward should be no surprise when the Presence of the Lord arrives. Paul fell to the ground when the Lord confronted him on the Damascus road (Acts 9:4). In the book of Ezekiel (1:28), when the Glory of the Lord appeared, and when Ezekiel saw it, he fell on his face. Neither of these examples is an exact replication of what is often seen in charismatic circles today. But that does not discount the authenticity that people today still fall to the floor under the Presence of the Lord.

The first time I was a part of a meeting where people were falling to the floor I was very suspicious; most likely because I was one of the few people still standing there as everyone around me was on the floor. Tonya was the first person to fall, and she fell forward. It was at a house meeting in our home, when the guest speaker was giving Tonya a prophetic word, she slowly fell forward. I watched, and noticed that she didn't bother putting her hands out to brace herself from the fall, she simply fell. Tonya was down on the floor for some time. Others fell forward, including the guest speaker.

There I stood, like a spectator wonder what was going on. In speaking with Tonya afterward, she knew the Presence of the Lord was upon her, and while she was on the floor, she was unable to move. I wasn't sure why I did not fall to the floor that evening. Since then, I have come under the Presence of the Lord and fallen to the floor. Each time I was aware that the power of God had come upon me, and once I was on the floor, I was unable to get up. Under the power of God, a person is usually down until the Spirit of the Lord has completed the work, or the Presence has lifted.

This is similar to bowing or abdominal crunches. I have experienced this several times. I have been standing either in prayer, or at an altar call, and felt a heavy Presence of the Lord come upon me. Perhaps similar, but less dramatic when the Glory of the Lord came into the temple (2 Chronicles 7:3), they bowed their faces toward the ground and worshiped. As the Presence of the Lord increases, I slowly bow toward the ground, as if I am unable to bear the weight of His Presence any longer. In these situations, I have either remained in a bowing position before the Lord or fallen to the floor. There have also been several occasions when my abdominal muscles began to contract as if I was doing abb crunches standing up. On one occasion, as a powerful prophetic word was being given over Tonya and me, I felt the Presence of the Lord so strong I began to bow, abbs crunching, tears flowing, and then I fell face first on the ground. In some charismatic churches, it would be said that I got "whacked" by the Spirit. I was so caught up in the Spirit, that I didn't even recall any of the prophetic word given. Fortunately, it was recorded.

Laughter in the Spirit or Holy laughter is one manifestation that I have not experienced. I have seen those who have experienced such laughter when the Spirit of God has come upon them. In most occasions where I have witnessed this manifestation, I knew the people involved and knew that unless they had been under the "influence" of the Holy Spirit, they would not have been laughing as they were. This manifestation is closely related to being drunk in the Spirit. Which is most likely one of the manifestations of the Holy Spirit that occurred on the day of Pentecost. Although tongues were the primary manifestation that all of the foreign visitors of Jerusalem recognized, some of the 120 must have appeared drunk to some extent.

Speaking in a foreign language usually has an appearance of being educated or cultured, but there were those observing that day who mocked the 120 and said they must be drunk. As I have experienced, someone can have more than one manifestation of the Holy Spirit at the same time. My guess is that they were so filled with joy, as they spoke the wonders of God in a foreign language (Acts 2:11), as the Spirit gave them the utterance. Perhaps it was the joy that gave them the appearance of being under the influence, even drunk.

Only once have I experienced being under the "influence" of the Holy Spirit. Tonya and I had been at a Randy Clark conference when the altars were opened

Life in the Spirit

up for prayer. I went forward, and as an altar worker prayed for me, I knew the Presence of the Lord had come upon me. The altar worker recognized it, and said: "There it is, the Presence of the Lord is all over you." I did not tear up, but could feel the weight of His Presence, and I slowly began to bow forward. This took several minutes, and I'm sure to anyone who may have been watching, I looked like a sunflower drooping as the sun sets. At some point, the altar worker who had prayed for me went on to someone else, and I made my way back to my seat next to Tonya. I felt fine as I walked back. But once I sat down all I could feel was euphoria. Tonya looked at me, and said: "Oh my, you're drunk!" Well, I wasn't exactly drunk, but I was definitely "under the influence" of the Holy Spirit.

There are those who have experienced a sense of electricity going through them when the power of God has come upon them. Although I have not experienced this manifestation, I was a part of it when "Andrea," the girl I had prayed over to receive the baptism in the Spirit. Andrea told Tonya and I later that she felt flaming arrows or electricity flowing through her as she was baptized in the Holy Spirit. In this particular situation, Andrea had been very frustrated that she had not received the baptism in the Spirit. For her, perhaps the Spirit chose to manifest in such a manner as to demonstrate to Andrea, that this is spiritual power flowing in, and through her (Acts 1:8). Since there are no recorded after-the-fact interviews conducted with the 120 on the day of Pentecost, we don't know whether or not they received any of the manifestations I have outlined here. I suspect that either they did, or many of those who had received the baptism in the Holy Spirit throughout the book of Acts did.

Although there may be even more manifestations of the Spirit, these have been the manifestations that I have personally experienced or witnessed. But as we read through 1 Corinthians chapter 12, Paul does not give us a comprehensive list of all the various ways in which the Holy Spirit will manifest while in operation. Nor does he provide us any explanation as to how the Spirit will manifest in various ministries or activities.

God is a personal God, who will speak to us in whatever manner that will best suit the situation, and meet the need in each of us as individuals; after all, God used a donkey to get Balaam's attention. The Lord, by His hand, caused a donkey to see the danger, and speak to Balaam. God then opened Balaam's eyes that he would also see what the donkey saw. This brought Balaam to repentance. Balaam then followed the Lord's command (Numbers 22:21-39). Incidentally, as I read this account of Balaam, I wondered if Balaam was so obtuse that he didn't question having a conversation with a talking donkey (v.28-30), or was the prophet so aware of the supernatural realm that he knew nothing would be too unorthodox? After all this is long before Mr. Ed.

MOVE FORWARD

Anyway, in the past, I would view the Bible more like a procedural manual. A reference book to be followed, step by step, which unfortunately takes away the personal nature of our God. Nothing is out of the realm of possibility with God (Luke 1:37). Although God will never violate what has already been given us in His written word, He certainly is not restricted in reaching beyond our understanding or our imaginations.

"Now to Him (Jesus), who is able to do immeasurably more than all we ask or imagine, according to His power that is at work within us." Ephesians 3:20

Let's return to 1 Corinthians 12:4-6. In these verses, Paul provides the reader with clarification, so they are not caught unaware that with the Spirit of God there are diversities of the gifts. There will also be different ministries and diverse activities of the Spirit of God. But all are from the same Holy Spirit. Although some manifestations of the Holy Spirit may be offensive to someone's theology, it does not mean it is not of the Holy Spirit. It usually means that the person has no personal reference for such a manifestation. Therefore, the manifestation has no place in a person's theology, they run the risk of missing an authentic move of the Holy Spirit.

Although some manifestations of the Holy Spirit may be offensive to someone's theology, it does not mean it is not of the Holy Spirit.

However, we will need to be able to discern the difference between a genuine manifestation of the Holy Spirit, and perhaps a person's zeal to be the focus of the Holy Spirit's attention. In such cases, the person most likely has a starving need which needs to be addressed. We have to discern the difference, and not take offense with the Spirit of God because of someone else who may be attempting to manufacture a manifestation or be the center of attention.

To hold an offense with an authentic move of the Holy Spirit because it does not conform to our understanding is to take the same position as the religious leaders did when they were offended by the great wonders and signs that Stephen had performed in Acts 6:8-9. Although we do not know what great wonders and signs Stephen performed, we do know that Stephen was a man full of faith, and the

Holy Spirit. We can be assured that the Holy Spirit was moving mightily through Stephen.

Whatever the religious leaders of the day observed, they took offense with what Stephen was doing (verse 9). However, they were unable to resist or counter the wisdom, and the Spirit by which Stephen spoke (verse 10). No doubt, they misunderstood an authentic move of the Holy Spirit and brought false accusations of blasphemy against Stephen. They were, in their religious zeal, committing the very thing they were accusing Stephen of - blasphemy. The religious leaders of Stephen's day attacked what they didn't understand since it was not in conformity with their theology, rather than recognizing a move of God in their midst. Such religious zeal will not only grieve the Holy Spirit (Ephesians 4:30), but could entangle a person into fighting with the One (Holy Spirit), who has been given to helps us.

There was a time when I also would have been quick to misjudge an authentic move of the Holy Spirit ...

"But they rebelled and grieved His Holy Spirit, so He turned Himself against them as an enemy. And He fought against them." Isaiah 63:10

There was a time when I also would have been quick to misjudge an authentic move of the Holy Spirit because it may not have lined up with my understanding. But the Lord has brought me tremendous growth in the area of spiritual understanding. Nonetheless, this is an area of spiritual discerning, and not a natural understanding. Kind of like having an argument with a donkey. The natural man does not receive the things of the Spirit of God, for they are foolishness to him, nor can he (natural man) know them.

Although our natural man may recoil at the things of the Spirit, we are responsible for discerning (make a proper distinction) spiritually of what manifestation we are witnessing (1 Corinthians 2:14). Since the Holy Spirit has been given to us as a helper (John 14:26), and teacher. As long as we remain in the Spirit we will be better able to properly spiritually discern. We do need to be careful not to default into our own logic. As we become more Holy Spirit aware, our own spirit will bear witness with the Holy Spirit (Romans 8:16).

"Beloved, do not believe every spirit but test (authenticate) the spirits whether they are of God, because many false prophets have gone out into the world." 1 John 4:1

MOVE FORWARD

The Lord has indeed brought me a long way in the ways of the Spirit, yet there are still times where I find myself fact checking both in my spirit and with the Lord as to whether I am in the presence of an authenticate move of the Holy Spirit. This is not to mean that I have the "spirit of suspicion" as I once did as a police officer. I have a desire to always be prudent, and test the spirits.

Whenever you are unsure, and your spirit does not bear witness with what may be assumed to be a manifestation of the Holy Spirit, especially in a setting that you are not familiar with, I recommend seeking the wisdom to know the difference (James 1:5 & 3:15). At times you observe an overly dramatic "manifestation," and you may suspect that it is more of the person's actions (their flesh) rather than an authentic work of the Holy Spirit. People can get so caught up in the "moment" the Spirit has come upon them that they overplay the work the Spirit was doing. In such situations use discernment. It may just be prudent to just step away.

Though I will advocate a measure of caution, we need not be given to fear. Being in fear of receiving that which is not of God is to suggest that we lack the confidence that the Lord has our best interest at heart.

"For God has not given us a spirit of fear, but of power, and of love, and of a sound mind. "2 Timothy 1:7

The Spirit that we have been given by the Lord is the Holy Spirit. This is the power (Luke 1:35), as well as the love of God (Romans 5:5). We have also been given a sound mind. The fruit of the Spirit includes self-control, which will help keep us from allowing our mind to run off in a direction of constant concern. Jesus has also assured us that when we are seeking the Holy Spirit, He will not give us a counterfeit (Luke 11:11-13). As I mentioned before, our spirits will bear witness (furnish evidence) as to whether we are in the Presence of a manifestation of the Holy Spirit, or another spirit. In chapter 5, I touched on Mark 16:17-18.

> **And these signs will follow those who believe; in My name they will cast out demons, they will speak in new tongues, they will take up serpents, and if they drink anything deadly, it will by no means hurt them, they will lay hands on the sick, and they will recover.**

For many, it's not difficult to understand Jesus affirming that those who believe, can cast out demons and lay hands on the sick and they will recover. But what does seem odd is the take-up serpents, and drinking anything deadly mention. Jesus was still speaking of the spiritual realm, or the supernatural when He said that "they" (believers), will take up serpents (handle them), and if they drink (ingest) anything deadly they will by no means be hurt. In other words, for those going about the commission of furthering the Kingdom of heaven you may, and most likely will, come into contact with "serpents" (demons), and they will attempt to

Life in the Spirit

get you to "drink" (absorb/ingest) what they have to offer. However, we need not fear, we are to simply "handle" them, and move on. This may be as simple as not coming into agreement with them because they have no part of us (John 14:30). Other times, your handling them will require you to cast them out, or rebuke them from interfering with ministry.

Some time ago, I had an opportunity to meet with Apostle Charles Green on one of my trips to Milwaukee. Apostle Green was one of the men of God who prophesied over us at the altar during GGG 2014. Apostle Green encouraged me to pray in the Spirit (tongues) every day. As we read in the book of Jude, verse 20 praying in the Spirit will build us up in the most holy faith. As we grow spiritually, we will be better equipped to discern spiritual matters, and effectively minister whenever the opportunity arises. Apostle Green shared with me during our meeting that on the morning of GGG 2014, he had awakened early in the morning, and began to pray in the Spirit. He told me that he prayed in the Spirit for four hours that morning. At the time we spoke I couldn't imagine that. However, since then, since I drive all over for my job, I pray in the Spirit most of the time as I drive. I've driven from Illinois to Utah, to Ohio, Iowa, and southern Illinois, all the while praying in the Spirit.

On one trip to far southern Illinois, 5 hours one way from where I live near Chicago, I prayed in the Spirit almost the entire time. When I pray in the Spirit (tongues), I don't just pray mindlessly into the air. It is with my spirit that I am praying, so with my mind, I was calling out to Holy Spirit to take me deeper. I did not want to just drive down the interstate in some form of mindless babble.

"For if I pray in a tongue, my spirit prays, but my mind (understanding) is unfruitful." 1 Corinthians 14:14

So, with my mind, or in my head, I prayed for Holy Spirit to enlarge my prayer language, to unlock more of Him in and through my spirit. Then, it happened. There was a distinct sweet fragrance. I had smelled it before. But that had been in a corporate worship where I knew the Presence of the Lord was rich in the atmosphere. There I was, all by myself, driving down the interstate, and that sweet fragrance welled up. Then my prayer language changed. There was a flow that I had not experienced since the anointing had come upon me when Andrea was baptized in the Holy Spirit. It was amazing. I just let my spirit pray with the Holy Spirit as I drove. The atmosphere was rich with the Presence of the Lord during that drive. Since then, my vehicle has become a worship center on wheels. It was ironic that it was Apostle Green, who when he prophesied, said that I was to spend much time in the Presence of the Lord. I didn't understand it then, but it is His Presence that I pursue more.

Growing spiritually will enable us to understand the gifts of the Spirit. When we are filled with the Spirit, we are then able to operate in any of the gifts of the Spirit. However, when we are baptized (filled) with the Spirit, it does not necessarily mean that we then possess all of the gifts of the Spirit. We do have access to each of the gifts, as the Spirit wills (1 Corinthians 12:11). We have been given the gift of the Holy Spirit (Acts 2:38).

The more time we spend with the Holy Spirit, developing a relationship with Him, not grieving Him, the more we understand His gifts and their functions.

Growing spiritually will enable us to understand the gifts of the Spirit.

We should all desire the Spiritual gifts (1 Corinthians 14:1). The word used here for desire, in the Greek, means to burn with zeal. Paul is passionate in his plea to the Corinthians (and us) here. "Pursue love, and desire the spiritual gifts, especially that you may prophesy." When we have the love of the Father, the gifts of the Spirit, and can hear the voice of God to deliver a word to someone, what an incredible impact we can have on the world around us. Freely we have received, freely give. Every Spirit-filled believer can operate in any of the nine gifts, as the Spirit wills (1 Corinthians 12:11). As we develop a relationship with the Holy Spirit, He will trust us to give what has been given, to whoever needs it, and we can deliver it with the love of God.

In 1 Corinthians 12:8-10, Paul gives us an outline of the nine gifts of the Spirit. However, he does not provide an in-depth explanation of the actual operation of these different gifts. I suspect, that was because the early church was so familiar with life in the Spirit and the gifts of the Spirit, that Paul was more concerned with bringing an understanding of an orderly assembly to the Corinthians when the gifts are in operation.

We will cover these spiritual gifts, but it will be an elementary explanation of each gift. I strongly encourage you to pursue a further study on each of the gifts, and be in an environment where the gifts of the Spirit are in practice on a regular basis.

The gifts of the Spirit.

The first of the nine gifts of the Spirit that Paul refers to is the word of wisdom, and word of knowledge.

"...for to one is given the word of wisdom through the Spirit, to another the word of knowledge through the same Spirit." 1 Corinthians 12:8

A word of wisdom is the spiritual revelation, by the Holy Spirit of the prophetic future. A word of knowledge is the spiritual revelation, by the Holy Spirit of an existing fact. These two gifts often work together and will accompany those who are moving prophetically. Often, the gifts will operate together since they complement each other. Together these two gifts may be valuable when ministering to someone. A word of wisdom or a word knowledge may also be given independently. There is always a divine purpose, which will meet a specific need for the person receiving a word. Whenever a word of wisdom or word of knowledge is received from the Holy Spirit, it is not for our own spiritual enrichment. Such spiritual revelation may be exactly what is needed to open a door for a person to receive from the Lord. A person who realizes that the Lord is giving a word of wisdom or knowledge may better receive that God cares about their life and their situation. It is often taught that the word of wisdom and the word knowledge is just that, a word. There may be an occasion when it is just a "word." That may be all that is needed. However, the "word" here is logos, and it means that which has been uttered by a living voice. In this case, by the Spirit of God, who is declaring what God has to say.

"... to another faith by the same Spirit, to another gifts of healings by the same Spirit." 1 Corinthians 12:9

The gift of faith is not easily defined since it is often difficult to recognize in operation. Each of us has been given a measure of faith (Romans 12:3), which is where each of us operates out of daily. We are also called to walk (live) by faith, 2 Corinthians 5:7. However, one who has been given the gift of faith has been given faith supernaturally by the Holy Spirit. The gift of faith is given to achieve a divine purpose. We often associate the gift of faith with something huge, which it could be. The gift of faith may also be given for a divine purpose that may seem relatively small but has great significance spiritually for the recipient. Do not despise small beginnings (Zechariah 4:10). Because, as a result of receiving the gift of faith, the person will be operating beyond their own measure of faith to achieve the purposes of the Lord.

The gifts of healings are simply, a believer possesses, by the Holy Spirit the supernatural ability to bring healing to someone who needs healing. I know that isn't very profound, but it's not any more complicated than that. Much has been made of the fact that many translations use the plural form. But of the nine gifts, it is the only one that Paul actually introduces as a gift aside from his introductory verse (4). I believe any Spirit-filled believer, can pray, and healings can occur (Matthew 10:8, Mark 16:18). However, there are those who, through the Holy Spirit have been gifted in healings. Over the years there have been some who have had amazing healing ministries. Some of which, over time, ventured into dubious practices, and their ministries fell. A reminder that moving in such an incredible ministry is to understand we, of ourselves, are not performing the healing; it is the Spirit within us and upon us. Always remember it is a gift. That gift is from the Lord, so when healings occur as a result of the laying on of hands, or otherwise in our midst, give all the glory and praise to God.

"... to another the working of miracles, to another prophecy, to another the discerning of spirits," 1 Corinthians 12:10 (a)

The working of miracles is the supernatural intervention by the Holy Spirit to do something that otherwise could not have occurred under natural, ordinary means. It is interesting that the word used here in the text is "dynamis." The same word used elsewhere as power. The spiritual gift is the working, or the affecting (a thing wrought), power (miracles).

Usually, when researching this gift, examples are given of the various miracles found in the scriptures. But since this is a manifestation of the Spirit, as are all the diverse gifts, it may be more accurately rendered as the gift of bringing power, to where the power of God is needed.

This would be a miracle to achieve the purposes of the Lord and the benefit of those who need the power of God to come upon them. Therefore, with the laying on of hands, when the Spirit of the Lord comes upon a person, and they are either slain, filled, delivered, or receive a reverse of a non-reversible physical condition, it would certainly be the working of a miracle. Categorizing the gifts of the Spirit by the results the Spirit works isn't always as definitive as we may understand. Nonetheless, it is all by the same Spirit.

The gift of prophecy is an inspired utterance of the Holy Spirit to either an individual or a corporate body. Of all the gifts, it is my take that Paul found moving prophetically to be the most coveted of all the gifts. Paul encourages us to desire spiritual gifts but especially to prophesy (1 Corinthians 14:1). It was Moses who announced that he wished that all of the Lord's people were prophets. Prophecy brings strength, encouragement, and comfort to those who receive a true prophetic word. A true prophetic word is a word from the Lord, and a word from the Lord is powerful. I believe that any Spirit-filled believer can prophesy. However, we each will prophesy in accordance with our level of faith. Each of us has a gifting as the Spirit gives (Romans 12:6). Those with the gift of prophecy will flow in the prophetic as one who holds the office of prophet (Ephesians 4:11).

Discerning of Spirits is the supernatural gift of the Holy Spirit revealing the spirits of the spirit realm. This will include the ability to comprehend the human spirit. This is not necessarily limited to the supernatural ability to discern demons, or the presence of the heavenly angelic beings. The gift of discerning of spirits will allow a person to distinguish with what demonic spirit they are dealing.

Jesus identified by name the spirit that possessed a man's son. "**...deaf and dumb spirit, I command you come out of him and enter him no more.**" **Mark 9:25.** Therefore, anyone who truly has the gift of discerning of spirits will most likely be able to identify the spirit with which they are dealing. More often than not, any Spirit-filled believer will be able to recognize that they are dealing with an evil spirit. The person who has the gift of discerning of spirits will have a supernatural ability to recognize the spirits at work in an about a person.

Also, the Holy Spirit is gifting someone with the ability to spiritually perceive someone else's spirit. This can be beneficial to accurately perceive if the person you are ministering to has a wounded spirit, a broken spirit or even a bound spirit. This, of course, may seem similar to a word of knowledge. But properly discerning the spirit you are dealing with, will lead you into the most effective avenue to minister a person.

The discerning of spirits is not having the "spirit of suspicion" so you can better gauge if a person is lying to you. Although you may be able to detect a lying spirit, that detection, may or may not be a result of you moving with the gifting of the discernment of spirits. In my job as an investigator, I often sense when a person is lying to me. It was not usually from a spiritual gifting. I have been trained to read both verbal, and non-verbal cues. In a ministry context, demons will often manifest at some point when they sense a threat of exposure. But that is another topic altogether. It is important to be to be able to properly discern the spirit you may be dealing with. Our response always needs to be one of love. We cannot recoil when we discern an unhealthy spirit. Most of us possessed a spirit of this world before the grace of God met us. So, push through, and love, even the unlovable.

Although the gift of discerning of spirits is a gift of the Holy Spirit, we can cultivate our spiritual discernment the more we become sensitive to the Holy Spirit and looking beyond the natural appearances of an individual (Hebrews 5:14). Looking beyond means that we discern what spirit the person has, and not judge solely based on their personality type, although someone's personality may reveal the person's spirit. Often a person's personality is actually masking the spirit. Hence, we need the Holy Spirit to give us discernment.

"... to another different kinds of tongues, to another the interpretation of tongues." 1 Corinthians 12:10(b)

The gift of tongues is the supernatural ability, by the Holy Spirit to speak in a "tongue" (language), not known to the person speaking. When researching the topic of tongues I've found that there still seems to be some confusion over this manifestation of the Holy Spirit. Paul, in the text, tells us, that by the same Spirit, there are different kinds of tongues or languages that will be manifested by the

Holy Spirit. Every Spirit-filled believer can speak in tongues. It is often referred to as the gift of tongues for the person who will publicly give a message in tongues. Such a message, as Paul outlines in 1 Corinthians 14:5, needs to be interpreted. Usually, this will be in a church setting as Paul is referring to in the text.

Speaking in tongues means that we are praying with our spirit, as the Holy Spirit gives the utterances. We are speaking "mysteries" because our spirit is speaking to God (1 Corinthians 14:2). This is also known as praying in the Spirit (Jude 20). Since our spirit is engaged in the praying, our mind is able to pray in our native tongue. Many people will have their personal prayer language which will become familiar to them. But there will be occasions when their "tongue" will change as the Spirit leads, for a specific purpose.

Tongues are often the initial evidence that a person has been baptized in the Spirit. We read in Acts 10:44–48, that while Peter was in the middle of his first sermon to an all Gentile group, the Holy Spirit fell upon them. The Jews who had accompanied Peter on this divine appointment, could not deny that even these Gentiles had been filled with the Holy Spirit because they too heard them magnifying God in their new tongue (prayer language).

I have heard the confusion over having a Spirit lead prayer language versus the gift of tongues because Paul does not initially distinguish the two as he outlines the nine gifts of the Spirit in 1 Corinthians 12. However, as we read the entire letter to the Corinthians it is apparent from the text that Paul knew his readers were familiar with the difference, and he was providing them with the proper operation of the gifts, and the proper place for their personal prayer language.

> *Every Spirit-filled believer can speak in tongues.*

In 1 Corinthians 14:2-14 Paul seems to address an issue of the body as a whole, filled with the Spirit, gathering together, and everyone wanting to speak in tongues. Of course, there is no understanding among them if they do so. Therefore, when they gather, if they speak in a tongue, let there be an interpretation. Otherwise, it would be better that they prophesy (verse 5). Paul then uses himself as an example that if he were to show up and all he did was speak in tongues, there would be no benefit (verse 6) to them as a body. So, Paul would rather give them a revelation, word of knowledge, prophecy, or a teaching. Paul reminds the church at Corinth, and us, that with our personal prayer language it is our spirit that prays, by the indwelling Holy Spirit, and even we do not know the words spoken (1 Corinthians 14:14).

The interpretation of tongues is just that, an interpretation of the unknown

Life in the Spirit

language given by someone else. Basically, the one interpreting is providing an explanation of the unknown tongue, as the Holy Spirit provides it. This is different from a translation which would focus on the linguistics of the language spoken, and perhaps take away the essence of what the Spirit has to say. Dreams, for example, are mostly parabolic (the language of heaven), which God gives the interpretation to the dreamer (Genesis 40:8 & 41:15). Whether we understand it or not, it is the wisdom of God who speaks in mysteries.

> But we speak the wisdom of God in a mystery, the hidden wisdom which God ordained before the ages for our glory .... But God has revealed them (mysteries) to us through His Spirit. For the Spirit searches all things, yes the deep things of God. (Read 1 Corinthians 2:7-10 for the complete context).

All of these spectacular and supernatural gifts of the Holy Spirit are given to do the work of the Lord, not serve one's own agenda. We should never operate in a fashion that shows we are blessed, or somehow "gifted." Desiring and operating in the gifts of the Spirit is always for the benefit of others. In chapter 12 of 1 Corinthians Paul explains that each may have a different gift, and that is the way it is supposed to operate as a fully functioning body (group of believers). Therefore, he uses the metaphor of how the human body functions, with all of its different, but necessary parts. Paul concludes the chapter with a plea to desire (burning zeal) for the best (those of the most service, or more advantageous) gifts (verse 31). The gifts given to us by the Holy Spirit are to be operated out of love, which never fails (1 Corinthians 13:8). In 1 Peter 4:8-11, Peter follows the same understanding as Paul. Peter reminds his readers that we are to be fervent in our love for one another, and each gift that we have received has been given to us, that we may minister to one another. Steward the gifts properly, which are given by His grace. As we speak, remember, speak not of ourselves, but of the oracles of God. All of the operations of the gifts and ministry are to be for the glory of God, the encouragement of the saints, and reaching the lost.

Whether we understand it or not, it is the wisdom of God who speaks in mysteries.

One Sunday I was driving home after church. As I left the church that day, I was feeling less than enthused. Something felt off, and I wasn't sure what it was. As I drove, a saw a homeless man standing on a street corner holding a cardboard sign. I hesitated, but drove by without stopping. I knew this was a divine appointment.

So, I made a u-turn and went back to the man. I grabbed a Bible from the box I keep in the car, got out to greet the man. In each Bible is a gift card for a fast food restaurant, and a simple typed page with Bible references outlining the plan of salvation in Jesus.

I explained to the man what I was giving him, and he told me that he knew Jesus as his Savior and Lord. I then asked if I could pray for him. As I prayed, I was given a word of knowledge about this man. Despite his apparent circumstances in life he still puts others before himself, and that he has a tender heart. I continued to pray for this man, and for the Lord's hand to be upon him and his life. When we concluded praying, the man said: "Wow, God really spoke to you." The man teared up, and then he explained how he had done certain things for the people in his life. As I drove away, I knew the Spirit of God dropped that in me, to give him. He left blessed, and encouraged that God sees him, as a person, and loves him. That man was uplifted (edified), and I was encouraged. God is so good. We had different circumstances, but both of us had been discouraged before God stepped in.

Anointings of the Holy Spirit.

Having an anointing or operating under an anointing is different from the gifts of the Spirit. Both are given to serve a divine Kingdom purpose. An anointing is simply the impartation of supernatural ability, strength, and even wisdom to do the work we have been called upon to do. As I wrote previously, I have experienced this on both mission trips Tonya and I had been on. An anointing may be as unique as the work God has called you to.

My favorite biblical example of an anointing can be found in Exodus 31:1-6 God spoke to Moses and told him that He had called Bezalel, by name to anoint him to do a specific work, for His purposes.

"...I have filled him (Bezalel) with the Spirit of God, in wisdom, in understanding, in knowledge, and in all manner of workmanship," Exodus 31:3

The text unfolds all of the various manners of workmanship Bezalel would complete under this anointing of the Spirit (Exodus 31:4-5). God also anointed others with wisdom that they also may complete the works needed for the furnishing of the tabernacle of meeting that Moses had been commanded to complete. When God calls us for a work, He provides the anointing to complete the work. We cannot fall back into the saying: "Well, if God wanted me to preach, witness, heal or cast out demons He would have given the anointing to do so." There are times, such as with Bezalel, that God will bring an anointing for a specific ministry. There are times, in our everyday walk when we do not sense that the Lord has poured an anointing on us. Nonetheless, we still walk and minister out of our authority we have in Christ. We are all called be witnesses for the Kingdom in which we are ambassadors. As such, we should be as an expert witness, as an expert who testifies in court. As we go, we testify of the Lord, present evidence of His Kingdom (signs will follow those who believe Mark 16:17-18), and everyone knows we too have been with Jesus (Acts 4:13).

Although the topic of anointings can fill an entire book, I think it is necessary to cover three basic anointings since I have touched on them throughout the book.

The Believer's Anointing

The believer's anointing is the anointing within an individual believer. This is the primary anointing that each believer carries. An anointing is a tangible measure of the Holy Spirit imparted upon, and to those whom He has chosen (Ephesians 1:4), in this anointing we are able to follow and serve Him. This anointing can be increased over time as we grow in faith, grace, and favor. The believer's anointing is the anointing that the other anointings are built upon.

> **But the anointing which you have received from Him abides in you, and you do not need that anyone teach you, but as the same anointing teaches you concerning all things, and is true, and is not a lie, and just as is has taught you, you will abide in Him. 1 John 2:27**

Therefore, we need to be careful to keep the "flies" (contaminates) out of the oil, so to speak. We are responsible to not allow the anointing to become stagnant, or be in danger of running low (Matthew 25:1-13).

The Ministerial Anointing

The ministerial anointing comes upon an individual for the purposes of ministering to others. If we minister to others out of our talents, intellect, or giftings, regardless of the fact that they are God-given, we are not operating under a particular anointing. The anointing is an impartation of His ability into, and upon us to do a work we otherwise would not be able to perform.

An example of this is when the ministerial anointing or the anointing for the gift of tongues came upon me when I was ministering to Andrea. Obviously, this was beyond my natural ability as the supernatural flow of tongues poured forth, and she was baptized in the Holy Spirit.

The Corporate Anointing

The corporate anointing is an anointing that falls or comes upon a group of believers. Such an anointing can come upon a gathering of believers during worship, a service, or a group on the mission field. Whenever there is an anointing, there is power. So, in a corporate setting, there is tremendous power. Such was the case when Peter and John had been brought before the religious rulers of the day (Acts 4:5-6), because a lame man had been healed (Acts 3:7). Peter, filled with the Holy Spirit preached to these leaders (Acts 4:8). Once released, Peter and John returned to their companions, praised the Lord with one accord, and entered into prayer. "They" (Acts 4:24) raised their voices to God and with one accord made declarations, praise, and asked God for a boldness (Acts 4:29), to speak His word. When they did so, the place was shaken and they were all filled with the Holy Spirit and spoke with word of God with boldness (Acts 4:31).

> *The corporate anointing is an anointing that falls or comes upon a group of believers.*

Although a large portion of what has been covered in this chapter has been manifestations (the phenomenon) of the Holy Spirit, we should never lose sight of the fact that the Holy Spirit is a Person. The third Person of the Trinity, God the Spirit. This is why, at times, Spirit, God, and Lord have been used interchangeably throughout the book. The Holy Spirit has been given to us that we may hear the voice of God, move in the power of God, and demonstrate the Kingdom of Heaven that others may see God working through the hands of His servants.

> **However, when the Spirit of truth has come, He will guide you into all truth, for He will not speak on His own authority but whatever He hears He will speak and He will tell you things to come. He will glorify Me, for He will take of what is Mine and declare it to you. John 16:13-14**

The Holy Spirit has been given to lead us into truth. He will guide us, and speak to us. To hear His voice, we need to develop a relationship with the Holy Spirit. As we do, we will hear His voice, know His prompting, know His impression, know His thoughts, and once we know Him, we can trust He is taking what has been given to Him, to give to us.

We live in the Spirit, and we walk in the Spirit. It's the life in the Spirit.

I would recommend the following three books in a further study of life in the Spirit.

- *The Gifts and Ministries of the Holy Spirit* by Lester Sumrall

Life in the Spirit

- *Power for All* by: Bill and Eva Dooley
- *Releasing Spiritual Gifts Today* by: James W. Goll

8

As You Go…

"And as you go, preach, saying that the Kingdom of Heaven is at hand. Heal the sick, cleanse the lepers, raise the dead, cast out demons. Freely you have received, freely give." Matthew 10:7-8

Driving across the country in January 2017, hitting a snow storm and dealing with horrible road conditions was quite a challenge. By the time I arrived at the hospital in Ogden Utah, I had been on the road for three days. The drive was much more difficult than I anticipated. Driving conditions in the winter through Wyoming and Utah were tough. I ran into a snow storm west of Rock Springs Wyoming. The snow was thick, blowing, and I could no longer see the roadway. Then ice pellets began to hit the windshield. I had to turn back and find a hotel in Rock Springs. As I laid there in bed that night, my entire body began to vibrate. At first, I assumed my nerves were "shot" from the stress of the drive. I began to read the Psalms as I laid there and vibrated. In Psalm 3:5 I read the following:

"I lay down and slept. I awoke, for the Lord had sustained me."

I eventually fell asleep that night, my body still vibrating. When I woke up in the morning, I was completely refreshed. The Lord had truly sustained me during the entire trip, and as I slept. I sensed that it was not my nerves that hit me when I laid down in bed that night. The Lord was doing a deep work within me.

I was stuck in that hotel in Wyoming for a day. All I could do was watch it snow, and it was really coming down. There had been several incidents during the drive that assured me that the Lord had given angels charge over me to keep me in all my ways (Psalm 91:11). The upside of the long drive was that I had spent a lot of uninterrupted time in prayer, both in the natural and in the Spirit. I had also been prompted by the Lord the day before I left to just remain in the moment. As the week progressed, I would better understand that this word from the Lord was more than just about the drive to and from Utah.

As You Go...

When I arrived at the hospital and saw my brother Jeff, he was not in very good shape. He had been in intensive care initially, but by the time I arrived at the hospital, he had been moved into intermediate care. Jeff was on three liters of oxygen and had a host of physical issues. He had severe pneumonia on top of the concerns for his heart, and possible organ damage from his lifestyle. Jeff and I spent time getting reacquainted but it was evident that the hospital staff had been waiting for my arrival to complete the administrative details. I met with his social worker, his nurse, and the administrator for financial eligibility.

Within the day, Jeff was transferred to the physical therapy floor to begin his physical rehab. Since each social worker at this hospital was assigned to a floor, the current social worker would no longer be overseeing Jeff's hospital stay.

Jeff's social worker, "Mike," gave me the final run down. When he was finished, I asked him if I may pray a blessing over him. He was very receptive to prayer. As I prayed for Mike, I sense there was genuine compassion within him. I prayed into what I believed the Lord was giving me for Mike and prayed for God to reveal Himself to Mike in a personal and powerful manner, and ended with a prayer of blessing over him.

During the week, I would find myself stepping into prayer with aides, visitors, and even the desk manager at the hospital guest house I was staying at.

By the conclusion of the week, I had a clear understanding of what the Lord was showing me about staying in the moment. Jeff's condition during the week was up and down. I had driven out to Utah with the idea that when Jeff was released, I would just drive him back to Illinois to stay with Tonya and me. However, it was apparent that Jeff was physically not able to make the drive. So, throughout the week, as I would talk with the nurses and with Jeff, there were times of planning and trying to figure out what to do with Jeff. In the past, I know I would have given into the pressure of "figuring" everything out.

I had a clear understanding of what the Lord was showing me about staying in the moment.

I tend to process and analyze everything, then devise a plan to determine the most efficient manner to execute that plan. There are times when such a process is tiring mentally. On this trip, there was little of that. That's not to say I didn't spend time staring out the window at the beautiful mountains wondering what I was going to do, but the pressure wasn't there. I simply gave the situation over to the Lord. I

MOVE FORWARD

was just in the moment, and trusting in the Lord to handle the details.

I was there on assignment, and my assignment was whatever and whoever was in need in front of me at the moment. There was never a time of wondering, "Gee, should I pray for this person, or what do I say next." All I had to do is step into what the Lord had put in front of me. It was awesome!

I had brought a book along with me to read, but I never had a chance to read it. By the time I would get back to the guesthouse at night, I would eat, and go to bed.

Ironically, the book I brought had the following quote in it.

> When God only gives us the guidance we need for the moment, it tends to keep us closer to Him. This helps us to learn the all-important lesson of dependence on God – a lesson that every single person marked by the favor of God has to learn."[1]

I wouldn't read that until returning from my second trip to Utah on the flight back to Chicago.

I also had many opportunities to minister to Jeff. Although Jeff had accepted the Lord with Tonya and me in December of 2015, I felt led to ensure his commitment one evening. I led Jeff in prayer, and he repeated out-loud his commitment to the Lord, as his Savior and Lord. Jeff had been through a lot over the years. Jeff had explained that before him falling and being brought to the ER, he had not eaten anything in a month. All he had been doing was drinking. It was reassuring to hear him profess his faith in the Lord.

I read Psalms over him one day when he was semi-conscience and not doing well. Whenever I could, I ministered love, declared life over him, and prayed for healing. By the end of the week, the staff had seen significant improvement with Jeff and scheduled a discharge date for the following Saturday. Where Jeff would go after being discharged still needed to be decided. While in Utah, when I had some quiet time, I reflected on Luke 12:22-34. Jesus was teaching His disciples about a lifestyle free from worry over the everyday needs of life. Also, Jesus taught that we should not have an anxious mind (verse 29). Rather, "**seek the Kingdom of God, and these things shall be added to you**" (verse 31). It is the Father's pleasure to give each of us His Kingdom (verse 32).

I truly believe that the Lord is concerned with all of the details of our lives. He even knows the number of hairs on our heads (Luke 12:7), which shows that He knows even the most trivial, or the most exact details of each of our lives. Therefore, I didn't give into the worry or spend the usual time pondering all of the

---

1   Face to Face with God by Bill Johnson pg. 50

possibilities of what to do about the situation. I remained, for the most part, in the moment. My focus was whatever the Lord wanted to be done with what was before me. As I remained there, I felt a definite ease, or flow. There was peace and joy. It was in this place, I also understood:

"Now the Lord is the Spirit, and where the Spirit of the Lord is, there is freedom." 2 Corinthians 3:17

As I prayed with those I encountered, there was a word of knowledge with each prayer. I sensed a complete ease just to move and allow the Spirit to work through me.

Each person seemed surprised afterward, as if they had not heard a prayer like that before. I was sure that everyone I had encountered had a Latter Day Saints background, and was unfamiliar with the freedom that the Spirit of the Lord brings.

That is not to say that there still wasn't a discipline for me. I read, and prayed aloud Philippians 4:4-8 daily. Although over the years, God has done a mighty work in Tonya and me, I find myself, even when I don't sense His Presence, to do my part at remaining well-grounded in Him and His promises. I don't allow myself to get side-tracked with secular TV or other distractions that could taint the anointing.

I consider it a blessing and a privilege to know there have been those who have prayed over me, and are still in prayer while I am away, and "as I go..." I'm about my Father's business.

By the end of the week, I would need to make the drive back to Illinois and then fly back to Utah the following week. In the meantime, I would be waiting for the Lord to give me a clear direction on how to best set up care for Jeff. Upon my return home, I checked with the airlines and found medical restrictions that would prohibit Jeff from flying back with me. So, I contacted his social worker at the hospital, and arrangements were made for Jeff to be transferred to a nursing home. The day before Jeff's discharge from the hospital, I flew back to Utah to be there for the transfer.

During the day, as I visited with Jeff before and during the transfer to the nursing home, everything seemed different spiritually. Everybody, myself included, seemed to be going about "their" business. At the nursing home, Jeff had been set up in one of the last rooms at the end of the wing. When staff would come in to get "things" situated for Jeff, I was largely ignored. In the past, this would have been my preference, but at this point I was confused. I certainly didn't sense that I was operating under the same anointing as I had on the previous trip. Since I had to run to the store for Jeff, I decided to make a pit stop at the guest house where

MOVE FORWARD

I had been staying, just to spend some time in prayer. As I arrived at the guest house, I felt the Lord remind me of Matthew 25:36.

"...I was naked and you clothed me, I was sick and you visited me"...

As I read and prayed, I realized that the assignment was different this trip. Of course, the circumstances were also very different. At the hospital, Jeff was attended to every 20 minutes. Either an aide or a nurse would come, take his vitals, or otherwise check on him. At the nursing home, once we got to the room and set up, that was it. So, the "divine" assignment, was to be there for and with Jeff. Jeff and I sat and visited together, as two brothers, for the first time in my memory. Jeff was alcohol-free, and it was great just to talk about anything, even memories.

As I read and prayed, I realized that the assignment was different this trip.

In Matthew 10, Jesus equipped and commissioned His disciples to gather the lost sheep of Israel. Jesus, the shepherd, sought to bring covenant people back into a right relationship with the Father. The lost sheep of Israel needed to accept their King, who had arrived. If they did, the nations of the earth would be blessed through Israel (Genesis 12:3). The message that the disciples delivered would be authenticated by miracles, as Jesus Himself did.

Although Jesus gave the twelve a specific assignment here, I believe we should model our lives after the simple, though profound instructions found in Matthew 10:7-8. This is not a structured checklist of what to do. Rather it is a way of life. Jesus had modeled this way of life to His disciples throughout His public ministry. It was a way of life for Jesus. Although not much is recorded about Jesus before His public ministry, we read in Luke (2:41-52), that even at the age of twelve Jesus was about His Father's business. Jesus told His disciples:

"For I have given you an example, that you should do as I have done to you." John 13:15

This example was of Jesus' entire life of being a servant, not just washing the feet of the disciples. For we are not greater than our master (Jesus). We are servants of the Most High God, and as such we serve. We serve those around us, and those we encounter along the way. **"For as we go, preach, saying that the Kingdom of heaven is at hand..."** It's living a life knowing that wherever we go, the Kingdom of heaven is truly at hand, within reach for anyone willing to believe, and receive. Jesus said that the Kingdom of God (heaven) is within us (Luke 17:21).

As You Go…

We have freely received of the Lord, so freely we are to give. We, as Christians, have the power and authority of the Kingdom of heaven residing in each of us. This is not for ourselves, but to share with those who are without.

As Peter exclaimed in Acts 3:6, when a certain lame man looked at him expecting to receive something. "Silver and gold I do not have but what I do have I give you; in the name of Jesus Christ of Nazareth, rise up and walk." Peter was aware of the anointing upon him. He had just been baptized in the Holy Spirit and had stepped into his role as a leader in the Church. He had freely received, so he freely gave. Perhaps this was the first healing that Peter had initiated on his own since Jesus had been crucified. Peter recognized the opportunity as he went about his business of walking to the temple that day with John, and seized it for the glory of God.

> *"As we go" about our daily business … we will need to look beyond our own business, and recognize the Kingdom opportunity*

It is really that simple. "As we go" about our daily business, we will run across a situation where we will need to look beyond our own business, and recognize the Kingdom opportunity, or purposes before us.

"But seek first the Kingdom of God and His righteousness, and all these things shall be added onto you." Matthew 6:33

"As we go," sometimes will require a course correction of sorts. Even though we may have the best of intentions, we have to be sensitive to what the Lord is doing in a situation or to a person's need. Being focused is great, but we have to properly discern the situation, as did Jesus when he encountered the Canaanite woman found in Matthew 15:21-28. Jesus and His disciples had withdrawn to a non-Jewish region assuming to have some private time. There is no indication that this was to be a missionary journey to the Gentiles.

Jesus Himself told the Canaanite woman, that His mission was for the lost sheep of Israel (verse 24). Although that was the divine assignment, this was not the only encounter Jesus would have where He would ultimately honor the request with a miracle. (See Luke 7:1-10 & John 2:1-11). We may conclude that Jesus was testing the Canaanite woman's faith since she was a Gentile. However, here as well as with other encounters, I believe Jesus was simply drawing out of the woman her need to express her faith verbally, to create the faith for the miracle, in this case, deliverance.

Jesus, who had been anointed by the Holy Spirit without measure would be able to heal regardless (Acts 10:38), but for the Canaanite woman, perhaps Jesus knew that she had some knowledge that Jesus could heal. She just needed to go to the next step, and believe in her heart that Jesus could heal her daughter.

The woman gave Jesus a Jewish greeting (v22) understanding His lineage, worshiped Him, and pleaded for His help. Did she really believe though? Jesus drew that out of the woman in her response in verse 27 using the appropriate analogy that a dog relentlessly awaits even a crumb from its master's table. In verse 28, we see that Jesus then commends the woman, on her faith, and her daughter was healed that very hour.

The point here is that Jesus may not have retreated to that region to bring healing to a Canaanite girl, but the Kingdom opportunity presented itself and Jesus discerned that there was more of a need than just a deliverance. Jesus declared to the Canaanite woman that she had great faith, and her desire had become a reality (verse 28).

This is an area that is still developing for me spiritually. I have a tendency to focus on the immediate, or the apparent, perceived need. There is nothing wrong with taking a moment to "wait" on the Lord to take us deeper when we are ministering to someone. Or even to ask questions that may lend better insight on something deeper that may need to be addressed.

Jesus remained focused on whatever the Father was doing. In John 5:19 we read:

"...Most assuredly, I say to you, the Son can do nothing of Himself, but what He sees the Father do, for whatever He does, the Son also does in like manner."

The word used here for "sees" goes beyond the natural eyesight. To see, as Jesus did with what the Father was doing, was to perceive, sense, and discern. Therefore, Jesus was aware of what the Father was doing in any given situation. He and the Father were in agreement with the response. Jesus was always about His Father's business. Therefore, as He went about His daily activities, He recognized more than the obvious need.

He also recognized the deeper work that may be needed in any given situation. Jesus' communion with the Father maintained His spiritual perception, not to be clouded or influenced by the surface need in the natural. Jesus recognized the greater need.

Another example can be found in Luke 18:35-43, a blind man was calling out to

Jesus. When Jesus commanded the blind man to be brought to Him, Jesus asked the blind man: **"What do you want me to do for you?"**

I would suppose that it was obvious, since the blind man required someone to bring him to Jesus, that the apparent need was for physical healing for his blind eyes. So, why did Jesus ask the question? Because there was a deeper need there in the man, who needed his blind eyes to be opened. From the text, I would say that Jesus knew the blind man needed to express his faith by requesting to receive his sight. In verse 36, the blind man heard the multitude passing by, and asked what it meant. He had heard of who Jesus was, and that miracles accompanied Jesus, so he began yelling out for Jesus to have mercy on him once he was told that Jesus was passing by. Once the blind man verbalized his request, Jesus replied: "receive your sight, your faith has made you well." By faith the man received his sight, and followed Jesus, glorifying God (verse 43). So, let us always be mindful that having a predetermined "ministry" agenda should always be subject to change. After all, it is the Father's business; we are the servants.

As I grow, I will better understand:

"If we live in the Spirit, let us also walk in the Spirit." Galatians 5:25 That is to be in harmony with the Spirit, who gives us a word of knowledge, word of wisdom, and the discerning of spirits, to better lead us as we minister to the needs of others. Since the Spirit of God is always speaking, we need to be sensitive to what He is saying, so we follow His lead.

Let's look at the action verb found in Matthew 10:7, we touched on "as you go." The action verb here is the word preach (kerysso), in the Greek. It means to herald, proclaim, as a public crier of the divine truth we possess. Some versions translate it as "teach."

So, "as we go," we possess within us a divine message that a struggling and even a dying world needs to hear. As we go about our daily lives, we will encounter Christians who need an encouraging word from the Lord. We will encounter those who are lost and reveal to them the love of God. We will encounter the sick, and those who need deliverance, and we will step into what the Lord has for each person. We will proclaim that the Kingdom of heaven is right here, right now for them.

"As we go," preaching the good news of the Kingdom of heaven, we will fulfill the very reason we were filled with the Spirit. We will be witnesses for Jesus (Acts 1:8), even to the remotest parts of the earth (where there are people least likely to hear the gospel). I am not necessarily referring to people on foreign soil, although that may be a call for some. I am referring to the highways and byways we travel in life, where we often come across the outcast or "forgotten" people. As I mentioned, it is not unusual for me to exit an expressway near Chicago or Milwaukee and come across a street person holding a sign. It couldn't be any more obvious, that these are opportunities to demonstrate the Kingdom of heaven to a person in need as the multitudes drive by in their own self-important worlds.

I am not one who ordinarily possesses a boldness to preach the message of salvation to everyone I encounter. I have been praying that the Lord would prepare me to meet whomever He has prepared to meet Him. This has become a daily prayer. When I say that I am praying to be prepared, I'm not referring to having all of the correct biblical answers to whatever I may encounter. I am referring to being in tune with His purposes, and what His Spirit has to say whenever the opportunity arises.

... being in tune with His purposes, and what His Spirit has to say whenever the opportunity arises.

I want to truly perceive what the Father is doing, and honor that, so the person He has been preparing for Himself, is lifting up into that place which will be a dynamic encounter with the Kingdom of heaven.

"Our Father in heaven, we honor Your holy name. We ask that your Kingdom will come now. May Your will be done here on earth, just as it is in heaven." Matthew 6:10 (The Living Bible).

Servanthood is to obediently ensure that our Lord's will is done wherever we may travel. The Kingdom of God is within us (Luke 17:21), and those around us should recognize this. Therefore, our heart's desire is to ensure that His will is done here on earth, as it is heaven.

Paul addresses servanthood to the Corinthians in 1 Corinthians 9:19-22. In this chapter, Paul is apparently addressing questions as to his apostleship, and other issues concerning his ministry.

He also addresses what it looks like to be a servant of Lord. Bearing in mind that Paul is accustom to dealing with "religious" people. He explains his freedom from the entanglements of men and their religious practices. Paul operated in the Spirit where there is freedom. He had chosen to be a servant to all, so that he may win them to the Lord. Although Paul is a servant to all, he did not compromise the gospel message. Paul's posture to seemingly adapt, and accommodate to those who he ministered to should not be construed that he tailored the gospel to appease people. Rather, Paul could find an area with each class of people to sympathize with, since he understood that each class came from a different perspective. The gospel message is universal, God loves each of us, and sent His Son to die for our sins. Paul tells the Corinthians that he approaches the presentation of the gospel this way that he may be a partaker (this ministry) with them, not apart from them. The Corinthians were Greek, Paul a Jew of Jews, yet he planted the church at Corinth. Paul was a servant of the Lord, and despite the troubles he had with the Jews over the gospel, he was still committed to sharing the gospel with them and everyone he could.

"As we go," we may encounter the homeless, the troubled store clerk, or the businessman with alcohol on his breath. Perhaps it is true that the predicament they find themselves in is a making of their own doing. So, we cannot relate to the situation they are in. Yet, we perceive the need in their life and look to the Spirit of God to be used in the moment to release what God has prepared for the person God longs to have a relationship with. We become, all things that we may win a soul for the Kingdom of heaven, a life can be forever changed.

When I stood on that front porch with a man who had struggled with crystal meth, I did not understand that particular addiction. However, I understood the struggle with substance abuse, and understood desperately wanting to change, but not being to able to on my own. In those few moments, the Holy Spirit gave me the direction to take, and before we parted that day, in a rural town in central Illinois, a man gave his life to the Lord, and I went about my business of investigating an insurance claim. Recently, the Lord has been emphasizing the urgency of proclaiming the gospel to the lost, hurting, and dying.

I usually don't encourage the sharing of dreams, since I believe scriptures reveal that dreams are for the dreamer. I will cover more of that in Appendix B. However, this dream will definitely illustrate the urgent desire of the Lord to preach to a lost world.

> *I usually don't encourage the sharing of dreams, since I believe scriptures reveal that dreams are for the dreamer.*

In the dream, I was standing at the driver's side of the car talking with two people who were seated in the car. There was a faceless, formless figure to my left. Even in the dream, I realized that this made no sense, since he would be where the windshield would have been. There was also another subject standing on the passenger side of the car, he was standing street side. In the dream, I was explaining that the Cubs would definitely win their

MOVE FORWARD

division this year (2017) but wasn't sure they would be able to repeat another world series title. I realized that the faceless figure to my left seemed to disagree with my assessment that the Cubs would win their division. Even in the dream, I thought to myself, "how could he possibly disagree with that?" Of course, the Cubs would win their division. As I continued to talk baseball, a truck came by and struck the man standing on the other side of the car. I simply walked around the car and found his remains in the roadway. He had been killed as we were talking.

When I woke up, I thought, as I often do, that the dream was nonsense. Later that morning I left for an appointment I began to pray as I drove. I asked for the interpretation. The Lord gave it to me immediately. As I am talking about nonsense, people are dying. That was sobering. Here I thought I was doing a relatively good job of being faithful in His work. However, I believe the Lord was showing me that **more** can still be done.

The faceless, formless figure was the Holy Spirit, who didn't care about whether the Cubs won their division or not. He was aware that I had an opportunity to share the gospel but chose to talk about baseball. In the dream, I had missed what the Holy Spirit was trying to tell me, and I allowed myself to get carried away in meaningless baseball talk. That's not to say that talking baseball or any benign topic is wrong. After all, it may be the avenue the Lord will use for us to share the gospel. Dreams are personal, and the Lord will speak to us about an area where we may otherwise be missing something.

For me, it was to be ever mindful, of what the Spirit of the Lord would like to do in any given situation. I do really like baseball so I could see myself getting sidetracked if I neglected to take those few moments, and ask the Lord to "prepare me for whomever He has prepared to meet Him." To be about the Father's business is to be as Jesus was, to perceive, sense, and discern the deeper need in any given situation.

"As we go," we preach the message of the good news not out of a religious obligation. It is for others to know the same freedom, and salvation that we know. As the Lord taught me during my trip to Utah, this life in the Spirit, a life in the hands of the Most High God, a life where Jesus leads as a good shepherd can be so free of the worldly entanglements. We should desire for everyone to enjoy this life, which ultimately is a life of peace. Our salvation is secure in Jesus, and as we set the Lord before us every day, we have the confidence of His abiding Presence _every day_, and _everywhere_.

> **I will bless the Lord who has given me counsel, my heart also instructs me in the night seasons. I have set the Lord always before me because He is at my right hand I shall not be moved. You will show me the paths**

As You Go...

of life, in Your Presence is fullness of joy, at You right hand are pleasures forever more. Psalm 16:7-8, & 11.

Let us look at Phillip, who is often referred to as Phillip the evangelist. Phillip was known as a layman, a deacon, and named as one of the seven selected to serve tables to the widows in the daily distribution of food (Acts 6:1 & 5). I think this is significant for us, who may not hold positions in full-time ministry. Phillip was selected to meet this basic need in the early church while the "big guys," the disciples gave themselves to prayer, and ministering the word (the real spiritual stuff) Acts 6:4. As we read in Acts chapter 8 we see what may seem like an extraordinary spiritual work surrounding Phillip, should really be a picture of the "ordinary" Christian life. Perhaps the disappearing at the hands of the Holy Spirit (Acts 8:39-40) is a one of a kind. That would sure be amazing.

We read that in the midst of a great persecution, Phillip went to Samaria. He preached Christ to them there (Acts 8:5). Those gathered to hear Phillip preach were heeding (taking notice). They were hearing Christ preached, and seeing the miracles brought forth by Phillip (Acts 8:6). How ironic is it that in the same chapter of the book of Acts, where Paul is persecuting the church, Phillip is preaching Christ, along with miracles. Paul himself would later write that this is how he (Paul) presented the gospel to a church he founded (1 Corinthians 2:1-5).

As Phillip continued in ministry, demons were cast out, the paralyzed and lame walked, and there was great joy in the city as a result (Acts 8:7-8). Phillip's faithfulness (Matthew 25:21), readied him for a specific, and important divine assignment. Phillip was ready and answered the call of an angel of the Lord, who gave him this divine assignment (Acts 8:26 & 29). Once Phillip arrived where the angel told him to go, the Spirit of the Lord gave him further instructions. "Then the Spirit said to Phillip, Go near and overtake this chariot." Acts 8:29. As a result of following the divine (supernatural) promptings, Phillip was able to preach Jesus to the Ethiopian eunuch from the scriptures. The man received Jesus into his heart and was baptized alongside the road. This entire encounter is a picture of what Jacob dreamed about in the book of Genesis 28:10-17. Jacob saw in a dream what it looked like to live under an open heaven, as Jesus explained to Nathanael the fulfillment of that dream.

"I tell you the truth, you shall see heaven open, and the angels of God ascending and descending on the Son of man." John 1:51

It was none other than Phillip, who had brought Nathanael to see Jesus, who spoke prophetically over him and told those gathered what they would see unfold in front of them as Jesus modeled the life under an open heaven. The disciples may not have actually seen the angels running back and forth from heaven to earth wherever Jesus was, but they did see the effects of living under an open heaven wherever Jesus was at. The Spirit of the Lord was upon Jesus, and remained upon him. The account we read about in Acts 8:5-40 of Phillip is a clear representation of how Jesus moved during his ministry.

"Then Phillip went down to the city of Samaria and preached Christ to them." Acts 8:5. As Phillip went, he preached Christ, and look at what unfolded. Prior to this, Phillip had been assigned to wait on the tables of widows in Jerusalem. My heart's desire is to become so aware of the open heaven available to me through Jesus that such divine assignments are apparent wherever I go.

What is the Spirit of the Lord telling us every day as we go about our business? I believe each of us can see past the routine affairs of our daily life, and "as we go," there is a divine assignment ready and waiting to be fulfilled. We do not have to strain to bring these assignments into focus. They are either there, or they are not. When they are, it takes courage to step into them. There will be times when we miss it. Trust me, there have been numerous times when I simply didn't see it in the moment. Unfortunately, as I went about my business, and the opportunity was lost, I later recognized that I had missed it. We can all get preoccupied with our own lives, and lose sight of the Father's business. There are even those times, we simply miss it because we are fallible.

> *... each of us can see past the routine affairs of our daily life, and "as we go," there is a divine assignment ready and waiting to be fulfilled.*

Be encouraged, even the Apostle Paul asked for prayer to have the boldness he needed to preach the gospel (Ephesians 6:19). It should be noted that the book of Ephesians had been written after the book to the church at Rome. Paul wrote to the church at Rome that he serves with his spirit the gospel of Jesus without ceasing (Romans 1:9). Paul continued that the Christians at Rome are not to be ashamed of the gospel of Jesus, knowing that it was the power of God for salvation to anyone who believes in it (Romans 1:16). Yet, the fearless Apostle Paul still desired to be lifted up in prayer by the believers in Ephesus.

"...and pray on my behalf that utterance may be given to me in the opening of my mouth, to make known with boldness the mystery of the gospel." Ephesians 6:19

As You Go...

Even the "giants" of faith need strength, encouragement, and the prayers of the saints for the Spirit of God to help usher in spreading the gospel. Therefore, never give into discouragement. That discouragement that may suggest we are not gifted enough, or do not have much of a testimony. Each of us has the testimony of Jesus, Christ in you, the hope of glory in us (Colossians 1:27).

I had been assigned to investigate an insurance claim of a residential burglary in Milwaukee. As I read through the claim notes, there were questions as to the circumstances which were all normal. As I reviewed the statement taken from the inside adjuster, there was a note that the wife had sickle-cell. There was no explanation as to why that note was in the statement. Once I contacted the husband and scheduled a date and time to visit them at the insured address, I committed the appointment to prayer. It had become my custom to pray over my appointments to ensure that whatever the Lord may have been working in the lives of the people I meet with, will be revealed to me, and that I may be better equipped to usher in the Kingdom of heaven while I'm there.

> *It had become my custom to pray over my appointments ...*

When I arrived at the insured's house in Milwaukee, I went through the usual investigative steps that I need to do. I inspected the reported damage to make sure it was consistent with a forced entry residential burglary. As I inspected the exterior of the house, I noticed that both vehicles in the driveway had handicap plaques hanging from the rearview mirrors. I suspected that they were there because of the wife. Although I did not know, at that time what sickle cell was, or what disabling effects it may have on a person. I took my photographs, had the husband walk me through the house and point out where the various items had been at the time of the theft. I completed a recorded statement with both the husband and the wife.

Although I had spent about an hour with the couple, I really did not get a "sense," or a prompting to step into anything. However, as we talked, it was apparent that the couple just wanted to live somewhere they could have peace. The husband especially expressed that he wanted to have peace of mind that his family was safe while he was at work since he worked the second shift.

So, without "sensing" an anointing, I chose to step out in authority and asked if I could pray a prayer of peace over the couple before I left. They both agreed. I don't recall exactly how the prayer started, but I did thank the Lord for the couple, and asked for His peace, that peace passes all understanding to be upon the couple. Then, the Holy Spirit showed up. As it was when I prayed over Andrea to receive the baptism in the Holy Spirit, a boldness came over me that I did not expect. The prayer was flowing, like a river of living water (John 7:38). At one point I grabbed the husband's right hand, and placed it upon his wife's shoulder, and placed my hand on top of his, then prayed for healing. I prayed that the red and white blood cells would regenerate, come into alignment with purposes that God originally intended. The husband was in complete agreement as we prayed. Although the wife was quiet, she was also in agreement, and began to weep. We prayed for several minutes. When we stopped, I had that same feeling I did after I had prayed for Andrea. The feeling of, "Oh did I just do that?" Once again, here I was in the home of an insured and had that instant thought that perhaps I had gone too far.

Although I may doubt myself at times, I knew there was a Kingdom purpose for this appointment. I had committed awhile ago to look past the insurance and see the opportunity. This was an opportunity to "preach," "proclaim" that the Kingdom of heaven was at hand. It was within this couples grasp, I was just the connector for them to know that God does care, and Jesus is only a prayer away. The couple was overwhelmed and very thankful. When there is a genuine move of the Holy Spirit, there is no denying His Presence. Later that evening, the husband had texted me and said that they had been so blessed by someone praying for them.

Two days later, the husband again texted me, thanking me. Their faith had grown, this couple experienced what the church looks like as a servant goes about his ordinary daily business. I never asked if the wife had received her healing. It would be encouraging to know, but at this point, I'm to remain faithful in my assignment. It's in these "ministry" moments that I find so exhilarating. Getting feedback like this is always very appreciated. However, I need to remain a humble servant regardless of the feedback.

"And as you go, preach, saying that the Kingdom of heaven is at hand. Heal the sick, cleanse the lepers, raise the dead, cast out demons. Freely you have received, freely give." Matthew 10:7-8

Ministry is not something we do, it's the life we live. Yet, our ministry or life should always remain humble. We should never operate from a position of pride. Jesus Himself, our model said: "I can do nothing of myself..." John 5:30. Jesus demonstrated complete dependence upon the Father. Regardless of how successful our "ministries" may become, or how many healings, salvations, deliverances or even miracles we are a part of, we are just the vessels. God is the one completing the work.

I believe that of all the sins that may cripple a Christian walk, or "ministry," it would be pride that is certain to bring ruin. God resists the proud (James 4:6). The first of the seven things that are an abomination to the Lord is a proud look. That is one who has an appearance of pride, which surfaces from a spiritual or attitude on the inside, and displayed upon the appearance. Remember, it was pride that surfaced in Lucifer (Isaiah 14:12-15), the most perfect, and anointed of cherub (Ezekiel 28:12-19) cause him to fall. He fell so fast, it was like lightning (Luke 10:18). "Pride goes before destruction, and a haughty spirit before a fall." Proverbs 16:18. We are to remain as humble servants of the Most High, and bear in mind that Jesus humbled Himself to bear a death on the cross (Philippians 2:8).

A few months later, I was in Cincinnati Ohio investigating a residential burglary. As I drove from the Chicago area, I prayed in the Spirit, listened to worship music, and a podcast of a sermon. By the time I arrived, there was a definite sense that I would be involved in "ministry."

During my years as a police officer, and in my travels as an insurance investigator, I have been in some pretty rough neighborhoods. As an insurance investigator, I have handled claims in the west and south sides of Chicago, as well as Milwaukee. As I arrived in a neighborhood in Cincinnati, it appeared to be completely out of control. I circled the block a couple of times which is what I usually do to survey the best place to park. However, this just brought attention to me that I didn't want. There was a dark-colored SUV pulled over it was obvious that he was dealing drugs out of the vehicle. The people sitting on porches were watching me. I assumed they were trying to determine if I was the police or just lost. After finding a place to park several houses away from the insured's address I walked down the street. There was a group of young kids in the back of a pickup truck. It appeared that they were looting the bed of the truck. They were throwing items everywhere from the truck bed. One of the boys asked if I had just come from church. I found that odd. I just laughed and said: "I did." Another boy began yelling at me, and demanded to know who I was. I refused to answer him, or the spirit that may be operating through him. As I kept walking, he yelled: "You better answer me." He was only about 10 years old, and was either so rebellious, or the enemy was already fully working through this kid.

Once at the insured's house, we went through the statement, and I conducted my investigation of the scene. Throughout the process of getting her statement, and discussing her claim, my heart ached for this woman, and her life's circumstances. I didn't have a word of knowledge or sense of direction, it was just an ache in my heart that I had never had before. I asked her if I could pray for her, and pray for her protection. She said that she would really appreciate that. As I began to pray, the Holy Spirit did give me words of encouragement, and insight for the woman. The Spirit of God had come upon her, and she began to weep. When we finished praying, we talked some more, and I learned that she had accepted to Lord years ago but had fallen away. I encouraged her to pursue her relationship with the Lord. Then we prayed again. She was very thankful and told me that she really needed that.

My heart still ached for the woman as I left. I knew that this had been a divine assignment and not just a "file assignment" as we call it in my company. It wasn't until sometime later that I understood the ache in my heart that the Lord gave me for this person. This person needed someone to just simply show her compassion. There was no one in her life, or around her, that would simply show her compassion and the love of Jesus. As we talked during the statement, I learned that this woman had fled from an abusive relationship, and now was surrounded by crime and chaos. As she told me, she was surviving. She was also wounded and needed to know that there is still love and God still sees her as important. So important, that through one of life's difficulties, He sent someone to her to bring compassion and encouragement.

Later that evening as I walked from the hotel through downtown Cincinnati to find a restaurant I came across a street person working a corner begging for money. He approached me and asked for $2.00 to get a burrito. I responded "$2.00?" and kept walking. I hadn't even crossed the street when the Spirit convicted me of my response. I was about to enter a four-star steakhouse that had been recommended to me. But I ignored a street person begging for $2.00. My dinner would be paid for by the company, and the person I just walked by may not even know if he would be able to collect enough money for his next meal.

Rather than enter the restaurant, I stood outside and watched this street person approaching people. Everyone did the same thing, they just ignored him and went about their business. I asked the Lord: "Well, what do You want me to do?" The response was: "The least that you do unto these you do unto Me." (Matthew 25:40). It would be a fair question to ask: "How could I be in 'ministry' only an hour earlier, then have such an obvious need approach me, and I have to take time to decipher the right course of action?" I, like many Christians, am ever growing. There have been times that I have simply missed the opportunity. There are other times, such as this, that I really need to allow the Holy Spirit to guide me. On this occasion, I was only thinking about getting my dinner after what had been a long day.

Everyone did the same thing, they just ignored him and went about their business.

I am careful not to be hustled by a street person. Over the years I have learned that there are people who have chosen to live on the streets rather than work or otherwise have chosen this street life. Such people all seemed to have a spiel, which

As You Go...

most of it is a rehearsed fabrication to get someone to give them money. Well, in this case, whether or not this street person was legitimately desperate or just trying to hustle pedestrians I knew the Lord was prompting me to demonstrate that the Kingdom of heaven is at hand. I approached this street person who told me his name was Isaiah. We talked for a little bit, and he told me his story of why he was on the street. I asked him if he knew Jesus as his Savior and Lord. Isaiah admitted that he had accepted the Lord years ago but had fallen away. He explained that he came from a line of preachers, and his aunt even has her own radio show in another state. We then discussed his need for Jesus in his life, and we prayed together. So, there we were, praying on the sidewalk in downtown Cincinnati with people just walking around us going about their own business. When we had finished praying, Isaiah remarked that he really needed that. We talked some more about his commitment to the Lord, I gave him some money for food, then Isaiah was on his way.

Ministry is not something we do, it's the life we live.

"As you go," know that ministry is not for a select few, it's for all believers. It's the life we live. Moving forward is a call to advance the Kingdom of Heaven wherever we go. Despite all that I have learned over the past three years, my encounter with Isaiah was a reminder for me to remain in the Spirit, all of the time; to live a life in the Spirit, and keep in step with the Spirit.

"If we live in the Spirit, let us also walk in the Spirit." Galatians 5:25

The Kingdom of heaven is always at hand in the life of a believer. As I stood there and spoke with Isaiah, there was something about his eyes. There was a soft, genuineness inside this young man. Although his life circumstances had him begging for money on the streets, he came from a line of preachers, made a commitment to the Lord years ago, but had fallen away. Nonetheless, he belonged to the Good Shepherd, and as one of His sheep. Isaiah may have needed that personal invitation to return to the fold, but I would have never known that had I just gone about my own business.

The lesson learned, even after all this time was a simple yet profound. I need to always be about my Father's business. There are a lot of "Isaiahs" in the world who have felt abandoned by the church, their families, and have no one to turn to. If each of us touches an "Isaiah" of the world with the Kingdom of heaven what an impact that would have. This walk as a Christian is a journey, and not just a destination. On this side of heaven, the Kingdom of heaven is within each of us. Therefore, "as we go" there will always be divine assignments where we can intercede for someone that they may know the Kingdom of heaven is truly at

MOVE FORWARD

hand.

Once inside the restaurant, I realized that it was going to be very expensive. As I looked through the menu, the prices were way too much for me to justify on an expense report. I politely told the waiter that I had a change of plans, which I did, that was to find a more reasonably priced restaurant. By the time I had gotten outside, Isaiah was nowhere to be found. This near miss encounter has had a significant impact on me.

Moving forward is a call for each of us know that our past has been dealt with at the cross. To move forward is to advance His Kingdom here on earth. Usually, when there is a call to advance the Kingdom of heaven, there is a tendency for Christians to mentally grab their armor (Ephesians 6: 11-17) and prepare for the impending battle with the enemy. I think of William Wallace from Brave Heart as he rides his horse back and forth getting his fellow countrymen ready for battle. Such was the case for the people of Jerusalem as their enemies conspired against them for an attack (Nehemiah 4:8). So, they prayed, set a watch as they built the wall, they were armed. There will be a time and place for us to stand firm with the whole armor of God when an attack is imminent. However, this call to move forward is to be prepared with a heart for God, His love, and His Kingdom, so we don't overlook the Isaiahs we may pass every day.

Ministry is not something we do, it's the life we live.

Appendix A

The Father is waiting for you.

God loves you, and regardless of your circumstances, or the life choices that you may have made, God always loves you (Romans 8:38-39).

God loves you so much that He gave His only Son to die for you, that you may have eternal life, and healing, it's called salvation, and salvation is in Jesus.

If you have never made a commitment to follow Jesus, and invite Him into your life as Savior and Lord, I encourage you to simply call out to Him, He is waiting to hear from you. Acknowledge that you no longer want to walk this life without Him, ask Him for forgiveness, and invite Him to be you personal Savior and Lord of you life.

"Behold I stand at the door and knock. If anyone hears My voice and opens the door, I will come to him and dine with him, and he with me. Revelation 3:20.

If you need to make a fresh commitment to the Lord because, like me you wondered away from Him or have otherwise found that the road you are on has left you battered, bruised and in need of a new life, call out to Him.

"Create in me a clean heart O God, and renew a right spirit within me." Psalm 51:10 "The Lord is near to those who have a broken heart, and saves such as have a contrite spirit." Psalm 34:18

Call out to Him, He will hear you, and heal you!

Look up the following Bible verses in this New Testament.

John 3:16 – For God so loved the world that He gave His only Son – Jesus.

Appendices

Luke 5:13 – As Jesus told the man full of leprosy, I am willing be cleansed. Jesus is willing to cleanse you of sin, and bring healing to you.

1 Corinthians 6:17 – In Jesus, you can be a new creation, the old things passed away.

Romans 3:23-24 – We all have fallen short of the Glory of God but through Jesus, we can be redeemed. God's grace, it is a gift.

Ephesians 2:8 – Salvation is by grace, give God thanks for this small gift, and ask Him for the gift of eternal life in Jesus. God knows what you need even before you ask (Matt 6:8), but He wants you to seek Him.

Take a moment to give God thanks for this gift card that you received, and ask Him for the gift of eternal life in Jesus.

Romans 10:9 – It is by our confession of faith in Jesus that you will be saved.

God really does love you!

Appendix B

Dreams and Visions

As far back as I can recall, I have had dreams. However, few come to memory prior to being filled with the Spirit in the summer of 2014. Except, there was one reoccurring dream that I had during that season of deliberate disobedience that I wrote about in chapter 3. The dream I would be driving on the toll way when a jet plane would be flying too low, and I knew it would crash. The plane would crash, and there was a tremendous explosion. However, each time, as the explosion occurred, I always found myself standing behind a concert pillar. All of the debris and effects of the explosion did not injured me since I was behind this concert pillar. I would wake up, scared to death. In my ignorance, I would dismiss the dream. I would say: "Oh, it was just a dream".

It wasn't until years later that I understood that the dream was a warning to me, and God revealing to me that it was only by His grace that I was being spared. The dream represented that the direction I was headed was the wrong way. It would only lead to disaster. For the time being, I was only protected by the stone, which I had been rejecting.

"The stone which the builders rejected Has become the chief cornerstone (the cement pillar)." Psalm 118:22 & Acts 4:11-12

God truly does speak to every person through dreams. That includes believers, and unbelievers. The bible documents that God spoke warnings to such unbelievers as Pharaoh (Genesis 41), and Nebuchadnezzar (Daniel 2). We will cover these two biblical examples a bit further shortly. This outline on dreams, and visions will be a very basic working understanding of the two. I encourage you to be very diligent in your own personal pursuit in the study dreams. Take the time to record them, and seek to understand all of your dreams. Dreams are not always non-sense from your subconscious. God may be warning you, giving you a word of instruction, or insights into areas of your life that may be a blind spot

Appendices

for you. God just might be speaking to you while you sleep. So, if it's important enough for God to speak to you, I believe it is even more important to seek an understanding of what our Father is saying.

Dreams from God are powerful. They are instructions, warnings, and encouraging glimpses into what is about to happen. Dreams from the Lord bypass our natural sense of understanding and logic. Therefore, Godly dreams are a supernatural experience. God descended from heaven in a pillar of cloud, and spoke the following to Aaron and Miriam:

"Hear now My words, if there is a prophet among you, I, the Lord make myself known to him in a vision, I speak to him in a dream." Numbers 12:6

A prophet can receive a word from the Lord in dreams. But not all dreamers are called to be prophets. Dreams are a chosen method of communication to everyone. So, if you are a dreamer, this does not mean you are more spiritual than a "non" dreamer. As an avid dreamer myself, it may mean that God has to resort to dreams to get your attention in the mist of a busy life.

Before we cover more on dreams, let's look briefly at sleep. Sleep is one of the methods God uses to speak to all of us. The reason why God chooses to speak to us while we are asleep is simple. In essence He has our full attention. We generally view sleep as a way for our physical bodies to get rest, and rejuvenate our bodies. Well, sleep is that, but it is also a time that the distractions of the day should not have us so preoccupied. During sleep, it is a prime opportunity for the Lord to get a word to each us. Therefore, while we are asleep, God has a captive audience. Although our body is asleep, our spirit is still awake, and able to receive a word from the Lord. God Himself does not sleep.

"Behold He (God) who keeps Israel shall neither slumber nor sleep." Psalm 121:4

When we have finished the day's activities, God is there for us. It is believed that on average we will sleep one third of our lives. I believe God has designed it as such that as we are at rest, we are to wait upon Him (Psalm 37:7). David tells us further that we are to meditate within our heart on our bed, and be still (Psalm 4:4).

Since the beginning of recorded biblical history God has used dreams to communicate to people. As we will cover, dreams are generally for the dreamer. Dreams are given as warnings, instructions, and even insight into the direction we should pursue. When we are asleep, our pride (soul) is in a sense unplugged, and out of the way. A person may receive the best of advice, or instructions but dismiss it because of their pride. When we are asleep, our spirit is not influenced by our pride. Therefore, the instructions can be better received.

MOVE FORWARD

> For God may speak in one way or in another, yet man does not perceive it. In a dream, in a vision of the night, when deep sleep falls upon men, while slumbering on their beds, then He open the ears of men, and seals their instructions. In order to turn man from his deed, and conceal pride from man, He keeps back his soul from the pit and his life from perishing by the sword. Job 33:14-18

It had been through a dream that the Lord warned the Magi not return to Herod after visiting baby Jesus (Matthew 2:12). Then God chose to warn Joseph, the man responsible for the upbringing of the Savior of the world, through a dream to flee to Egypt (Matthew 2:13). God, being God could have chosen a Prophet to deliver these warnings as He had warned His people before. God chose to speak to the Magi and Joseph in dreams. My point is, for God, speaking to us through dreams is a valid method of communication to people. Before we cover some more biblical examples of dreams, we also need to understand that not all dreams are from God. Dreams can originate from three sources.

Our subconscious (soul) is a active source for many dreams. Since these dreams originate from our subconscious, they bypass the normal self defense mechanisms we each have, and the preconceived notions we have about ourselves. Often times, we have our own blind spots where we do not see our strengths or weaknesses as accurately as we should. In addition, what may lay within our hearts, may be revealed in our dreams. Therefore, do not disregard dreams that portrays oneself as being involved in behavior that is obviously less than God. Especially behavior that seems absolutely "out of character" for oneself. This may be a revelation of an area in your heart that may need to be repented of that one may refuse to admit openly. Generally, if a distasteful behavior appears in a dream, and is an area that needs attention, it will come up more than once.

Dreams of the subconscious will also reveal that which is pressing upon our minds. There are a volume of examples that could be given. We can all be preoccupied with our families, jobs, and our life circumstances. As a police officer, I had a recurring dream that, I would later learn was very common among police officers. It would involve a deadly force situation, where I would pull my duty weapon, and shot at the bad guy, but the bullets would either not work, or my gun would malfunction or some other tactical mishap would occur. I would wake up, and think "great"! Something is going to go wrong, and I'm going to end up shot. It wasn't until I heard Lt. Col. Dave Grossman speak at a conference that I discovered this reoccurring dream was very common among police officers and soldiers. He explained that it was the subconscious reminding those who are involved in potential combat situations that there was concern about their tactical proficiency. All they needed to do was get to the range, log in some training time, and that subconscious concern would disappear.

Appendices

The fact was, I was not tactically proficient at the time. I had spent too many years riding a desk as a detective. At the time of this reoccurring dream I had been promoted to sergeant, and was back in uniform. I then made it a practice to be on the range about once a month. In time, with the amount of range time and training I did on my own, this reoccurring dream did stop. This was a deep seated concern that I harbored, but would never have admitted it. Through my subconscious it came forth in my dreams. Of course there are numerous examples of a deep seated concerns, hidden sin, or the trials of life, that the subconscious may bring forth through a dream. Though not necessarily divinely inspired, many of these dreams may need to be examined, and corrective steps taken.

False dreams as they are know can originate from the deceptive imaginations of a person's heart or be from a demonic influence. False dreams, and visions will be contrary to God's word, and will usually be for the purpose of deceiving the dreamer, or others into believing a lie.

"Behold I am against those who prophesy false dreams, say the Lord, and tell them and cause My people to err by their lies and by their recklessness..." Jeremiah 23:32

False dreams can originate from the deceitfulness of the false prophets heart. For most of us, hopefully, this will not be a problem. If you are sincerely seeking the Lord, and diligently seek to understand your dreams, the Holy Spirit will teach and guide you through the process. A concern for all of us is that last portion of Jeremiah 23:32. "By their recklessness." We need to be prudent in the sharing of our dreams. As I mentioned, dreams are generally for the dreamer, even if familiar people are in the dreams. I strongly recommend that you have an accurate understanding of a dream before you share it with someone, and suggest that the particular dream was given to you to warning them. This may fall into the "recklessness" portion of the verse, and thereby qualify you as a false prophet.

Daniel, a dreamer, and one who received visions, is an excellent example to follow. Daniel, who after receiving the interpretation of his troubling dream during the first year of the reign of king Belshazzar (Daniel 7), kept the matter in his heart v28. Daniel had not been instructed to share this dream publicly. For me, the only dreams that I am willing to share publicly, such as through this book, will be dreams that I know I have been given the understanding and interpretation.

Dreams can either originate or be influenced by the demonic. Since there is an authentic voice of God to people through dreams and visions, Satan and his minions will attempt to counterfeit this form of communication. The enemy will, whenever possible attempt to destroy or derail the work of the Lord in our lives. But we need not be fearful that every strange, or even frightening dream has originated from the enemy. The word of God needs to dwell richly in our hearts so we always have wellspring of biblical understanding to draw from whenever the enemy tries to deceive us. We need to be discerning, and have an established understanding of what an authentic word from the Lord, through a dream or vision looks, and sounds like.

There are two obvious examples of demonic influence in dreams. Known as Incubus, and Succubus. These are commonly referred to as evil spirits who will entice a person to have sex during the dream. Also known as a wet dream. The Incubus is known as a "male" spirit, and the Succubus is known as the "female" spirit. Not all "wet" dreams may be related to the infiltration of an evil spirit into your dream world. Such dreams can of course be the product of one's subconscious. Nonetheless, if these are frequent dreams, it is an indicator that this is an area of your life that needs attention. At times, when either an Incubus or Succubus spirit is involved, they will usually appear as a sexually attractive person. But once the dreamer has committed to having sex, they may reveal themselves as a grotesque figure or sickly person. We need not be ignorant of the enemies devices (2 Corinthians 2:11). If this has happened to you, just know that none of us are immune from an attack from the enemy. Simply bring the matter before the Lord, and commit your sleep time to Him.

Before I go to bed each night, I commit that time to the Lord. I ask for His protection while I sleep, and seek to hear His voice, and "hear" what He has to "show" me during the night. There is no need to be concerned, we just need to discern. I believe that each of us abides in a real measure of protection from the Lord everyday (read Psalm 91). There may be times when the enemy gets the best of us, but we operate, even when we sleep from place of triumph (2 Corinthians 2:14). I don't bother giving the devil more attention than he deserves. So, neither should you. I wanted to touch on the enemies tactics merely so you are aware of them. When you lie down to sleep, sleep in peace (Psalm 4:8).

A couple great biblical examples of dreams given by God are found in Genesis 40, with the baker and the butler, and Pharaoh's dream in Genesis 41. In Genesis 40 a baker and butler, who had offended the king found themselves in prison with Joseph. One night both the baker and the butler had dreams. What is interesting is that the reason both men were sad was that they didn't think there was anyone available to interpret their dreams since they were in prison. Apparently they were familiar with dreams, and having someone available to interpret dreams. It would be assumed that in Pharaoh's palace it would have been the magicians on staff who would have been providing the interpretation. Although, these magicians may have received their sense of interpretation from divination, what we can learn is there was a familiarity with receiving a dream, and having it interpreted. Joseph then explains to both the baker and the butler that a true interpretation of a dream is from God (Genesis 40:8).

Appendices

What is significant here in both dreams, is both the baker and the butler there was a representation of the number 3. For the baker, there were three branches which was a prophetic representation of three days. For the butler, there were three baskets which also prophetically represented three days. The baker was to be restored to his position in three day. However, for the butler, he would lose his head in three days. Three represents completeness in the bible. In these dreams, three established when the fulfillment of each dream would occur. It has been my own experience that when dreams come in three segments, they are without a doubt a word from the Lord. What is also very significant from this example, is that the interpretation comes from God. Using dream dictionaries for the common symbols can be a useful tool but to truly understand what has been given to you in a dream requires supernatural revelation.

As we see from the examples of the baker and the butler, the dreams given, were for the dreamer. Each was specific to them, and there circumstances. Joseph provided the accurate dream interpretation by revelation from the Spirit of God (Genesis 41:38). Dreams are very subjective. Although there are many common symbols found in dreams such as cars, planes, roads, different animals, each may have a unique meaning to the dreamer. For example, someone who loves dogs, and in there dream walk into a house where there is a dog in every room will sense that the house is inviting since there favorite animal is in every room. But the person who is scared to death of dogs the same dream would be a nightmare. That person would sense that the house was filled with what they feared.

Two years later, in Genesis 41 Pharaoh had a dream, and Joseph interpreted the dream. By all accounts, Pharaoh was not a God fearing ruler, nor is there any record that he worshiped the God who would ultimately give him the interpretation. What we find in Pharaoh's two dreams is how God speaks a warning, to unbelievers and believers in a parabolic or symbolic language. Cows for example are not water bearing animals, let alone rise from a river. Cows also are not carnivorous, and would not devour or eat another flesh bearing animal. Wheat of course does not devour other stalks of wheat. But there are clues in each dream. These clues however, in of themselves do not give a complete understanding of the dreams. Once the interpretation is brought forth, the clues make sense.

What is relevant for this basic teaching on dreams, is that even Pharaoh knew there was a meaning and a purpose to the dream. So much so, that it troubled him, and he was angry because he could find anyone to interpret his dreams. Joseph discloses to Pharaoh (Genesis 41:15-16), that it is not him that gives the interpretation of the dreams, but God. Nonetheless, Joseph also moves in wisdom (James 3:17), that none of Pharaoh's staff could match. The dream given to Pharaoh was obviously a warning to him as the ruler of his nation to prepare for a coming famine. Joseph, in the Spirit of wisdom provides the solution on how to prepare for the coming famine. In doing so, Joseph is given favor. He is then appointed to rule over Pharaoh's house, and his people (Genesis 41:40). As a result, Joseph will then be able to fulfill his dream that he had so many years ago.

What I find amazing is that Joseph had been in prison when he was given the interpretation for the baker and the butler. Then, a forgotten Joseph was remembered two years later. Yet, he still had a prophetic connection with the Lord to be used for the interpretation of Pharaoh's dreams. As we read in Genesis 39, Joseph had found favor with God, and prospered in all that he did. Joseph did not take this favor for granted, and he demonstrated his integrity in not giving in to the adulterous advances of Potiphar's wife. Joseph knew that he had been blessed of God (verse 5), and such a sin would be considered wickedness before the Lord (verse 9). This apparently did not discourage Potiphar's wife, for she continued after Joseph day after day (verse 10). Yet Joseph was faithful to God, and his master in his duties and did not fail either. Therefore, I suspect, that while Joseph remained in prison for two more years, he continued to be faithful to the Lord in his relationship with Him. No doubt there were day where Joseph probably didn't understand why he was still in prison. But when the appointed time arrived, Joseph, because of his continued faithfulness, was able to step into his divine assignment.

Daniel, a prophet who declared God's present and eternal purposes to the Gentile and Jewish world, is an example on how we can handle dreams. In Daniel 7:1, Daniel had a dream, and wrote down the main facts. This is key to anyone who has dreams. Write them down. I know this can be a laborious task, if like me you have multiple dreams during the night. It is important to record them by date so you can look back when you understand that a dream has come to pass. I did this recently after understanding what a symbol in a dream was that I had had over a year before. It was a dream that I had forgotten about until I had the key. Once I had the understanding of a key symbol, looked at the date, and the events surrounding my life then, I had the interpretation. It all made sense.

The topic of dreams obviously could cover an entire book. However, I am simply not qualified to provide that much of a comprehensive study to dreams. As I live this life in the Spirit, I am pursuing a better understanding of the dreams I have. I believe that each of us need to seek the understanding, and interpretation of our dreams. They may contain valuable insights from the Lord.

"It is the glory of God to conceal a matter, but the glory of kings is to search out a matter." Proverbs 25:2

Don't be discouraged as you embark on this wonderful adventure to understand what God may be saying to you in dreams. When I first began making the effort to understand the dreams I was having I found it frustrating at times. I thought

Appendices

why can't God just spell it out plainly so even I could understand what He is trying to tell me. Rather than getting frustrated, we are to search out the matter. The parabolic language that God uses in dreams, is the language of Heaven. God also speaks very personal through dreams. He will use what may be familiar to you, and would not make any sense to someone else. When you can't make the connection of what He may be telling you, seek Him.

"**Call to Me, and I will answer you, and show you great and mighty things, which you do not know." Jeremiah 33:3**

God is always speaking to us, and dreams are one of the ways He has chosen to speak to each of us. Pursue your dreams.

Visions

As you may recall from chapter 1, the first vision I ever had was while I was seated at my work station typing up a use of force investigation in 2014. The vision was a clear snap shot of a future work the Lord had for Tonya and I to step into. It was two years after that first vision, that Tonya and I met the toddler in a white dress, named Kenisha. On the mission field in Jamaica in 2016, we met Kenisha, and the Lord provided a word for her as the vision was fulfilled.

A vision is a supernatural appearance, similar to a dream. Yet, they can offer more clarity, and often times be more literal. Generally, visions will show the recipient a future event. Visions can also simply be, God allowing the recipient to see through the veil, and into the spiritual. Visions can be parabolic like dreams. When given in the parabolic language of heaven, there may be a quick work of understanding given.

> Then the Lord answered me and said, "Record the vision and inscribe it on tablets, that the one who reads it may run. For the vision is yet for the appointed time, it hastens toward the goal and it will not fail. Though it tarries, wait for it, for it will certainly come, it will not delay. Habakkuk 2:2-3

The vision of Kenisha, the appointed time for that vision to be fulfilled was two years. Visions provide a glimpse, from the Lord, into a future work. They offer encouragement, and reassurance that there is a goal, and it will not fail. When Tonya and I were considering going to South Africa the Lord gave me a vision. The vision was the confirmation for us that we were to go, since we had been praying about whether or not to go. In addition, the vision, again showed me a future work that I would be involved in. When the Holy Spirit came upon me one morning during church, I clearly saw that I was preaching a message of God's love to an audience of all black youth. A few months later, as I stood on a desk in

MOVE FORWARD

a courtyard of a high school in Cape Town South Africa, I recognized that I was fulfilling the vision the Lord had given me. That was so awesome!

As I was giving my testimony that morning in South Africa, Tonya and the other team members were lined up along a wall behind me facing the audience. Tonya told me later that as I was speaking she was "seeing" a glow around the head one young man. At first assumed it was the somehow from the sun since we were outside, and the students were standing in the sun. But Tonya said that this glow was just around this one particular person. Tonya tried to re-focus to make sure she wasn't seeing anything. But the glow remained on this one person. As I was still speaking, Tonya went to the team leader, and told him her observations. He then granted Tonya permission to call out the young man, since the Lord was highlighting him among all of the other students in the crowd. During the alter call this young man, "Sam" along with numerous other students gave his life to the Lord. Afterwards, Tonya and I had the privilege to pray with "Sam", and help sow the seeds that God wanted planted in that young man's life.

What Tonya experienced that morning is what is known as an "open" vision.

An open vision is where the Lord, supernatural pulls back the veil of the natural, to allow a person to see what is going on in the spiritual realm at that moment. Tonya has had several of these open visions. One open vision Tonya had was quiet frightening. While we were at church, a homeless man came in, and sat at the rear of the church. Myself and another person ministered to him, and when he was about the leave, he asked us if he could hug us. Tonya was standing nearby. Tonya told us afterwards that when the guy hugged us, she clearly saw a demonic reptile like figure upon the man, and it was as if both the man and the demonic had hug each of us. Neither myself or the other person ministering to the man sensed the actual demonic presence, we both sensed that there was a spirit of homosexuality upon him. Tonya's glimpse into the spiritual realm confirmed that there was a demonic spirit although we were unable to see it with our natural eyes.

In 2 Kings chapter 6, Elisha asked that the "eyes" of his servant may be opened to see into the spiritual realm to calm his fears.

"And Elisha prayed, and said "Lord, I pray, open the eyes that he may see" Then the Lord opened the eyes of the young man, and he saw. And behold, the mountain was full of horses and chariots of fire all around Elisha." 2 King 6:17

There is a very real spiritual reality all around us, whether we "see" it or not.

Peter was given a vision while he had been praying. For Peter, the vision was needed to Peter to understand an assignment that the Lord had for him as a patriarch of the early church. It was through two visions that the Lord used to usher in the Gentiles to the church, and receiving the Holy Spirit. In Acts 10, we read

Appendices

that Cornelius, a devout God fearing centurion was given a vision that lead him to send three men to Joppa to locate Peter. Peter later recounts his vision as a way of explanation to the other apostles, and brethren at Jerusalem as to why he to the uncircumcised men and ate with them.

"I was in the city of Joppa praying, and in a trance I saw a vision, an object descending like a great sheet, let down from heaven by four corners, and it came to me." Acts 11:5.

For Peter the vision was instructional, and prophetic. Peter needed the Lord to show him that it was God's will to take the message of Jesus to the Gentiles, and God sealed the work with an out pouring of the Holy Spirit.

If you have a vision, it will usually be apparent that the Lord is showing you something. Most likely it will be of a future work. My experience has been, as Habakkuk writes, the vision is for an appointed time.

Jim and Tonya Coursey

Jim and Tonya Coursey are the founders of Psalm51Ministries.com

The couple have a dynamic testimony of what the love of God can do in an individual's life. Although Jim had been a Christian for 30 years, he had little understanding of the love of the Father until Jim met Him at an altar during a tent revival. Just as the father in the parable of the prodigal son (Luke 15:20) met his son, Jim encountered the Lord in a powerful and undeniable manner under the prophetic anointing of two ministers. During this encounter with the Lord, He created a clean heart, and renewed a right spirit within Jim. As a result, Jim and Tonya's marriage was restored, and new life was birthed.

Jim and Tonya now understand what is to be a new creation in Christ Jesus. They are eager to share what the Lord has done in their lives. Their testimony and enthusiasm for the Kingdom of heaven will help in the equipping of the saints for the work of ministry. "Ministry is not what we do, it's the life we live!"

Learn more at: *https://www.psalm51ministries.com/*

www.ingramcontent.com/pod-product-compliance
Lightning Source LLC
Chambersburg PA
CBHW060518100426
42743CB00009B/1363